C8000000

D1485550

A BRIDGE AT ARNHEM

Operation Market Garden: a massive airborne strike designed to open a corridor through Nazi-held Holland, by-pass the Siegfried Line and crush the 1,000 Year Reich before Christmas. Despite the gallantry of the elite First British Airborne Division – the Red Devils – who were to seize the key bridge across the Lower Rhine at Arnhem, the Operation ended in a resounding victory for the Germans. This is the story of this epic battle, the commanders who planned it and the units who paid for their mistakes.

A BRIDGE AT ARNHEM

by

Charles Whiting

Magna Large Print Books
Long Preston, North Yorkshire,
BD23 4ND, England.

British Library Cataloguing in Publication Data.

Whiting, Charles
    A bridge at Arnhem.

    A catalogue record of this book is
    available from the British Library

    ISBN   978-0-7505-2668-5

First published in Great Britain in 1974 by
Futura Publications Ltd.

Copyright © Futura Publications Ltd. 1974

Cover illustration © The Mary Evans Picture Library

The moral right of the author has been asserted

Published in Large Print 2007 by arrangement with
Eskdale Publishing

Magna Large Print is an imprint of Library Magna Books Ltd.

Printed and bound in Great Britain by
T.J. (International) Ltd., Cornwall, PL28 8RW

ACKNOWLEDGEMENTS

I should like to thank the following for their assistance in writing this book: Sir Kenneth Strong, Group Captain Fred Winterbotham, Mr Thixton and Messrs Dukes, Pennock, White, Burrows, Howden, Walton – all of the First Airborne Division.

In Germany I owe thanks to General Student, Colonel Giskes, Hans Freuhauf (late the Hermann Goering Division) and H. Matz (ex-Ninth SS Panzer Division).

My greatest debt, however, is to one of the few who survived the Battle of the Bridge at Arnhem – Eddie (Mick) Tucker. With his Irish gift of the gab, it was not difficult for the writer to learn what happened during that terrible fight on the Bridge by Frost's Second Paras. If I may borrow your old war-cry, Mr Tucker – 'Whoa Mahomet!'

CONTENTS

PRELUDE TO A BATTLE
(September 10–17, 1944)

'I think we may be going a bridge too far'.
*Gen. Browning, Deputy Commander Allied
Airborne Army, to Field Marshal Montgomery
(10th Sept. 1944)*

1

As the early morning mist began to clear
away that Sunday morning the soldiers
clambered stiffly out of their foxholes to
begin another day of war. Behind them in
the villages, little whitewashed Belgian
houses burned here and there. Somewhere
in the far distance, there came the persistent
dry crack of an M-1 rifle followed by the
high-pitched hysterical burr of a German
spandau; and, as always, the heavy guns
rumbled stolidly, opening the new day with
the ever-present background music of war.

But the young soldiers of General
Hodges's victorious First US Army had no
ears for the guns, nor eyes for what was
taking place behind them in the territory
which they had conquered from the enemy
during the previous day's headlong rush
through the Ardennes. Their gaze that hazy
September morning was concentrated on
the valleys below with their long lines of
concrete 'dragon's teeth', backed by the
silent expectant bunkers of the West Wall,
running from north to south as far as the
eye could see.

As the bells began their joyous peal of

triumph and liberation in the onion-towered Baroque churches of Old Belgium, the officers blew their whistles, the NCOs bellowed their hoarse commands and the drab olive line started to move forward again. From the Luxembourg–German frontier, through Belgium, right up to the border of Holland with the Third Reich, facing the old Imperial city of Aachen itself, the great American steam-roller commenced to roll once again.

In a valley dominated by the great ruined castle of Viaden, once owned by the Delanoy family, forefathers of the American president Franklin Delano Roosevelt, Sergeant William Holzinger prepared the infantry patrol which would give him the brief fame of being the first Allied soldier to set foot on German soil. Further north in a Belgian orchard, still sparkling with morning dew, a young artillery captain of 'Lightning Joe's' 7 US Corps set up his 105mm 'Long Toms', with which he would soon start pounding a lonely cross-roads in the woods just outside Aachen. And above the little border village of Raeren, lying half in Belgium and half in Germany, the tankers of General Rose, the son of a Jewish Rabbi, prepared their attack on Raeren. An attack which would make the Jewish Commander of the Third Armoured Division the first invader since the time of Napoleon to conquer German territory.

The Western Allies had finally achieved what some of them had been awaiting for five long, bitter years: they had reached the border of National Socialist Germany. The end was in sight at last. On that warm, autumn Sunday morning as the young victors moved forward confidently into the final battle – or so they thought – a decision had to be made: what form would the last offensive take, which would deal the death blow to the Thousand Year Reich?

The man who had to make that tremendous decision was in a bad mood that Sunday morning. With his leg propped up on a chair, the Supreme Commander, General Dwight D. Eisenhower scowled out of the window of his headquarters in the aptly named 'Villa Montgomery' at Granville, some 400 miles behind the far-off front, and glared at the grey-green waters of the English Channel, washing around the Mont-Saint-Michel.

A few days before his little L-5 scout plane had been forced to make an emergency landing on the beach in front of the villa. In helping the pilot, Captain Dick Underwood, to push the plane out of the way of the incoming tide, he had twisted his 'good' knee. His 'bad' one had been injured years before as a cadet at West Point. Now he was confined to his chair with his knee fixed in 'some sort of a rubber gadget' just as his armies were moving into Germany and he was vitally needed 'up front'.

During August his men had at last broken out of their landing area in Normandy and flooded into Brittany under General 'Blood and Guts' Patton, or the 'Green Hornet', as Eisenhower was wont to call him. Further north, General Montgomery's combined British, Canadian and American troops had barrelled through Belgium into southern Holland to the borders of the Reich itself. Now Eisenhower's three top commanders, General Patton, his chief General Bradley, the bespectacled commander of the 12th Army Group and Montgomery, wanted a decision from him – and wanted it fast. Indeed, Eisenhower knew as he brooded in his chair, smoking yet another of the sixty 'Luckies' and 'Camels' he chain-smoked a day, the sharp-faced Britisher wanted the decision from him that very Sunday. Three days before, on September 7th, 1944, Montgomery had written to him, stating: 'My maintenance is stretched to the limit. First instalment of 18 locomotives only just released to me and balance still seem uncertain. I require an air lift of 1,000 tons a day at Douai or Brussels and in the last two days have had only 750 tons total. My transport is based on operating 150 miles from my ports and at present I am over 300 miles from Bayeux. In order to save

14

transport I have cut down my intake into France to 6,000 tons a day, which is half what I consume, and I cannot go on for long like this. It is clear, therefore, that based as I am at present, on Bayeux, I cannot capture the Ruhr. As soon as I have a Pas de Calais port working I would then require about 2,500 3-ton lorries plus an assured air lift averaging a minimum 1,000 tons a day to enable me to get to the Ruhr and finally to Berlin. I submit with all respect … that a reallocation of our present sources of every description *would* be adequate to get *one* thrust to Berlin'. And 'Ike' knew who would insist on commanding that sole thrust to Berlin, the heart of the Reich. No other person than Bernard Law Montgomery.

Over the last three years Eisenhower had come a long way. When he returned from duty in the Philippines in 1940 he was an obscure colonel of forty who had never fired a shot in anger or even commanded a battalion. He had not seen a battlefield until he went to France in the late twenties to prepare the official US Government guide, and in 1940 he had thought his career was over. Then the war came and he shot up the ladder of promotion as the protégé of General Marshall, enigmatic head of the US Army, and was made Supreme Commander of all Allied troops in Europe above the

15

heads of 366 other US Generals senior to him.

In spite of the popularity he enjoyed among the rank-and-file of his 4 million strong command, there were many in high places who disliked him and felt he was not fitted for the Supreme Command. Field Marshal Sir Alan Brooke, Chief of British Imperial General Staff thought: 'Being no commander, he has no strategic vision, is incapable of making a plan or running operations when started.' Churchill, the British Premier, thought he 'was a good fellow who was amenable', and 'could be influenced'. Even in his own camp, he was not spared criticism. Patton sneered at him as 'the best general the British have', snorting with remarkable foresight (for 1944) that 'he'd make a better president, than a general', while Vice-President Truman, the obscure, former Missouri haberdasher, whom Eisenhower would succeed as president one day thought 'he was very weak as a field commander'. The General, whom Truman was wont to call 'that son of a bitch', was 'incapable of making a decision' and 'had to be led every step of the way' by General Marshall. For many British and Americans, Dwight D. Eisenhower, whom his former boss, General MacArthur, had called, 'the apotheosis of mediocrity', was 'the military manager, the front office man, for whom the title of manager was something of an anachronism' (to use the words of Eisenhower's biographer Marquis Childs).

But on this September Sunday he was obliged to make a decision, for in his letter of the 7th, Montgomery had written, 'It is very difficult to explain things like this,' and wondered if it would be possible for Eisenhower to come and see him. And Eisenhower had agreed to fly to Montgomery's Brussels-based TAC HQ to discuss the problem that very afternoon.

In essence, there were four invasion routes available to the Allies: through the Lorraine Gap in Northern France, where Patton commanded; through the Ardennes, where General Hodges was in charge; through the Maubeuge–Liège area, a joint Hodges–Montgomery responsibility: and through Belgium–Holland where Montgomery was in sole command. All four had their pros and cons, but the man ploughing his way through yet another pack of cigarettes thought the two northern avenues were the best; firstly because the major concentration of enemy troops was there and secondly because an attack in that direction would not only capture the vital supply sport of Antwerp, 'a permanent and adequate base' for operations within the Reich, but also position the Allies for the final thrust into the 'belly' of National

Socialist Germany (the Ruhr) and its 'heart' (Berlin).

But Eisenhower also thought there was room for a secondary thrust by Bradley's main commander Patton, through the Lorraine Gap, into the Eifel and Saar areas of Germany. After all, Bradley, 'the GIs General', as Ernie Pyle had called him, had suffered enough under Montgomery's command in the past. Soon, indeed, he swore he would resign rather than serve again under the little Britisher (who had been in charge of all land forces in Europe till September 1st). Eisenhower, always conscious of publicity and public relations – that new aspect of total war which every general after him would have to learn to live with and like – knew that Bradley could not be left out in the cold. He would have to have part of the spoils of final victory.

The 'victor of Alamein', who had just been promoted to the rank of field marshal, thought otherwise. For Montgomery, the war could only be won rapidly by 'one powerful full-blooded thrust across the Rhine and into the heart of Germany backed by the whole resources of the Allied armies' – 'the forty divisions' he was dreaming about continually. He demanded that his front should be given the sole priority for men and supplies so that he could force the West Wall and 'bounce' a crossing across the Rhine

18

while the Germans were in full retreat.

But on that Sunday when Intelligence was confidently predicting that total German collapse was imminent, and the German armies in the West were in full flight across their own borders, national and personal prestige had begun to emerge as the decisive factors. Soon they would become more important than the problem of winning the war quickly and economically. As his red-headed 'secretary-driver' Kay Summersby (the British ex-model for whom he would soon be prepared to divorce Mamie, his wife, and sacrifice his Army career) began to help him to get ready for the flight to Brussels, General Dwight D. Eisenhower felt he must somehow find a nice balance between what he knew 'Monty' would demand and what he had to give 'Brad' for the sake of the US Army and the 12th Army Group's personal prestige...

2

The newest Field Marshal in the British Army walked briskly from the big Humber staff car flying the Union Jack, casually acknowledged the salutes of the MPs lining the runway, and entered the Supreme Commander's personal Dakota followed by his Chief Administrative Officer, General

Graham. He nodded to Air Marshal Tedder, Eisenhower's deputy, a man he didn't like and who didn't like him. Bending slightly he shook hands with the seated 'Ike', enquired perfunctorily about his injured leg and got down to business at once in that typical no-nonsense manner of his.

He asked Eisenhower to get rid of his British admin officer Sir Humphrey Gale before the conference began. Montgomery mistrusted all British officers working at Supreme Command Headquarters and he did not want too many hostile witnesses to hear what he was going to say to Eisenhower. He could not ask Tedder to leave, but at least Tedder was only RAF and could not report directly to Montgomery's own direct superior 'Brookie'. Somewhat startled, but used to Monty's idiosyncrasies by now – hadn't the Britisher told him to put out his cigarette at their first meeting two years before? – Eisenhower dismissed Gale and waited for what must come.

It came with a violence that was new even to Eisenhower, who had suffered rough treatment enough at his subordinate's hands in these last years that they had worked together. His face flushed and angry, the Field Marshal dragged out a sheaf of signals which he had received from Eisenhower over the last seven days and launched into a bitter attack on his superior's conduct of the war.

He told the American that the German V-2 rockets had already begun to fall on London and that something had to be done at once to capture the German bases from which they were fired, before London's morale broke down completely. He, Montgomery, wanted immediate permission to carry out his attack on the Ruhr with 'absolute priority' for his command. As the British general wrote himself after the war about what he told Eisenhower that afternoon: 'I said so long as he (Eisenhower) continued with two thrusts, with the maintenance split between the two, neither could succeed... There were two possible plans – Bradley's and mine. It was essential to back one of them. If he tried to back both, we couldn't possibly gain any decisive results quickly!'

Eisenhower listened in stony silence, his face revealing nothing. But when Montgomery paused in his tirade to take a breath, he leaned forward and placed his hand on the Britisher's knee. 'Steady Monty,' he said quietly. 'You can't speak to me like that ... I'm your boss, you know.'

There was an awkward silence while Tedder, in his shabby creased RAF battle-dress, sucked his unlit pipe and stared at the two of them reflectively. Montgomery bit his lip and said finally: 'I'm sorry, Ike.' The crisis had been overcome. The vital meeting could continue on a much calmer level.

Montgomery went on to detail the strategy which he thought would win the war in Europe and bring the conflict to an end before Christmas. As he saw it, he must be empowered to strike through Arnhem, Holland, where he would 'bounce' across the Rhine, the last great natural barrier into the Reich and circumvent the vaunted West Wall, Hitler's pre-war fortified line which ran along Germany's frontier with France and Belgium for five hundred miles. From there he would push forward on a narrow front into the heart of the Ruhr itself.

Tedder watched Eisenhowser's reaction. It was one of utter amazement. The broad-shouldered American from the mid-west had been working with Montgomery for two years now but he had never experienced anything like this before from the British officer. As Tedder recalled later: '(Ike thought) it was fantastic to talk of marching to Berlin with an army which was still drawing the great bulk of its supplies over the beaches north of Bayeux.' On that same day, Eisenhower confided to his office diary similar thoughts: 'Monty's suggestion is simple. *Give him everything, which is crazy!*' Thus the conference, which Montgomery had thought would decide the conduct of the rest of the war in North-West Europe, dragged on. But Montgomery's pleadings for his command to be given absolutely priority over Bradley's were in vain. In his account, written the same day to Chief of the Air Staff, Sir Charles Portal, Tedder summed it all up with: 'Montgomery made a great play over the word "priority", he insisted that in his interpretation, the word implied absolute priority, to the exclusion of all other operations, if necessary. Argument on such a basis was obviously futile, Eisenhower made it clear that he did not accept such an interpretation. Our fight must be with both hands at present, the moment for the left hook has not yet come and cannot come till Northern Army Group maintenance is securely based on the Channel Ports.'

Just before the two men parted, however, Eisenhower gave the British Commander a last chance, which he seized upon eagerly. General Eisenhower authorized Montgomery to go ahead with Operation MARKET GARDEN, saying that 'successful operations in that direction would open up wide possibilities for future action.'

The die had been cast. Eisenhower had approved the most bold and uncharacteristic operation the British Field Marshal had ever planned since he had first come into the limelight with his great victory at El Alamein; Britain's first in three long years of war. The airborne attack on Arnhem was on.

'Had the pious teetotalling Montgomery wobbled into SHAEF with a hangover, I could not have been more astonished than I was by the daring adventure he proposed!' was General Bradley's reaction when he first heard the news. 'For in contrast to the conservative tactics Montgomery ordinarily chose, the Arnhem attack was to be made over a sixty-mile carpet of airborne troops'. Although he was soon to object to it violently, because he felt it would cripple his own drive into Germany, he conceded that 'Monty's plan for Arnhem was one of the most imaginative of the war'.

In essence, Operation Market Garden – 'the springboard for a powerful full-blooded thrust to the heart of Germany' – as Montgomery called it, envisaged capturing the five bridges spanning the two canals and three rivers barring the road to Arnhem. From the present British frontline based on the Meuse–Escaut Canal, the attackers of the British Second Army would have to fight their way across the Wilhelmina Canal, twenty miles beyond the Dutch frontier, and the Zuid Willems Vaart Canal ten miles further north. Thereafter they would be faced by the Maas, the Waal and the Neder Rijn rivers. This was the 'Garden' part of the daring plan.

'Market' was even more ambitious. It visualized the dropping of three airborne divisions along that attack route: the US 101st Airborne, veteran of the Normandy landings, were to drop between Sindhoven and Uden to capture the two canal bridges and open up the road between them; the US 82nd Airborne, the USA's most experienced airborne division, once commanded by Bradley himself in 1941, to capture the Maas Bridge at Grave and the Waal Bridge at Nijmegen; while a third – the British 1st Airborne Division, which had taken such high losses at the Sicily landings the year before – would be dropped at Arnhem itself, sixty miles beyond the Second Army front to capture and hold the bridge across the 150 yard wide Neder Rijn.

It was a tall order, especially for the 'Red Devils', as the maroon-bereted paras of the 1st Airborne fondly believed the Germans called them. Ten thousand of them would land sixty miles deep within German-held territory at a spot that the Germans had to defend to the utmost if they did not want their whole border defensive system to crumble. But Montgomery had told Eisenhower specifically that he wanted the 1st Airborne to carry out the task (and not the US 101st as had been planned first). His reasons were obvious.

As Eisenhower told his Public Relations man, former radio executive Lieutenant-Commander Butcher later when the disaster

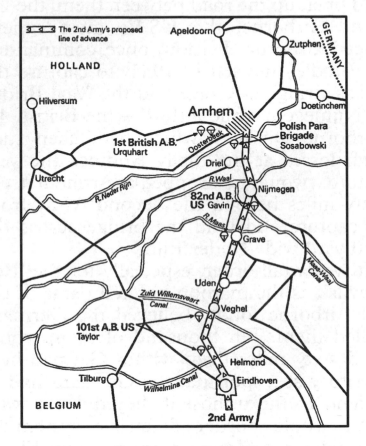

The 2nd Army's proposed line of advance

HOLLAND

GERMANY

Apeldoorn
Zutphen
Hilversum
Doetinchem
Arnhem
1st British A.B. Urquhart
Oosterbeek
Polish Para Brigade Sosabowski
Driel
Utrecht
R.Neder Rijn
R.Waal
82nd A.B. US Gavin
Nijmegen
R.Maas
Grave
Maas-Waal Canal
Uden
Zuid Willemsvaart Canal
Veghel
101st A.B. US Taylor
Helmond
Tilburg
Wilhelmina Canal
Eindhoven
BELGIUM
2nd Army

'I think we may be going one bridge too far ...' – Lt. Gen. 'Boy' Browning, Deputy-Commander Allied Airborne Army to Field Marshall Montgomery (Sept. 10th 1944)

had already occurred: 'The British had voluntarily insisted that their Airborne Divisions take the toughest and most advanced assignment. What would be the American reaction if either our 82nd or 101st Airborne had been assigned by Monty to the tough spot given the British airborne?'

In other words, if there was going to be a massacre of the troops on that last bridge, for the sake of US public opinion it would have to be of British troops and not American.

But then on that sunny Sunday afternoon, Field Marshal Montgomery was desperate. Time was running out, both for his country and for himself as a great commander. He was prepared to make the most terrible sacrifices to rescue the position.

Every war produces its own heroes; but it had taken three years of British defeats before Britain had produced this particular and peculiar military hero, with his austere habits, strange uniforms (the King himself had taken him to task for the sloppiness of his appearance) and even stranger attitudes. And it was these years of bitter defeat which had magnified Montgomery's status as a great captain in the eyes of the British people and himself after El Alamein. Now the non-smoking, non-drinking Bishop's son, whose appointment as Field Marshal had been signed by the King ten days earlier in

Churchill's bedroom, wanted the kudos of the final victory. He was to be the general who would lead the triumphant drive into the enemy capital. But it was not only personal ambition which drove Montgomery to take the decision that would risk the lives of 10,000 of Britain's most elite soldiers – so unlike his usual careful husbanding of his human resources. The most political of the Allied generals, he knew that Britain could not afford many more months of war. His political and military masters – Churchill and Sir Alan Brooke – had both made it quite clear to him that the manpower barrel was virtually scraped clean. Already he had been forced to 'cannibalise' one division to provide infantry reinforcements, and soon he would have to do the same thing to one of his best divisions, the 50th, which had served with him in the desert. And in the political battles to come after the shooting war, the British Premier, concerned to keep the Russians as far as possible out of Western Europe and maintain the British Empire, wanted to have the 'big battalions' on his side when it came to a showdown with his erstwhile allies, the Soviet dictator Stalin and the US President Roosevelt. Churchill, who had sworn that he had not become the 'King's First Minister' to 'preside over the dissolution of the British Empire', wanted the war in Europe finished by the end of 1944.

Thus when Montgomery faced the man who was to command the great new attack from the air that afternoon, there was no doubt in his own mind that if the British 1st Airborne Division were to be sacrificed, then it would be done so for the highest personal and political reasons.

Montgomery outlined the plan to him, then asked ex-Guardsman Lieutenant-General 'Boy' Browning, Deputy-Commander of the newly formed Allied Airborne Army: 'What do you think?'

The General, who was called by his 'Red Devils' the 'Father of the Airborne' because he had been connected with the British paras right from the start, asked how long his men would be expected to hold the Arnhem Bridge.

Montgomery did not hesitate. 'Two days,' he snapped briskly. 'They'll be up with you then.'

Browning hesitated for a moment and touched his trim Guards' moustache. 'We can hold it for four, sir,' he replied. 'But I think we might be going a bridge too far...'

3

Early that Sunday the First Airborne Division, spread out over the flat terrain of Lincolnshire and East Anglia, had stood down from Operation Comet, yet another plan of the sixteen for which they had been alerted on that hot, exciting, frustrating summer. Now the church parades were over and the men had thumbed their way down the neighbouring towns – Grantham, Spalding, Uppingham, Melton Mowbray – to enjoy the limited pleasures of English provincial towns in wartime.

Those who had been lucky enough to get 'their feet under the table' with some local girl or wife of a worker on Sunday shift were in bed or in the fields, as soon as possible, snatching the fleeting brief pleasures of war with greedy hands. Those less fortunate, went to the local 'Sally Ann' or YMCA canteens and stood in line for 'char and wads' and 'bangers and beans'. For some, who had gone to towns where the watch committees had relaxed their pre-war 'blue laws' sufficiently to allow the local cinemas to open to five, there was the opportunity to join the long afternoon queues waiting to see Noel Coward*'s This Happy Breed* in 'gorgeous technicolor' or Ann Ziegler and Webster Booth in *Demobbed;* 'a good hearty laugh for all'.

Everywhere, the middle-aged local police kept an eye on the maroon-bereted soldiers. They were universally well-liked. But they had a reputation for a rather carefree attiude to other people's property, as well as habit of going looking for 'Yanks' to beat up when they had a few pints of the weak, flat, wartime beer.

'Whenever there was a car or taxi missing in Grantham,' Corporal Wooten, a paratrooper regimental policeman recalls, 'the police would come out to our camp looking for it. Once a local bus inspector told a group of our chaps there was no bus to take them back to camp. So they simply pinched his bus and parked it on the square. Naturally there were charges all round, but when Boy Browning heard about it, he'd freed the lot of them in ten minutes. He said, "They're trained to get from point A to point B the quickest way possible. So they stole a bus." And that was that.'

But on this lazy Sunday afternoon, after forty-eight hours of being 'stood to', the young men of the First Airborne were in no mood for trouble. They were glad to be out of their guarded camps, where security was much tighter than anywhere else in the British Army, and enjoying themselves, even in the antiseptic atmosphere of the local 'Sally Ann' canteen. They savoured this time out of war.

Their officers were little different. Major 'Boy' Wilson, the tough, middle-aged CO of the 21st Independent Para Company, the élite unit which would guide in the rest of the Division, had nipped off home to take

31

lunch with his family. Lieutenant-Colonel C.B. Mackenzie, GSO I(Ops), the divisional commander's chief of staff officer, had gone boating on the Thames with a group of other staff officers. At the three brigade headquarters, the brigadiers enjoyed a lazy lunch with their staffs, talking over the current fighting in far-off Belgium and cursing their own division, which had not seen action since the invasion of Sicily and the follow-up in Italy the previous summer, but seemed fated to sit out the rest of the war in the flat peaceful reaches of Eastern England. And then suddenly the telephones started to sound the alarm everywhere. Excited dispatch riders roared down dusty lanes bearing their urgent summons. Jeep drivers careened into country drive-ways at impossible speeds to fetch their masters. All staff officers and senior commanders were required back at Divisional HQ at once. The First Airborne had been given a new operation by no other person than Field Marshal Montgomery himself!

They met at General Roy Urquhart's tactical headquarters at Moor Park, in the sparsely furnished but elegant pillared clubhouse, which had been built by a successful specu-lator in the 18th century South Sea Bubble. Two American para generals, the tremen-dously fit and experienced General 'Slim

32

Jim' Gavin, the commander of the 82nd Airborne; tough-looking General Taylor, one day to be head of the US Army, ambassador to France and adviser to President Kennedy, now head of the 'Screaming Eagles', the 101st Airborne; and General Roy Urquhart, a big 42-year-old Scot who had taken over the First Airborne at the beginning of the year although he'd never made a paradrop in his life and was inclined to air sickness.

'Boy' Browning did not waste time. Swiftly he sketched the various roles which would change all their lives dramatically. For the Americans the operation would set the seal on their professional-competency and put them on the road to the highest offices their Army could offer; for Urquhart it would mean an end to his professional career and the lifelong, nagging thought that somehow or other he had failed.

But on that Sunday evening, with no sound from outside save the tread of the sentries who had sealed off the whole area, there was no time for such considerations. Time was of the essence and much had to be done in the next few hours. When he had finished with the two Americans, Browning drew a grandiose circle – his third – on the talc-covered map of Holland and fixing Urquhart with his hard, direct gaze, he snapped; 'Arnhem Bridge – *and hold it!*'

The big Scot nodded, but said nothing.

But as Browning continued with his exposé, Urquhart glanced at the two American generals sitting beside him and wondered if they were surprised as he was that such a hazardous plan should have come from the cautious Montgomery. Apparently they weren't; or if they were, their tense faces revealed nothing of it. Accordingly he congratulated himself on the fact that his own division had been picked for the most dangerous assignment and listened to the rest of Browning's clipped explanation of Market.

Just before the meeting broke up for the generals to start briefing their own staffs, already assembling outside, Browning informed Urquhart that he had persuaded the RAF to agree to a daylight operation. Although the head of the First Airborne welcomed the chance to land his Division by daylight instead of at night, there was a catch. Because of the limited number of aircraft available, the 101st and 82nd would go in one lift, but his own Division would be forced to do the op in three lifts – 'in penny packets', the dread of all British commanders ever since they had learned the danger of such tactics at their first staff college course. When he had recovered from the shock of the announcement, Urquhart protested against Browning's decision, only to be told firmly: 'It's got to be bottom to top, *otherwise you'd stand a chance of being massacred'*. They were to be prophetic words.

On Tuesday evening, September 12th, the popular Divisional Commander, who had been so surprised when he had been offered the First Airborne nine months before, assembled his brigadiers and their staffs for the initial briefing on the Arnhem operation. There were four of them: Gerald Lathbury, languid but extremely intelligent, the CO of the First Parachute Brigade; Pip Hicks, the oldest man in the Division at 49, a solemn, stolid infantryman who commanded the First Airlanding Brigade; and Shan Hackett, an ex-Hussar, who had come to the paras from the special forces in the desert, a sharp, alert personality, with a taste for collecting university degrees and – in contrast – with the pug nose of a boxer. There was also the commander of the attached Polish Para Brigade, Sosabowski, a keen-eyed, moustached former professor of the Warsaw War Academy, who was to become the plan's sharpest critic. As he observed his British colleagues, the one whose reputation would be destroyed before the month was out, the other who would be paralysed, and the remaining two who would become hunted fugitives from the German enemy – he could not help thinking that Urquhart and his British brigadiers were unduly confident. As he wrote afterwards: 'Most of them sat nonchalantly with legs crossed, looking rather bored and waiting for the conference to end.'

But Urquhart could not deal with them as quickly as Browning had dealt with his divisional commanders. The elegant ex-Guardsman had posed the problem very simply, but the answers to that problem were anything but simple. He knew, for instance, General Gavin's maxim that 'it is in general better to take landing losses and land on the objective in order to reach the objective': a maxim which had been proved in Sicily the year before, when the First Airborne had taken heavy losses because of a poor choice of landing zones having been made.

As he told his commanders, he was concerned to get as much of the division down at Arnhem 'all in one piece and able to function properly on landing', particularly as the First would be 'functioning some 60 or 70 miles away from our nearest troops'. But that desire was frustrated by the lack of aircraft. He would have to drop Lathbury's 1st Para Brigade and land most of the 1st Air Landing Brigade's gliders under Hicks on the first day. They would be followed by Hackett's 4th and the rest of the Air Landing Brigade on the second day. Sosabowski would come in on the third day.

Hackett, who had already warned his three battalion commanders to expect heavy casualties, frowned but said nothing as

Urquhart went on to explain the second major problem facing the division. He said he would 'have liked to put in troops on both sides of the river and as close as possible to the main bridge'. But there was a catch. The RAF had reported that the flak about the bridge was 'almost prohibitive' and they could not drop troops there. In addition, agents of British Intelligence and the Dutch Resistance had pointed out that the low-lying polderland around the bridge was swampy and cut up by deep ditches: both hazards for paratroopers and gliders. Hence he had decided that the division's dropping zones would have to be on the high, dry ground to the west of the town of Arnhem, and seven miles away from the objective!

Even the most humble of General Urquhart's paras remember vividly the shock they received when they heard the distance from the DZ to the Arnhem Bridge. Thirty years later ex-Corporal Dukes of the 1st Parachute Battalion, confined today to a wheelchair, recalls: 'When I heard that from the CO, I thought *Christ!*' Ex-RSM 'Chalky' White of the 10th Parachute Battalion had similar feelings. 'My battalion never even got into Arnhem, not to mention never seeing the bridge itself'. The regular soldier, whose reward from Arnhem was a bad wound, eight months in a German POW camp and on his return, the offer of a transfer to the

Pioneer Corps or a discharge from the Army, says today: 'And no wonder, the distance we dropped from the objective!'

But in the crowded ops room that Tuesday evening, the assembled brigadiers and their staffs did not seem to notice the distance. As Urquhart records: 'Generally, the brigadiers appeared not unhappy with the task confronting us'. Yet one problem did worry all of them: the lack of intelligence. In spite of the prophetic warnings from Urquhart's namesake at 1st Allied Airborne HQ, Major Brian Urquhart, that the Division could expect stiff resistance, the Headquarters thought that there was no 'direct evidence that the area Arnhem/Nijmegan' was 'manned by much more than the considerable flak defences already known to exist'. Everything pointed to the area – a main German Army training ground – being defended by 'nothing larger than a brigade with a few guns and tanks'.

Privately, Urquhart knew that Montgomery's experts in Brussels dare include nothing in the Intelligence picture which might tempt Eisenhower to cancel the daring operation or even simply 'mar the optimism prevailing across the Channel' (as the big Scot was to write much later). So, knowing that his own intelligence staff were feverishly 'scratching around for morsels of information' on the enemy without too much success and that his men were impatient for a fight after a year without any action, he allowed himself to accept his Headquarter's optimistic assessment of the expected German resistance.

Thus, as the conference came to an end, the enemy was conveniently forgotten, just as it had been at the discussion of Market's predecessor when General Sosobowski had vehemently interrupted Headquarters' unrealistic appreciation of the situation on the ground with a heavily accented, passionate 'But the Germans, General ... the Germans!'

As the commanders filed out followed by their staffs into the warm autumn night, 'that particular animal' – the name they liked to use for the German enemy – seemed to be the least of their worries. It was to be a fatal oversight, which they would pay for in shame, disgrace and blood.

4

Almost as the conference in England ended, a 30-year-old Dutchman, with the arms of a giant and the diminutive torso of a child, which had gained for him the cover-name of 'King Kong' in the Dutch Underground, swaggered into the German Headquarters at Vught with the greatest piece of information of his long and dirty career as a double agent for both the British and the Germans: he had learned from his sources in American-occupied Liège that the British Second Army was standing by to push into Holland. Indeed his new masters, the Allies, had sent him through the lines at Eindhoven, with an order in his pocket for the head of the Dutch Resistance there to go into action early on Sunday morning, the 17th September: the day on which the British would begin their attack. But the agent, whose own German spymaster described as 'a double-dyed and dangerous menace, on whom it is impossible to rely', knew more than that. He had information that British and American para-chute divisions were standing by in England for a big airborne operation.

'King Kong' had met the Third Reich's arch spymaster, Colonel Giskes, the tall, sar-donic, humorous and most successful spy catcher of the whole *Abwehr*, in Brussels six months before.

'King Kong', whose real name was Chris-tiaan Lindemans, was a Dutch civil servant from Rotterdam and an important member of the Dutch Resistance. But in March 1944 he wanted to change sides, for, as he told the man who had been hunting him for so long: 'I have worked for the English Secret Service since the spring of 1940. For the last six months I have brought in my youngest brother to assist in getting English airmen out of the country. He has been discovered, arrested by the SIPO (German Security Police) and is now under sentence of death pronounced by a German military court. I feel myself responsible for my bother's fate, since it was I who introduced him to this work. If you can arrange to have my brother freed, I am ready to hand over the whole of my knowledge of the Allied Secret Services. I know the Underground from the North Sea to the Spanish frontier. You may assume that after five years of work for the Allies I have experience and contacts which will be of great value to you.'

Hermann Giskes, the former wine sales-man who had been doing deals like this since he had bribed Hooper, a naturalised Brit-isher to betray the Continental agents of the MI6 to him, looked at Christiaan's fists, which lay on the table in front of him 'like a pair of blacksmith's hammers', and then flashed a look at the Dutchman's expectant blue eyes beneath a 'broad, low, heavy fore-head'. 'I do not know your brother's case,' he began at last. 'If he has been sentenced simply for the crime of helping prisoners to escape, I think I can promise you that we can have him set free... If you can satisfy me that you are playing us no tricks and if the information which you give us proves that you are the man you make yourself out to be, you may rely on it that your brother will be free in a week, at the latest.'

'King-Kong', whom Giskes code-named 'CC' by doubling the initial of his Christian name, proved he was genuine enough. Three days later 'CC' produced a report that was a convincing picture of every kind of secret Allied operation within Occupied Europe. Courier-lines, safe houses, frontier crossing spots, agents' names by the hundred: the whole escape network. Giskes had been convinced. 'CC's' brother had been released and 'CC' assigned to Major Wiesekoetter – Giskes' second-in-command – as an agent.

Thereafter 'CC' worked as hard for the Germans as he had done previously for the British until the 1st September 1944 when Giskes met him during the great German retreat eastwards and ordered him to remain behind in the Belgian city of Liège. There he was 'to establish contact with the Intelligence of the advancing English army immediately after the occupation of the capital'. The spy and his old fox of a master agreed that 'CC' should get himself employed by the English as a forward agent, so as to enable him to get back to Germany through the lines at the earliest possible moment, using the code-word 'Dr Gerhardts'.

Now 'CC' had appeared on the German front running along the Meuse–Escaut Canal shouting the password. It had taken him rapidly to a German Army headquarters, located in a country cottage at Vught, south of S' Hertogenbosch. 'CC' could not have found a more suitable place to deliver his vital information; for the headquarters belonged to no other a person than General Kurt Student, the Father of the German Airborne, the Conqueror of Crete and the man, who in 1940 had done exactly what Urquhart's paratroopers hoped to do – capture the vital bridges over the waterways barring the ground forces' drive into the heart of Holland. By sheer chance the double agent had found the German general best able to fight off an airborne landing.

Today we do not know what 'CC' told Student's staff officers, or whether they believed what they heard from the repulsive-looking Dutch giant. We do know that he passed on his key information to his chief Major Wiesekoetter the following morning, but by the time Giskes received the latter's report, 'CC' had vanished again. One month later he would vanish for good, probably put to death – slowly – at the hands of the Belgian Underground men who captured him on 23rd November 1944.

For his part, General Student maintains that he learned of the operation from a captured plan found on the body of a dead American officer a few hours after the landing had taken place. Conveniently enough for the Hero of Crete, the glider concerned came down just near Vught and deposited the dead officer virtually on his own doorstep. But whether General Student was trying to protect 'CC' or not, it was becoming quite clear in German quarters that something was in the offing in the Arnhem area.

On the early afternoon of that same day when 'CC' made his last report to Wiesekoetter a young German radio operator of the Luftwaffe Radio Interception Service started getting a lot of 'traffic' on an RAF network which he had not previously encountered. He was experienced enough to realise what he had picked up: a 'tuningin' test of aircraft radio sets, preceding an operation. It was clear that the RAF was preparing for another large scale mission. The problem was where.

But even that problem was solved two hours later for German Intelligence in the Arnhem area. Around two o'clock, two British aircraft appeared over both Nijmegan and Arnhem, and began a lengthy reconnaissance of the bridge area. In itself, their appearance would not have aroused the German's suspicions, save for one thing. During the whole course of their flight, they were protected by over thirty Marauders of the US Air Force.

Later the German Command in Holland was to attribute this tremendously strong escort to the fact that a personal reconnaissance of the area was being carried out by the commanders of the attacking divisions. If this were really the case, General Urquhart of the First British Airborne was not with them. On that Friday afternoon, while his troops were beginning to be briefed for the great operation on their airfields and the gliders were being loaded, he had taken out his golf clubs and was playing a few of the holes still usable at Moor Park. He was just about to putt at one of them when his Chief-of-Staff Lieutenant-Colonel Charles Mackenzie appeared at the edge of the green looking worried. But he seemed prepared to wait until his CO had finished his putt.

'Well, what is it, Charles?' Urquhart asked. 'Go on talking.'

Hurriedly Mackenzie explained that there had been a reduction in the number of gliders which could be used in the drop and that the Division would have to cut the load taken on the first lift.

Urquhart's reaction was immediate: 'Whatever is to be sacrificed, Charles,' he told his subordinate, 'it must not be anti-tank guns.'

As Urquhart was to write many years later: 'We would need every anti-tank weapon we could lay our hands on.' He did not know until it was too late how overwhelmingly right he was. For unknown to him, that day the tanks and self-propelled guns of the Second SS Panzer Corps, commanded by General Willi Bittrich, a stiff-backed regular officer, were already in position in Arnhem itself and in the woods to the north-east of the Dutch city. Now when the British did begin to drop from the skies – wherever it might be in that part of Holland – Field Marshal Model, billeted in a white-washed hotel in Oosterbeek, would not only have Student's First Parachute Army to bar the advance of Montgomery's second Army from the Meuse–Escaut Canal, he would also have under his command Bittrich's highly mobile, experienced and élite two SS divisions. The situation was building up for a disaster.

5

But German Intelligence was not alone in its successful spotting of an impending large scale land-and-airborne operation somewhere in Holland. British Secret Intelligence (MI6), that mysterious espionage organisation run by 'C' from its white stucco headquarters in Queen Anne's Gate, had already noted the German build-up in the Arnhem area. 'Zero C', Head of Air Intelligence, Group Captain Winterbotham, who had been in the MI6 for nearly fourteen years, remembers today: 'I saw from the agents' reports from Holland that a number of units were refitting in the vicinity of Arnhem. They mentioned the 9th and 10th Panzer Divisions which had been at Falaise. SHAEF separately received reports of parts of Panzer Army from Falaise in Arnhem area. All this information must at once have been passed to 21st Army Group.'

But agents' reports were notoriously unreliable and old hands like 'C' and 'Zero C' would not have paid too much attention to them, save for one other thing. Britain's greatest war-winning Secret Intelligence unit, code-named 'Ultra', the full details of which are still classified to this day, had already reported in the first week of September – even before Eisenhower had accepted Montgomery's bold plan – that the escapees from Falaise were retreating towards Holland, and that there were thirty thousand of them. And 'Ultra' was never wrong.

'Ultra' began by sheer chance. In 1939 a disgruntled Polish mechanic, who had been working in a Berlin factory, reported to Polish Intelligence in Warsaw that he had been employed making coding machines, before he had decided to come home. The Polish officers listened politely to his story and then sat up with a start when he mentioned the name of the coding machine the factory was manufacturing. The Enigma.

The mechanic had actually worked on Germany's most highly guarded secret: the coding machine which was being issued to all German commands, from division right up to Hitler's own headquarters, for the foolproof encoding of top secret messages. Furthermore the mechanic, who for security reasons had only been allowed to work on one part of the top secret machine, had kept his eyes open and believed now that he could reconstruct the whole machine. But by this time, the Poles, already working closely together with their future British intelligence allies, were uncertain about their own security. Admiral Canaris's *Abwehr* agents were everywhere in Poland. As a result they appealed to 'C'.

'C' reacted immediately. The Pole was smuggled out of Poland and taken to Paris, where under the supervision of the MI6's Parisian resident Bill Dunderdale, he reconstructed the Enigma in wood. But 'C' was not completely satisfied with the model which reminded 'Zero C' of a 'pianola' when he and 'C' viewed it for the first time in Queen Anne's Gate. He wanted the real thing. Therefore, as time began to run out, and the German threat loomed ever larger, the Polish Secret Service and their Swedish helpers in Berlin set about stealing a complete Enigma. Amazingly enough, they succeeded, and in the summer of 1939 the coding-machine was handed over to the MI6 representative who had come to a lonely Polish castle to fetch it.

That man was a Scottish ex-school teacher called Lieutenant-Commander Alastair Denniston, who had been working in Intelligence, primarily de-coding enemy messages, since 1914 when he had left his teaching job as Osborne. Now his experts of the Government Code and Cypher School, nicknamed 'the Golf Club and Chess Society', located at Bletchley Park, Buckinghamshire, went to work to break the Enigma's secrets. The results were disappointing. They told 'Zero C' it would take five months under existing circumstances to decode a single message. 'Zero C's' response was: 'Why not attempt to invent a machine to decode what another machine encoded?'

The suggestion was taken up. In the first winter of the Phoney War post office engineers worked feverishly to invent such a machine – one of the world's first computers – and in February 1940, the first decoding machines were available in London. Now Prime Minister Churchill who was to use the Bletchley operation as his most successful secret source of information throughout the war, was in a position to know what Hitler was going to do, before even the most senior

Nazi generals – as long as operational orders were encoded by the Enigma (and the Germans relied exclusively on the supposedly foolproof machine right to the very end).

Just before Montgomery was sent out to Africa in 1942 to command the Eighth Army, he was let into the secret of this tremendous source of information – information restricted to Army commanders only. He was deeply impressed and demanded that the information supplied by the 'Ultra' should be given to him exclusively. In the end Churchill had to intervene and make it clear to the future hero of El Alamein that this could not be. Although 'Ultra' supplied Montgomery with the complete, detailed German Order-of-Battle prior to El Alamein, he lost enthusiasm for the whole operation, leaving his Chief-of-Intelligence to deal with the 'Ultra' station which was attached to his own headquarters. But there is no doubt that he and his most senior subordinate commander General Dempsey, the head of the British Second Army, were well informed of the progress of the Second SS Panzer Corps as it passed from Amiens to St Quentin, and from France into Belgium near Albert, on the 1st September 1944, until it finally halted at Arnhem for refitting with new tanks.

On the 10th September, the very day on which Montgomery convinced Eisenhower that the great plan should be put into operation, 'Bimbo' Dempsey went to Montgomery's Brussels 'CP' to warn him of German resistance and suggest that the new offensive should be directed eastwards to the Rhine near Wessel, instead of northwards. Montgomery turned down the alteration, although he knew the Second SS Corps was there. In his own words: 'The second SS Panzer Corps was refitting in the Arnhem area, having limped up there after its mauling in Normandy. *We knew it was there.*' (My italics.)

Why then did the British commander allow his lightly-armed paras to drop so far ahead of the Second Army, when he had certain knowledge that German armour was present? Why indeed? His own lame explanation is that 'We were wrong in supposing that it could not fight effectively; its battle state was far beyond our expectation. It was quickly brought into action against the First Airborne Division.'

Why, too, did he not inform General Brian Horrocks, commander of the second Army's leading corps, which was to attempt the sixty-mile link-up dash to Arnhem? For the latter was to write: 'Quite unknown to me, and, as far as I can make out, also to our own Intelligence service, a few days before the 9th and 10th SS Panzer Divisions had arrived in the Zutphen area to refit.'

51

The reason is obvious. On the 11th September he had wired Eisenhower: he had not sufficient supplies to ensure an early start of Market Garden. Alarmed, Eisenhower had sent his red-headed, evil-tempered Chief-of-Staff Bedell Smith, who often boasted that 'someone had to be a sonuvabitch around these headquarters' to see the British Commander. At Brussels Bedell Smith had promised Montgomery all possible support for his operation and the Britisher thereupon agreed to begin his daring attack on Sunday 17th September. On the next day (13th Sept) Eisenhower confirmed Smith's offer, adding:

'Naturally, these measures are emergency ones and must be temporary but I am willing to give effect to them for a limited time to enable you to cross the Rhine and capture the approaches to Antwerp... The arrangement can continue until about the first of October; by then it is anticipated you will have reached your initial objective.'

Eisenhower's letter must have filled Montgomery with both elation and apprehension. He had got his way with the Allies' major supply and military effort being directed to his front for the push to Arnhem, but the measures taken were 'emergency ones and must be temporary'. What if he were forced to cancel Market Garden because of the new opposition reported by Intelligence? Would not Eisenhower, already under pressure from the Bradley-Patton team, turn to other solutions within the 12th US Army Group's area of operations? Might he not be left out in the cold, with the kudos of final victory going to those American generals whom he despised as new boys and amateurs? What was he to do? In the end he did nothing.

6

At ten thirty on the morning of Saturday 16th September, the brass of Thirty Corps jostled each other outside the dilapidated cinema in the little Belgian mining town of Leopoldsburg to show their passes – even the highest ranking of them – to hard-eyed, suspicious redcaps.

But the officers of the Guards Armoured Division, with the eye in its shield divisional patch that was supposed to wink when it saw a virgin 'and it hasn't winked yet', and those of the 43rd Infantry Division, called the 'Wessex' from its 'W'-shaped patch, were not lining up to see a film. They were running the MPs' gauntlet to hear their Corps Commander General Horrocks explain the details of Second Army's hush-hush new plan – Garden.

Horrocks – 'Jorrocks' to his men – the tall, lean general with his large beak of a nose dominating his ascetic, almost ecclesiastical face, arrived promptly at eleven. As he stood in front of a map of North Belgium hanging from the screen that had once amused miners with the pre-war goings-on of Pepe Le Moko, alias Charles Boyer, and French workers who turned out to be Jean Gabin, he launched into his exposé with characteristic style.

'This is a tale you will tell your grandchildren,' he announced prodding the map with his pointer, 'and mighty bored they'll be!'

His audience, including General Thomas of the 43rd and General Adair of the Guards Armoured, laughed dutifully. 'Jorrocks' was in fine form, they told themselves, using his usual mixture of hard facts, theatricality and personal hypnotism to convince his audience of the one hundred per cent certainty of his plans.

In that rapid manner of his, complete with a large number of un-English gestures with his hands, Horrocks detailed the tasks facing the Corps. The Guards Armoured Division would open the attack, with the Irish Guards in the van. It would be the Micks' job to cross 'Joe's Bridge', captured six days before and start the drive to the Dutch frontier where they would link up with the first airborne unit, Taylor's 'Screaming Eagles'.

Horrocks allowed a moment for the

information to sink in. Most of the regular officers present were not used to his quick nervous way of speech; it contrasted strongly with their own languid, tongue-tied style of presentation. The Guards, he added, would be given twelve hours to achieve the link-up.

The advance would continue to Nijmegen, where it was hoped the 'all American Division' – Gavin's 82nd – would have already captured the bridges across the Meuse and Waal undamaged. This stage would take a further twenty-four hours. If the key bridges were undamaged, Horrocks explained, the Guards followed by Thomas's 43rd, would race for Arnhem. There, in the area between Nunspeet and Apeldoorn, the Guards would cut West Holland's connections with the north of the country while the 43rd would pass over the Arnhem bridge and establish a bridgehead on the east bank of the river. The estimated time for this last stage would be a further twenty-four hours. Thus, Horrocks concluded, 30 Corps would link-up with the First Airborne Division within two days of starting Garden, which would commence as soon as Colonel Joe's Micks spotted the Airborne's first planes heading for their dropping zones.

Even if the bridges were blown, 30 Corps was prepared. Thirteen hundred vehicles were already busily engaged bringing bridging equipment from the Normandy dumps and depositing it in the very town they were presently meeting. They had even dismantled bridges across the River Seine to provide sufficient material.

Statistic followed statistic, emphasized by a tap of the big pointer on the map or a dynamic wave of Horrocks' free hand. 'River Meuse Group ... 878 vehicles ... Meuse-Waal Canal – 483 vehicles ... River Waal Group – 380 ... River Neder Rijn – 536 ... 766 of these vehicles earmarked for the advance beyond Arnhem...' And all of them to drive down one single *pavé* road, bordered by flat marshy, heavily wooded country which could be easily defended by mere handfuls of determined men. As the writer of the Guards Armoured history, who was present at that tremendous *tour de force* given by the Corps Commander on that Saturday morning, was to comment much later about the Irish Guards' chances: 'On the whole, it would be easier for a rich man to get into heaven...'

The Moor Park Airborne HQ was virtually deserted now. The staffs had dispersed to the battalion areas and airfields, where the paratroopers were already confined to camp to ensure complete security. In the heavily guarded intelligence nissen huts of the First Parachute Brigade, the 'Red Devils' viewed the photos and mock-ups of their objectives: for Frost's 2nd Battalion and Major Freddie Gough's Reconnaissance Squadron, it would be the key bridge itself, supported by Colonel Dobbie's 1st Para which would make for the high ground north of the town, while Colonel Fitch's 3rd would take the higher road from Heelsum into Arnhem, move on the bridge from the north and strengthen the bridge defence on the north east.

The capture of the bridge then depended upon silver-haired Freddie Gough's 'recce boys' and Colonel Frost's veterans of the 2nd Battalion. But the men of 'JD's' command thought there 'was nothing in it'. They were tough, well trained and completely convinced that the CO would see them through. Hadn't he said to them on parade, the day before, as they had lined up in the park of the house outside Grantham which had once belonged to Sir Isaac Newton: 'I know you'll do it, men?' No more was needed from the six-foot tall, slow-speaking, slow-moving Colonel who had been with the paras almost from the start.

His men adored him. Ulsterman and regular soldier Private Tucker, who had joined the Airborne after Dunkirk because 'they got an extra bob a day', thought he was 'one of the best'. A few weeks before when Tucker had beaten up two 'Yanks' who had tried to get fresh with his girl in a

Grantham dance-hall, RSM Strachan had marched him in front of the CO for sentencing. Frost had listened attentively, then asked: 'Did you win the fight?'

Puzzled, the dark-haired, quick-tempered Ulsterman had answered: 'Yessir.'

Frost had smiled slightly: 'Fine – seven days! But if you'd lost, Tucker, I'd have given you fourteen days.'

They were eager to go, too. Private James Sims remembers how, when the Battalion had heard at a RAF Regiment camp (where they were going over an assault course) that their rivals, the British Sixth Airborne Division, had jumped into France on D-Day, we 'rioted and protested at not being there. Only the assurances of our officers that we were being kept for something special mollified the angry paras. The "something special" turned out to be Arnhem'.

But if the men of the key battalion – the 2nd – were not worried about the task before them on the morrow, some of the others were. Sergeant Major 'Chalky' White of the 10th Battalion, belonging to Brigadier Hackett's Fourth Parachute Brigade, was, for one. Since the Battalion had returned from Italy in December 1943 it had never trained together in anything stronger than a company. Nor had it any experience of fighting in the type of country it would soon encounter – built-up areas and woods. It was used to the wide-open vistas. But the stocky ex-Rifleman with twelve years service behind him, consoled himself with the thought that the op might yet well be called off, as so many had been in these last few months. As he told anxious enquirers that day: 'Believe nothing until I tell you to prime your grenades'. But he would have worried more if he had known just how badly briefed most of the men in the 4th Parachute Brigade ('not an easy command' as Urquhart himself admitted) were. As one of them, another regular soldier, Corporal Burrows remembers today: 'We were all ready to go. Tremendously keen. The CO had told us the armour would link up with us within 24 hours. But we knew nothing. We had to depend upon the officers completely.'

What would happen, however, if and when those officers were no longer there to guide and lead them? No one in the sealed-off encampments of the 4th Parachute Brigade apparently cared to ask that question, in spite of their commander's warning to his battalion colonels to expect 'heavy casualties'.

Thus they waited – the 10,000 picked men of the 1st British Airborne Division, volunteers all and the cream of the British Army – cleaning and oiling their weapons, sharpening their fighting knives, changing into clean underwear in case they were hit and tucking metal issue shaving mirrors into the left-hand pockets of their camouflaged jumping smocks. For they had all heard the tale of the squaddie in another battalion – it was always another battalion – whose mirror had saved him from a 'Jerry bullet with his number on it'. Sometimes it was a Bible, but not often. They prepared and waited for their own particular rendezvous with destiny.

General Urquhart spent the last afternoon flying down to the West Country where his own take-off field was located. Looking out of the window of his Oxford in the fading light, he could see the airfields from which his men would be flying in the morning. 'The tugs and gliders with their freshly painted white stripes across wings and fuselage,' he thought, 'resembled swarms of patient bees.'

On landing, he played a game of bridge and a game of poker before retiring to sleep soundly for the night.

ONE:
THE BATTLE OF THE BRIDGE

(Sunday, 17th Sept, 1944–Thursday, 21st Sept, 1944)

DAY ONE

'This seems a pretty quiet area. Suppose we get out here!'

*Maj. 'Boy'Wilson, CO 21st
Independent Para. Company.*

Sunday. The weather was warm and sunny. Over the DZ the forecast was excellent. Clear and light winds: excellent dropping conditions.

On their score of fields, the paras lolled on the grass, backs resting on their chutes, smoking, chatting quietly and reading the Sunday papers. The *News of the World* informed them that Hitler's batman had been captured at Ghent the previous day. He had told his interrogators that his former boss 'alternates between kindness and brutality and is very nervous ... and he is not averse to blondes. One of them is a typist who visits him in a special car.' *The Empire News,* being the newspaper it was, steered clear of the sex stories which were a feature of the what the paras called 'Part Two Orders'. It reported that 'Monty's pullover, lost in the withdrawal of 1940', had been just returned to him at

63

Louvain. He was now 'wearing it again'. For those officers who were inclined to higher things, the *Observer* warned that 'returning evacuees had been hit by flying bombs' and that motor shares had fallen.

Here and there the exhibitionists and company jokers tried to raise a laugh. 'Guv Beech', the PT instructor of Colonel Dobie's First Battalion, walked down the flight line at Grantham Field, wearing 'his well-known opera hat which he kept taking off à la Winston Churchill' and bowing to the men lying in the dry dusty grass on both sides.

The only Canadian officer of the same battalion Lieutenant Leo Heaps was chatting with the American major who was going to fly them to Arnhem.

'I'll be taking you in about seven hundred,' the Major explained, 'and I'll give you the green light about six hundred and fifty. You should all be out at four hundred.' He smiled and added: 'I've been on lots of drops before and I haven't missed my target yet.'

Confident that the pilot meant what he said, Lieutenant Heaps and his stick sat down on the grass again. Photographers from the US Signal Corps were beginning to snap shots of them now for the papers and the official record. The admiring USAF ground crews started to pester the soldiers with all sorts of questions. To Heaps 'it all seemed like a football game before the kick off'.

Private Cardale of the Second Battalion – one day to be a clergyman – was worried, however. About his pipes. Cardale, who had only been informed the night before that he was going on the op, knew that drops played hell with pipes. For that reason he was taking two with him, plus fourteen ounces of tobacco, boiled sweets, ration chocolate and two twenty-four hour compo ration boxes, holding 'dog biscuits', as the paras called them, dehydrated meat, pressed oats and teacubes. Nor was Private Cardale, who had worked the 2nd's switchboard, the only one in the Battalion who had not expected to be there that pleasant Sunday morning.

Another was Private 'Smudger' Smith. A veteran of Sicily, he had proclaimed back in the UK he had had enough of 'Hermann's Big Beefy Bastards' and had gone 'on the trot' to Blackpool. Finally he had surrendered himself to the MPs and had been given eighty-four days' detention. But now, as he was proclaiming loudly to anyone who cared to listen: 'That bastard Browning pulled us out of the glasshouse!'

Just as the Third Parachute Battalion at Saltby was being issued with two cheese and bully sandwiches plus a cup of tea – not many of them had touched their early breakfasts – General Urquhart started to look over his men at his own field. Although he had not liked it when Horrocks had first remarked – 'your men are killers' – this lazy Sunday morning, they did look like 'a force that would be capable of big things against the enemy' in their camouflaged jump smocks and leaf-covered crash helmets. He walked over to Major 'Boy' Wilson, whose 21st Independent Company, which included twenty-five German-Jewish refugees, would be the first to drop. Urquhart knew that the ebullient, grey-haired 'Boy' Wilson was much too old for jumping and that he had a defective ear, which really should have kept him out of the paras; but Wilson simply exuded confidence and assertiveness. When Urquhart had first met him, he'd said:

'Ah Wilson, I understand you bounce off everybody.' With the typical aggressiveness of a small man, the CO of the 21st path-finder force had replied,

'Yessir. I have an independent unit and I'm considered to be rather independent.'

Now the 45-year-old Major, whose 186 men had captured the Italian port of Bari, was his usual buoyant self. Indeed that morning the Divisional Commander felt he 'was positively boyish now that he was about to set off in the van of the armada'.

As the C-47s, which would take Wilson's force started to rev up their twin engines and here and there paras began chalking slogans

66

on their planes 'Up with the Reds!... Up with the frauleins' skirts!' Urquhart strolled over to Colonel Mackenzie. As a precaution he mentioned to his chief staff officer that if he were knocked out, Brigadier Lathbury should take over. If he were hit, then Pip Hicks and Hackett would succeed in that order. A chance decision, but one which was soon to cause a great deal of trouble.

A little later he climbed into his Horsa glider, piloted by Colonel Iain Murray, commander of one of the two glider wings involved. Hancock, the little Cornish batman who had been with Urquhart since 1941, handed him his shoulder pack before he strapped himself in and swallowed his anti-airsick pill. Suddenly Urquhart felt a tug as the glider took the strain. Hancock flung an anxious glance at his master. General Urquhart knew what it meant. Hancock was worried that the commander of First British Airborne Division was going to be violently sick.

In Holland it was midday. At his headquarters in Oosterbeek, soon to become the 1st Airborne Division's dropping zone, the waiters, white jackets over their field-grey uniform, were setting the tables for lunch, while Field Marshal Model, who commanded Army Group B, enjoyed a preluncheon drink with his officers in the

Kasino. Colonel-General Kurt Student, commander of the 1st Para Army, whose balding head still bore the red scar of the wound he had received during his own airborne capture of Rotterdam four years before, had already commenced lunch in his whitewashed cottage at Vught.

Colonel Harzer, acting divisional commander of the *Hohenstaufen,* one of the two divisions belonging to Bittrich's 2nd SS Panzer Corps, was making a presentation to Major Graebner of the Division's Reconnaissance Battalion at Veluwe. Graebner had won the Knight's Cross in France before the debacle and now the 500 strong unit was lined up in front of its recce cars and half-tracks to hear a speech in which Harzer, a tough determined man, praised the 'bravery of the troops and their commander Graebner', before pinning the coveted black and white decoration on his breast. Soon they would go off to the *Kasino* to eat the traditional Germany Army's lunch of green pea soup. If they were lucky, they would have a few chunks of pork in it. A soldier always needed 'something to grease his ribs'.

'It was a sunny day,' Colonel Walter Harzer was to recall many years later, 'a typically quiet and peaceful Sunday.'

The twelve RAF Stirlings – converted bombers – carrying Boy Wilson's pathfinders, six officers and 180 men, had already crossed the Dutch coast now. Sitting with the pilot in the first flight, Wilson thought 'everything looked so peaceful. There were cows feeding quietly in the fields and peasants going about their work. Not a sign of fighting or war. Not a glimpse of the enemy'. In his usual cocky way, Wilson turned to the RAF man and joked:

'This seems a pretty quiet area. Suppose we get out here?'

Before the moustached pilot could answer, flak started exploding all around in black frightening bursts, but the Stirlings sailed on majestically in strict formation. Five minutes later the old, old drill began. The paras, laden with up to 80 lbs of gear and weapons, stood up and faced the door, now open. Automatically they checked the man's chute in front of them. The red light had changed to green. Time to go. The first man poised at the door. Below at a mere five hundred feet, the russet-green heath flashed by at a tremendous rate. Tracer stitched the air in white and red morse. The lead man took a deep breath and went. It was as if an invisible hand had reached inside the aircraft and abruptly dragged him out. Next instant his chute opened and his terrifyingly rapid descent stopped with a sudden jerk. Now man after man followed him in swift succession.

A machine gun bullet struck a pathfinder and as the man descended to the ground, the first casualty of the many to follow, his head slumped to one side. He hit the ground with a crash, and a sudden cloud of dust. When it had cleared, he was still lying there. He was dead.

But their only casualty did not spoil the pathfinders' mood of confidence, symbolized in the best battledresses, metal and boot polish most of them had brought with them for the victorious entry into Germany. Wilson, their commander, was too concerned about the bottles of whisky, gin and sherry he had stowed in his 75 lb leg-bag, which he was going to use to entertain the Dutch Resistance leaders.

Next moment, as he struggled out of his para harness with the blue sky above him blossoming with the white chutes of his men, a German came running towards him, hands above his head yelling. But the word he was yelling was not a war cry, but one of surrender. As Wilson finally freed himself, the German led him to the rest of his section who also wanted to give themselves up.

Wilson had no time for prisoners. He told them to 'hang on', while he organised his men. Swiftly they formed a defensive screen while their comrades began to put out the smoke signals and yellow marker beacons to indicate to the planes fifteen minutes behind them that this was the DZ. He contacted the outlying platoons by radio and ordered them to release their pigeons. The trained birds would carry the first news of their successful landing to the War Office in London. But once released, the pigeons fluttered up to the roof of a nearby farmhouse and refused to move, cooing and billing as if there was no urgency whatsoever. At last someone shouted hoarsely: 'Throw a bloody stone at the daft buggers!' and they rose and winged their path westwards, back the way they had come. The message was on the way to London: 'Landing completely unopposed.'

Now the gliders were coming into sight. Sergeant Louis Hagen, a German Jewish refugee and now a glider pilot, sweated with the strain of managing his plane as it tossed about in the wash of hundreds of tugs flying in the same formation. But the sight of the Lower Rhine and the DZ – two small squares of wooded land pieced together at one corner only – took his mind off the sheer physical effort of fighting the engineless plane with its heavy load of men and equipment. This was the moment to cast off.

'Hello Tug… We're getting ready to cast off now… Thanks for the wizard ride.'

'Best of luck, Matchbox,' the pilot's voice crackled over the radio. 'See you soon.'

'Okay, Tug… Same to you.'

The pilot pulled the lever which released the cable from the big wooden glider's wings. Free flight. A wonderful hushing silence. Now they were losing height gradually. As they swooped silently across the river, Hagen could see the bridge at Arnhem, their ultimate objective.

Now the gliders came sweeping in – some 350 of them – landing on the fields of Reyescamp Farm and Renkum Heath. Suddenly all was chaos, or so it seemed to the amazed Dutch farmers, who had been disturbed so rudely over their lunches. Gliders slithering, skidding, careening, crashing to a halt. Noses flung open to disgorge men or canvas hacked apart by axes for the same purpose. Six pounders rushed out and hooked to the waiting jeeps. Vehicles driven straight through hedges. Panicked animals rushing wildly with farmers and excited soldiers in a strange khaki uniform in pursuit. Smoke and dust everywhere. But not one single German soldier.

A glider took evasive action to avoid over-shooting the DZ. Its wing tipped the scored earth. It swung round, brakes screaming furiously, churning up the field even more, before it ripped apart and lay still. Wilson ran forward to help. Glider troops staggered out, shaken and bruised. Nothing serious.

Then the CO of the pathfinders recognised the pilot, an ex-Guardsman and an old friend.

'Come along to my HQ,' he urged. 'I'll give you some water.'

In the farmhouse HQ, Wilson opened his treasured bottle of Scotch and gave the glider pilot a stiff shot. The man swallowed it in one go, then turning his blackened, scratched face to Wilson, exclaimed: 'My God, this Dutch water's good!'

General Urquhart's Horsa glider landed gently. He jumped out and left his batman Hancock and the rest to get on with the unloading of his personal jeep. Civilians and soldiers were everywhere. In their midst the farmer whose fields they had descended upon so surprisingly was pointing out the way to Arnhem; and already some of the Red Devils were setting out in small groups towards their objective.

'Here they come!' someone shouted.

The big General turned, startled. It was the 1st Parachute Brigade dropping only four hundred yards away. Urquhart saw that their Dakotas were right on target. As their white parachutes started to open everywhere, he noted to his satisfaction that very few of them were off target. He told himself it was 'turning out to be a textbook drop'.

Private Cardale of the Second Battalion

thought so too.

'It was perfect outside,' he recalls, 'and no Ack Ack! At last the green light and someone shouted "Go!" Our platoon officer pushed his bicycle out first and followed it, a matter of seconds before I went also. Soon we were all in the air. It never dawned on me that it was dangerous and I enjoyed every second of the flight down after my chute had opened. I was loaded with gear plus a rifle on a cord twenty feet long which lightened your final descent by landing first. Weather was perfect. Landed and dazedly got up.'

A few moments later he was facing a sergeant operating a movie camera. It was only then that he looked for his new pipe. It was broken in two pieces.

Private Tucker of the same battalion also found that all was not well when he finally hit the deck; this time, however, the defect was much more serious.

'Smudger' Smith had just come running up, red beret perched on the top of his blond, curly hair, prodding a group of terrified German prisoners in front of him. 'What the hell are you doing here?' Tucker yelled above the roar. 'I thought you was in the glasshouse?'

Smudger spat angrily into the dust. 'That bastard Browning pulled us all out for this op.' He dug his bayonet into the nearest prisoner. 'All right, move your arse!'

The prisoner 'moved his arse'. Smudger vanished – Tucker wouldn't see him again – and the Ulsterman occupied himself with his 18 set. An officer helped him to put it on net. And then the Battalion signaller made a discovery that signallers were making everywhere in that moment. The soft boggy ground and the presence of wooded areas made it impossible for him to receive or send signals.

At first Tucker thought it was his particular set. 'I assumed it was on the blink. So when I spotted a jeep – unattended – with another 18 set in the back, I nicked it.'

But when Tucker tried again with the new set, he realised that it was not just his 18 which was 'on the blink', but *all* 18 sets: 'the first intimation of a snag that was to grow and bedevil us almost to the end,' as General Urquhart, who had soon lost contact with most of his units, was to write much later. Now the 2nd Battalion, which was to make the advance to the vital bridge, was cut off from the rest of the Division.

But thee men of the Second were not worried. Signal failures and a general 'ballsup', as they were wont to phrase it in their tough, careless way, were typical of airborne ops.

Lieutenant Heaps, who had landed safely, together with his batman Watts, near the Amersfoort to Arnhem highway, felt it was 'unbelievably quiet on this Sunday afternoon'. All he could hear was an occasional shot. Together with a lost corporal, he and Watts marched to the Wolfhezen Hotel, where several excited Dutch people rushed out and pointed to twenty meek and defeated Germans, who came forward, hands on their heads. Without being ordered to do so, they began emptying their pockets for their surprised captors.

Heaps, who had already been wounded in Normandy before he had joined the paras, decided to ignore them. As he said later, 'it was much too nice an afternoon to worry about things like war'. Handing a rifle to one of the Dutchmen and ordering him to stand on guard, he, the lost corporal and Watts accepted the hotel proprietor's invitation to join him for tea...

2

The Commander of the First Parachute Army, Kurt Student, whose élite Seventh Para Division had virtually conquered Holland single-handed in May 1940, had been brought out onto the balcony of his cottage by the noise of the German flak around Vught. Now putting on the glasses which he hated wearing in the presence of his troops, he stared upwards at the immense stream of planes and gliders passing over his head in awed fascination, unconcerned by the danger to his own person. A moment later his Chief-of-Staff joined him on the balcony. All that Student could remark was: 'I wish I had had such powerful means at my disposal!'

Erwin Kirchof, the German war correspondent on the spot, experienced a similar feeling. After the war he wrote: 'The cinemas in the small Dutch towns were slowly filling up, and the streets and highways, along the canals and small streams, were crowded with young people on bicycles. And then out of the blue sky, roared several hundred enemy fighter-bombers.

Their aim was to attack the German defensive positions and locate the flak positions. Hardly had they disappeared beyond the horizon when, coming from the west across the flooded coastal areas, appeared the planes and gliders carrying regiments and brigades of the enemy's airborne army... The first parachute landings were made on a front of about seventy kilometres and approximately a hundred kilometres behind our lines. The troops bailed out from a very low altitude, sometimes as low as sixty metres.

Immediately after that the several hundred gliders started to land. In those first few minutes it looked as if the downcoming masses would suffocate every single life on the ground.'

Walter Harzer, acting commander of the Ninth SS Panzer Division, the Hohenstaufen, named after the Holy Roman Emperors of the Middle Ages, was not particularly worried by that fact.

'As the troops were moving off to their quarters, and the officers and myself were making for the officers' mess for lunch,' the big, burly Colonel remembered later, 'we saw the first parachutes over Arnhem in the sky... It could not be deduced at this stage that a large-scale operation was under way and we sat down quietly to lunch.'

Field Marshal Model never finished his Sunday lunch that day. He had just sat down to enjoy the meal – and the Field Marshal who had gained the name 'the Fuhrer's Fireman' for his stonewall defensive stands in Russia, liked his food – when the news reached him that 'Tommy paras' had landed only four kilometres from his Tafelberg Hotel HQ in Oosterbeek. Model rushed to his room to pack his case. Down below everything was sudden confusion. Outside, his driver was sitting tensely in his dark grey Mercedes, sounding the horn urgently.

Model clattered down the stairs in his gleaming jackboots, monocle screwed tightly into his eye. He could not risk the terrible ignominy of being captured so far behind the front. As he ran out into the open, his case burst open, scattering his underwear onto the cobbled road. But he did not stop to pick it up. Dropping into the rear of the car, he ordered the driver to drive to Arnhem to General Kussin's Area Command HQ.

There he ordered the General, who a few hours later, would be mown down by a burst of machine-gun fire from a para of the 1st Brigade, to radio details to Hitler's East Prussian 'Wolf's Lair' immediately.

It caused a sensation. Hitler immediately broke off the planning for the last great offensive in the West, the attack which would one day be known as the 'Battle of the Bulge', and immediately started to discuss the news. The Fuhrer thought that the whole 'business is so dangerous – that you must understand clearly.'

He looked directly at Colonel-General Jodl, his pale-faced, cunning chief adviser.

'What if such a mess happens here? Here I sit with my whole supreme command.' He swung round the assembled dignitaries. 'Here sit the Reichsmarshal the OKH Reichsfuhrer SS and the Reich Foreign Min-ister– Well then, this is the most worthwhile catch, that's obvious. I would not hesitate to risk two parachute divisions here if with one blow I could get my hands on the whole German command.'

But Field Marshal Model, who had survived the drop, only to commit suicide in a lonely German forest some eight months later, was not concerned with his Fuhrer's reaction. Now he urged his nervous driver to get him to General Bittrich's HQ at Doetinchem at once.

Of all the senior commanders that afternoon, SS General Bittrich, a cultivated, humorous man, was the calmest. Like a spider spinning the web for its victim, he began rapping out orders to his command.

The Frundsberg Division (the 10th SS) was to march to Nijmegen at once to stop the link-up, which he had guessed must come, as soon as the Luftwaffe listening posts had informed him the landings were taking place. A little while later he ordered a reconnaissance battalion of the Hohenstaufen to follow them and defend the same narrow road from the south.

Using the civilian telephone network, he alarmed Harzer's HQ (Harzer himself was still absent with Graebner's unit) and placed the division on 'alert stage one'. A few minutes later Harzer himself was informed of the new measure and immedi-

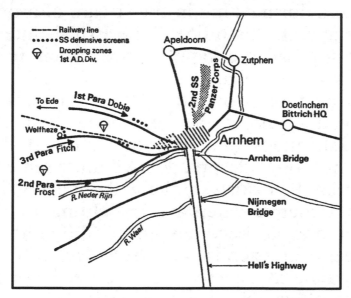

DAY ONE: 'Almost before the British had touched the ground, we were ready to defeat them.' – General Bittrich, Commander, 2nd SS Panzer Corps

ately he ordered Graebner's armoured car unit to drive into Arnhem and block any advance into the centre of the city.

Bittrich was under strain, but confident. He had immediately guessed what the British were up to. As he told one of his staff officers during a lull in the stream of orders issuing from his office: 'The British intend to bridge all the gaps between their front line and the Reich.'

As he took a breath of fresh air outside with the officer, he explained that the 'British attack (would) not be too daring and not too widespread... We must remember that the British soldier will not act on his own initiative when he is fighting in the town and it becomes more difficult for officers to exercise control. He will be incredible in defence, but we need not be afraid of his offensive capabilities.'

The staff officer guessed that his chief was playing a dangerous game. Bittrich was obviously going to defend only those places where the Tommies were actually attacking or were going to attack. The rest of them would be left to their own devices until they proved themselves a danger too by attacking. And it was pretty clear where the enemy was going to attack: the bridge at Arnhem.

Bittrich's finalized order to the 9th SS Division confirmed his guess. It read: 'The Division (is) to go immediately into action, occupying the Arnhem area and destroying the enemy forces which have landed west of Arnhem at Oosterbeek. *Immediate attack is essential. The aim is to occupy and firmly hold the bridge at Arnhem.*'

But if the Commanding Officer of the 2nd SS Corps had known the situation at the Arnhem Bridge at that particular moment, he might not have been so confident. A few minutes before, the twenty odd men manning the flak guns, defending the 150 yard iron bridge, had fled in panic at the approach of the great airborne army. Now the structure, which ten thousand élite soldiers were prepared to give their lives for, was guarded by one lone, middle-aged and somewhat bewildered Dutch policeman, Constable van Kuiyk.

3

While Generals Horrocks and Adair took up their positions on the factory roof over-looking Joe's Bridge, armed with their bino-culars, the lead squadron of the Irish Guards – Number Three – began to rattle over the makeshift structure in their battle-worn dusty 30-ton Shermans. It was now exactly 1.45 pm.

At precisely 2 pm the 300-gun barrage

began. It continued for thirty minutes. Just before it ended for the commencement of the two-division strong mortar bombardment, word was passed down the line of waiting tankers, nervously smoking a last 'free issue' Woodbine: 'H hour is fourteen thirty-five!'

Now the barrage grew in intensity. The obscene belch and soft plop of the 3-inch mortar stonk, followed seconds later by the great ear-splitting roar of the exploding shell.

It was 2.32. Two hundred and forty 25-pounder guns joined in. Three minutes to go. The big black-bereted Irish Guardsmen, mostly from the north of England and 'neutral' Eire, stubbed out their cigarettes hurriedly. Everywhere they began to 'button up' for the battle to come. In the turrets the gunners tested the electric turret motors that would send their long-hooded 17-pounders swinging swiftly from side to side. The commanders checked their radios. The barrage was reaching its terrible crescendo now. 2.34 pm. In the lead Sherman Lieutenant Keith Heathcote kicked his driver's shoulder below and yelled: *'Drive, advance!'*

The great link-up operation, which Montgomery would use to advance into the heart of the Reich itself before Eisenhower could stop him, was on. As the creeping barrage moved forward at a speed of 200 yards a minute, tank after tank disappeared into the thick yellow clouds of dust. Above them the cannon-firing Typhoons of the waiting 'cab rank' lost sight of them immediately. In the woods on either side of the road, the Devons, an infantry battalion, moved forward cautiously to protect the Guards' flanks.

Five minutes passed. The Shermans rattled rustily along the dead-straight, embanked road, without opposition. The thick pine woods on either side were silent and mysterious. Not a German in sight. Ten minutes. Up on the factory roof, the two Generals, vainly trying to penetrate the dust-and-smoke clouds with their binoculars, were informed by a panting aide: 'Number Three Squadron reports, sir – advance going well!'

Horrocks beamed at Adair and focussed his glasses once more.

The lead Sherman crossed the frontier. Although his angle of vision was confined to the thirty degree arc of his periscope, young Lieutenant Heathcote knew that he had passed into Holland by the different sound of his tracks; they were now running on Dutch concrete instead of Belgian *pavé*. A moment later a bullet-pocked sign, hanging at a crazy angle, confirmed it. It read *'Naar Valkenswaard'*. It was Holland all right.

And then suddenly it happened. The German 88mm gunners opened up. A flat dry crack, followed a second later by a tremendous tearing sound like a piece of canvas being ripped apart. The first Sherman came to an abrupt halt. For what seemed an age nothing happened. Then a thick cloud of white smoke started to rise from the 'ronson' – as the Guards nicknamed the Sherman tank because of the ease with which it caught fire. Next moment the thirty-ton monster was burning fiercely, and its crew were running for their lives.

Now the woods on both sides of the high road came to life. SS men and paras, clad in camouflaged capes appeared everywhere in the ditches. Hard-bitten old sweats from the Wehrmacht's Penal Battalion started firing bazookas into the trapped tanks at fifty yards' range. One after another the tanks were 'brewed up' by the German gunners with systematic *Gruendlichkeit*. The Sherman commanded by Sergeant Capewell fired a whole belt of Browning into a German armed with *Panzerfaust*. He flung up his arms and fell screaming. But it did not stop his comrades knocking out Capewell's tank. To his rear, Major M O'Cock – 'a good Mick name', as his men used to chortle behind his back – watched with horrified fascination as the killing shells came closer and closer to his tank. Before him now, nine Shermans lay burning or crippled in a space of half a mile, while their crews lay dead or pinned down in the ditches on both sides.

Up on the factory with the horrified Generals, a staff officer groaned: 'Oh my God, they won't get through!'

But back at his Brussels HQ, the commander who had dreamed up this tremendous operation on 'Hell's Highway', as the Americans came to call it, was undismayed by the initial set-back. He knew that the sheer weight of the drive he had ordered would break through what his intelligence officers considered was the 'hard crust' of the German defence, into the void beyond it. Indeed Montgomery must have been a happy man that day as he received his rival General Bradley at his CP, and told the Missourian that 'Ike' was considering letting him have full priority of the whole Allied Army for the drive, which in the end would head for the enemy's capital – 'the main prize' in Eisenhower's words.

But if Montgomery was pleased, Bradley certainly was not. As soon as he got back to 'Eagle Main', his own HQ, he called his favourite general in great excitement.

'Blood and Guts' Patton came to the telephone at once (although Bradley had once been his own subordinate until Patton had slapped a shell-shocked GI in Sicily and had lost his command in the resultant scandal). Bradley swiftly filled in the 3rd Army's Commander with the details of what 'Monty' was about, making no attempt to conceal either his anger or concern. Patton told Bradley not to worry. His own opinion of the 'Field Marshal', as he had been calling Montgomery contemptuously ever since his promotion to that rank of the 1st, was low; as it was of Eisenhower, who was now being called by Patton's staff officers: 'the best General the British have.'

'I'll get so involved, Brad,' he said, 'that they won't be able to stop me. Eddy (a Third Army corps commander) will start tomorrow morning for the West Wall and then we'll be off running. So play it dumb, Brad. Don't call me till after dark on the 19th. After that,' he concluded cynically, 'we won't have any reason to worry about Monty's *daggerlike* thrust.'

With that Patton put down the telephone, leaving his Chief in no doubt about his intention. Using his traditional 'rock soup' method (a tramp asks a housewife for water to make a soup. He puts two rocks in it, then requests some meat and a few vegetables, which the housewife, mystified by how he would make a soup with two rocks, brings. He begins to make soup), he would build up an armed reconnaissance into a minor skirmish. The skirmish would develop into a small battle and from that into a full-scale conflict. So that in the end Eisenhower's hand would be forced, as it had been by the same method before. The 'best general the British have' would have to give Bradley's armies the same kind of priority as Montgomery was getting in the north.

In essence, the malicious story which Patton had gleefully related to a group of correspondents a few days before when he had first heard of the Arnhem operation, would come true. 'You see,' he told the smiling newspapermen, who knew that 'Old Blood and Guts' was always good copy, 'yesterday, the Field Marshal *ordered* SHAEF to have Third Army to go on the defensive, stand in place and prepare to guard his right flank. The Field Marshal then announced that he will, after regrouping, making what he describes as a lightning dagger thrust at the heart of Germany. "They will be off their guard," the Field Marshal predicts, "and I shall pop out at them," he paused to give full effect to the punchline, "like an angry rabbit!"'

4

The commanding officer of the 2nd Parachute Battalion faced up to the problem immediately. The transport gliders, bringing in the Recce Squadron's jeep with which they would make the first dash to the bridge, had not turned up. Therefore Major 'Freddie' Gough's recce boys would not be able to carry out their *coup de main*. Colonel Frost, the veteran of France, Africa and Sicily, did not hesitate. He worked out a quick plan to do the job himself. It was simple but effective. His 'A' Company would move off in the lead, straight to the bridge. 'C' would follow, seize the railway bridge – if it were still intact – cross it and attack the main bridge from the other side. His 'B' Company would be the last of the three with two possible objectives of opportunity. It would capture the pontoon bridge across the Lower Rhine (if it existed). If it didn't, they were to seize Den Brink, an area of high ground, which controlled the entrance to Arnhem from the west.

He explained his plan quickly to Brigadier Lathbury. Lathbury approved it and said he would accompany the 2nd Battalion, while Dobie's 1st and Fitch's 3rd pushed along on parallel roads to Frost to carry out their tasks.

It was now 3 o'clock. The race between Frost's paras and Bittrich's SS for the capture of the vital bridge had begun.

But it was not Frost's battalion which hit the first real German resistance; it was Dobie's First. Led by the Colonel himself, the Red Devils strung out in single file on both sides of the tree-lined main Arnhem–Ede highway, made rapid progress. In spite of the tempting offers of food, water and kisses by the cheering Dutch civilians, Dobie urged them on at a rapid pace. For to their right he could hear the characteristic high-pitched, hysterical bursts of German spandau fire. Obviously the 2nd and 3rd were running into trouble, he told himself.

And then he ran into it himself. Mark IV tanks appeared on their flank, almost like Indian scouts in the old Hollywood western, shadowing them, heavy with impending menace, but not yet attacking.

The afternoon passed. Dobie began to have doubts of achieving his objective – the high ground to the north of Arnhem. He halted the Battalion while he considered, with two companies deployed at both sides of the road, facing a wide expanse of ploughed field, which looked to him pretty 'dicey'. The other company – R – had moved into a small wood further away to the right. It was an unfortunate choice of position, for the wood contained the first real opposition the First Airborne Division had met all that long afternoon: *Sturnbannfuhrer* Krafft's 500-strong SS Training Battalion. And the SS officer lived up to the meaning of his name – 'strength'. His theory of how an airborne attack should be dealt with was brutal in its simplicity. As soon as the drop was reported to him, he declared: 'The only way to draw the teeth of an airborne landing is to drive straight into it.'

At the head of his teenage trainees, commanded by the hard-bitten veteran NCOs of the Russian fighting, he did exactly this. Within the hour R Company had suffered fifty per cent casualties and the wood was full of their dead and dying. Temporarily at least, Colonel Dobie's Battalion had come to an abrupt halt.

It was six o'clock now. Constable van Kuijk, tramping up and down alone on the debris-strewn bridge, with the sound of the battle still far away, was suddenly alarmed by the roar of many motors approaching at speed. The next instant the first armoured car bearing the double runic SS of Harzer's 9th Panzer Division roared into view. Hastily, van Kuijk waved it on. The driver, his young face set and grim, nearly ran the lone Dutch policeman down as he raced over the bridge heading south towards Nijmegen. Behind him clattered the half-tracks of the reconnaissance battalion, filled with heavily-armed panzer grenadiers, weapons on the alert. Vehicle after vehicle. But still there was no sign of the advancing British paras.

Another hour passed. The sound of the small arms battle in the town grew louder.

Now the bridge was empty again, a kind of no-man's land in the middle of German-held territory. It was not even prepared for demolition. The light began to go. Colonel Frost's HQ group, which included the 1st Parachute Brigade Major Christopher Hibbert, were perhaps half a mile away from their objective. They had been delayed by a brush with a German recce patrol. But now the Germans lay dead, sprawled out in the street, and the paras were advancing again.

Major Dover's C Company, however, was closer to the railway bridge, approaching it cautiously along the banks of the Lower Rhine. But the Germans had spotted them. While a German corporal rushed into a cafe where the demolition crew was billeted, the men on duty were already preparing the explosive charges. Just as the leading Red Devils came within sight, a NCO pressed the plunger of the exploding device. There was a blinding flash of fire. Lieutenant Barry and his platoon halted abruptly. Corporal Roberts, a medic, saw how the railway bridge 'seemed to curl back on us'. Then the mid section sagged into the boiling water below and the air was full of fist-sized pieces of flying metal. Barry went down. Another man followed. And another. Suddenly Corporal Roberts had no more time for the bridge now. He set about tending the casualties.

Light was fading rapidly now. Frost

pushed on determinedly although he had lost contact with his B and C companies. It was just before eight o'clock. He must reach his objective soon. And then there it was. Looming up, stark and black against the darkening sky, with German transport racing across it southwards. The bridge, still intact. Trying to contain his excitement, he ordered his men to advance on it as quietly as they could.

'It was easier said than done,' 'Mick' Tucker remembers today. 'The road we were advancing along was cobbled, with glass and debris everywhere. And we all had on our ammo boots, complete with the regulation thirteen hobnails. God, did they make a row! You would have thought we would have woken up the dead.

'I slung the second 18 set. It was a dead loss, though I did keep the useless field telephone for another day. Now pulling out my Colt – it was as useless as the 18 I was to find out later – I tagged on to 'Mousy' Mousell's Vickers machine-gun platoon. We passed a pillbox, making a hell of a racket. But there was nobody in it. Thank God! There were still Jerry trucks on the bridge, but they didn't spot us – not yet at least. Finally we made it to one of the houses overlooking the bridge.'

Swiftly the machine gunners began setting up a defensive position under the command of the young lieutenant who had gained his nickname on account of the moustache of which he was inordinately proud. They smashed in the windows and posted two machine guns there. Hurriedly they filled the bath with water just in case and then began searching the house.

'We hadn't got far though when this young signaller, who I'd thought was a bit windy back on the plane,' Tucker recalls, 'came rushing in to say that there was an old lady in one of the back bedrooms and she was refusing to go. In the end she stayed and the young signaller risked his life a dozen times to feed her.'

All through the terrible fight to come, she remained in that back bedroom, 'never turning a hair at it all.' Astounded by her courage, it was only just before she died that Tucker learned 'she'd been as deaf as a post all along!'

Frost, too, had a brief respite from the grimness of war at that moment of great triumph. Looking out of the upper window of the house he had chosen for his headquarters in *Markstraat*, he spotted a uniformed figure at the end of the darkened, silent street. He told himself that the figure might be that of another policeman like van Kruijk, whom they had taken into their HQ, or a member of the Dutch resistance. Hastily he dispatched a para to find out. After several the man came back.

'Well?' Frost demanded.

'Oh, he's not Resistance, sir,' the para answered casually. 'He says he's Panzer SS.'

But the time was running out for laughter. Frost had to organize his defences quickly. 'The atmosphere at this time,' an eye witness reports, 'can only be described as a trifle crazy. We would knock upon the door of a house and be instantly met by the earnest prayers of its inhabitants not to billet ourselves on them. Seeing our preparations for defence, they would say most politely, "surely you are not going to fortify this house?" To which I would reply, equally politely, "I'm afraid I am."'

In the middle of these frenzied preparations for what must surely come soon, Major Tatham-Warter, commanding the 2nd Battalion's A Company suggested a platoon should cross the bridge to secure its southern end. Frost agreed hastily and Lieutenant Grayburn, a smiling, pleasant-faced young officer was given the job.

Grayburn begun his assault with bold determination. But he had not advanced more than a dozen yards across the bridge when a multiple 20mm flak cannon opened up, supported by an armoured car. Suddenly the air was full of shells. Almost at once, John Grayburn was shot through the shoulder, as his men began to drop all around him. In spite of the fact there was absolutely no cover on the bridge, he pressed home his attack. But it was no use. His casualties were too heavy. Dragging their wounded and dying with them, the A Company started to fall back, with Grayburn, blood pouring from his shoulder, covering them the best he could. In forty-eight hours time he would be dead, and the first of five men in the Division during the next seven terrible days to win his country's most coveted honour – the Victoria Cross.

While Grayburn positioned his men in a nearby house, Frost seized time to assess his position. The Arnhem Bridge was bigger than the usual sort of English bridge with a similar breadth of river to span. Because the low-lying Dutch polder countryside usually floods in winter, its builders, like all Dutch bridging engineers, had raised the roadway on both ends above the ground. This was carried on a massive ramp for some distance before it met the section which actually spanned the river itself. And in order to lower the total weight, this span was made of open girderwork. As a result there was virtually no cover for any attacker from whatever side he came. Attack would be suicide, therefore. Defence was everything. Yet as Frost realized when he stared the length of the bridge, now silent again after the failure of young Grayburn's attack, his men were very thin on the ground: not more than five hundred of them at the most. At that moment, the question uppermost in the big Colonel's mind was: 'Where is Fitch's Third Battalion?'

At about the same time that Frost reached the bridge, Fitch's Third had run into serious trouble in the shape of two Tigers from Harzer's 9th SS Panzer, the *Hohenstaufen.* He tried to side-slip them and ran into fresh German armour. He began to take casualties. A self-propelled gun rattled up the road and barred the advance.

The Captain leading the first platoon, young Jimmy Clemison, renowned throughout the Battalion for his fierce and spreading moustache, whose men had already ambushed and killed General Kussin, Arnhem's Commandant, swiftly tried to organize a 'stalk'. He and his company commander, Peter Waddy, would each take a platoon up the sides of the road and attack the SP from its flanks. In the meantime a six-pound anti-tank gun would tackle the German vehicle on the road itself.

But the *Ferdinand* reacted quicker. Its great hooded gun boomed. The crew of the anti-tank gun disappeared in a ball of ugly yellow flame. As the paras started throwing their grenades and bombs at the German, the crew of the *Ferdinand* picked up one of the wounded anti-tankers and draping him across their front as protection, ran the gauntlet in safety.

Waddy and Clemison advanced again, only to be swept by German spandau fire. They fell back on the Hartenstein Hotel, where they had already helped themselves to the *hors d' oeuvre* laid out on the long table for the Hotel's German guests who had led in alarm earlier. There, in the company of the Divisional Commander, who had lost virtually all contact with his Division and Brigadier Lathbury who was in a not much better situation, they were fated to spend most of the night. The 3rd's advance to the bridge had bogged down, among the stolid Dutch bourgeois surroundings of the Hartenstein Hotel.

But not all of the 3rd had come to an abrupt halt. C Company, which had apparently vanished – or so Fitch thought – leaving behind a few dead Germans and burning ammo trucks, was very much alive, although it had taken casualties. Indeed it was now passing through a virtually deserted Arnhem towards the Bridge. As Sergeant-Major Mason of that company recalls: 'It was now dusk, so we proceeded down the railway cutting until we reached Arnhem Station. A recce was made by 8 Platoon and when they returned, we moved off towards the bridge... The town was deserted except for two Dutch policemen who gave us a great welcome.'

Thus they crushed their way across broken glass down the darkened streets, weapons at the alert, hearts beating faster at the knowledge that behind the barred windows and doors of the silent, yellow-brick Dutch houses, there were equally tense men and women. Perhaps even Germans waiting to open fire upon them as soon as they had passed.

As the first 88mm shell slammed into Private Tucker's house – and failed to explode – Private McKinnon of C Company stopped on his way to the bridge, where Frost was waiting for him and the rest of the 3rd so anxiously. He had spotted a butcher's shop and he was hungry. But the Dutch butcher was unable to offer him meat. Instead he regaled him with bread and cheese and wine. With the help of the wine, the conversation, carried out with the help of much hand waving and gestures, became easier. Finally the beaming butcher asked McKinnon a favour: could he bring his daughter down to meet the first 'Tommy' she would ever see in her whole life. A happy McKinnon agreed.

A few minutes later the shy twelve-year-old was pushed towards the unshaven begrimed para to utter the one hesitant line of English she knew: 'Many happy returns after your long stay away...'

DAY TWO

'A grossly untidy situation'.
— *General Hackett.*

Dawn on Monday. As usual in the British Army, Frost's paras on the bridge were standing to. During the night they had had little rest. Twice the Germans had attacked and been driven off. But now for the moment, there was a brief respite.

In the house occupied by part of 'Mousey's' Vickers machine-gun platoon, the floor was already littered with gleaming yellow cartridge cases, its walls riddled by German bullets, Mick Tucker slumped against the wall cleaning his Colt pistol with oil he had found in a tin of sardines. Dust from the ceiling had got into it and it wouldn't work. But after cleaning, the pistol still wouldn't work. He thrust it into his holster with a curse and picking up a German rifle from a German shot during the night, watched curiously as the young signaller prepared a soup from one of their

101

issue meat cubes for the old lady in the bedroom.

A couple of houses away, Captain Mackay of the attached Royal Engineer section, made a quick survey of his strength. He had fifty men – seven wounded – armed with their personal weapons and six Brens. Not much, he told himself, but they did have plenty of ammo and grenades. Food was virtually gone, however, and the only water they had was that contained in their water-bottles. He decided, as he recalled much later, 'to fight the battle from the first floor, merely holding the basement and ground floor, and to observe from the attic'.

Colonel Frost was also assessing his position that dawn. He did not have exact figures because his command was so strung out and it was damnably dangerous to leave the cover of the houses – they had not begun to burrow like moles from one house to another yet – but he guessed he must have between 300–400 men on the bridge. With that number, he was confident that he could hold it until the rest of the Division came up. Indeed as the first ugly white of the false dawn began to creep into the eastern sky, his only one real fear was that the Germans would attempt to obtain a foothold on the southern end of the vital bridge. Accordingly he ordered that Lieutenant Mousell – now proudly sporting a captured Luger – should build up his machine-gun defence in the upper storeys of their houses in order to beat off any attempt to rush the other end of the bridge. 'Mousey' hurried away to carry out his orders and the Colonel, settled back to await the first German attack of the new day.

It came for Mick Tucker in the shape of a mysterious rippling of the wallpaper above his head as he lay slumped against the wall. For a moment he could not understand what was happening. Then he got it. German machine-gun fire. As the enemy machine-gunners started to soften the British defences prior to the attack, he raised his head cautiously above the shattered window sill. He caught a quick glimpse of a red beret. But the face beneath the cherished para headgear was not British. 'Jerry,' he cried to the others, as the German 20mm flak cannon joined in the 'softening up'.

Tensely the machine-gunners waited for the German sniper to appear again; then they fired. 'After that he was still wearing the red beret,' Mick Turner remembers today, 'but he certainly wasn't going anywhere in it!'

Captain Mackay's men in the Van Limburg Stirumschool also spotted the enemy in their midst as it got lighter. They were located in a house only twenty yards away, from which the Engineers had been driven a few hours before. It was a matter of moments for the young captain to form a plan to deal with them. He ordered one of his Brens to open fire on them from north, firing it by remote control. Immediately the over-confident Germans started firing back at it. They were soon to regret their over-reaction. From their flank Mackay's two Bren gunners poured a vicious hail of fire into their unprotected backs. They went down like broken dolls.

Now the Germans went over to the attack. Three heavy enemy trucks, filled with men, started to rumble ponderously over the great span of the bridge. Urgently Frost told his men to hold their fire. Tensely the machine gunners followed their progress through their sights as they got closer and closer, while the bombers held their Gammon anti-tank grenades in sweat-sticky hands. Close and closer.

'Bloody hell,' someone breathed in awe, 'they've even brought the shite-hawks with 'em!' Indeed they had, for the centre truck was obviously what those who survived and were taken prisoner to Germany were going to learn to call 'the honey-dew cart': the big container on its back was used to pump out military 'thunderboxes'. The remark broke the tension, but it also seemed to serve as a signal for the Germans to stop. Perhaps Frost thought, 'they had seen our ugly eyes looking at them from the windows.'

If they had, it was too late now. 'Fire!' the command was rapped out on all sides. Bullets whizzed through the air. The Gammon grenades followed, lobbed hurriedly at the confused Germans. Within a matter of minutes it was all over. The wrecked trucks lay sprawled at crazy angles across the width of the bridge, the dead and dying soldiers all around them. Only two men survived to be captured, both badly wounded.

The first attack of the Monday had been beaten off, but a confident yet cautious Frost knew he had not heard the last of the Germans that particular morning.

At 7.30 that Monday morning, General Urquhart was reported 'officially missing'. Back at divisional HQ there were rumours that he had been killed, wounded, missing. All night Colonel Mackenzie had been attempting to find his missing chief. Without success. Now, working from a cluster of houses near a wood on the Heelsum road, he started making his own decisions.

He made his second-in-command send for the cheerful Canadian lieutenant from the 1st Paras who by now had completely lost his battalion, and order him to go on a vital mission. Major Newton-Dunn found Heaps and snapped:

'I have a job for you. Come with me quickly.'

Together they crossed the road where a jeep was waiting. The staff Major pointed to it and said:

'There's food and ammunition on it. You've got a radio set, a wireless operator and a driver. You must try to get through to the bridge. Our last contact with them was early this morning and at that time they had run out of food and had very little ammo left. When you reach the bridge contact us by wireless.' To emphasize the danger of the mission, he handed the dirty-faced young Canadian a bullet-proof vest. 'Here,' he said, 'you'll need this more than I will.'

Heaps set about his dangerous mission energetically. While Watts, his mild-mannered little batman perched himself on the crates of food next to Martin, the radio operator, the Canadian recruited a cadaverous-looking Dutch civilian named Labouchere, who was anxious to help and had volunteered to show Heaps the way. With an old-fashioned Dutch helmet on his head, the yellow band of the 'Oranje' Resistance organization on his sleeve and bundled into the bullet-proof vest over his tweed coat and plus-fours, he was placed beside the driver, Martin. Just before they left Heaps pressed a tommy-gun into Labouchere's hands and said: 'All you need to do is to press the trigger.' Thus the 'odd-looking expedition', as Heaps called it himself, set off on their journey into the unknown.

But Heaps was never to reach the bridge. Although told by his CO Colonel Dobie, who had stalled like the 3rd Battalion, that he would not be able to get through, the Canadian decided to park the jeep and make an attempt on foot.

After being pinned down on the river bank for an hour, he felt it was worth making a dash for it in the jeep. Returning to the little four wheel vehicle, he took over from Martin at the wheel. Then they were off. Heaps pressed down on the accelerator, hard. They roared through Dobie's foremost positions. They were on their way, followed by an angry burst of German spandau fire.

And then fate took a hand. The steering wheel came loose in Heaps' hands. He had no time to find out why. The jeep careened over towards the embankment. For a moment it hung on one wheel, as if it would overturn. But it stayed on that wheel, while the German gunner stitched a pattern of violet-sparking lead on the cobbles ten yards in front of them. With a crash, their supplies collapsed into the ditch. The radio followed. Their attempt to get through to the bridge was over, it seemed.

But in spite of being shaken and Labouchere wounded, Heaps was determined not to give up. Martin, the Dutchman and the radio operator hurriedly piled up the supplies – Watts had disappeared, never to be seen again – while Heaps found a bren gun carrier. Swiftly he convinced the soldier-driver to have a crack at getting through with the vital supplies. The man thought a moment. Then he spat in the dust, winked conspiratorially at the officer and swung the carrier round. The supplies and radio were quickly loaded and they were off again.

The Dutchman began to direct them eastwards, deeper and deeper into the heart of Arnhem itself.

Heaps recalls that strange journey through the empty shell of Arnhem: 'Telegraph lines lay on the streets. Telephone poles had been knocked down, and many of the houses around us were smoking and burning. All the buildings in the district were shattered. Shells were bursting everywhere now. We could see the flashes coming from the guns of German tanks, which were not more than two hundred yards down the road. The outlines of the German tanks were obscured by the thick pall of smoke which hung over everything. We turned down a driveway between two large houses.' It was just then that Heaps spotted a British uniform. A strange lieutenant ran up to him and asked:

'Are you a Canadian officer?'

Puzzled, Heaps answered, 'Yes.'

'Follow me,' the other man ordered.

Heaps dropped over the side of the bren

carrier and followed him. They stepped over the dead body of a para major sprawled across the house steps to be confronted the next moment by a big smiling general, who, to Heaps, seemed 'as cool and collected as if he had been to afternoon tea'. Swiftly he explained what he wanted Heaps to do. He was not to attempt to drive to the bridge. Instead he was to get back to Divisional HQ with vital messages and the information that the General was still alive. Before Urquhart could elaborate, Brigadier Lathbury, carrying a rifle, came up with his bodyguard, and told the Commander that they had to move off. Just before Heaps did the same, a carrier loaded with five dirty unshaven paras drove up, one wounded in the eyes, the other in the shoulder. A begrimed lieutenant got out wearily. 'Bloody filthy battle,' he breathed as he passed Heaps, abandoned it seemed with Lebouchere in the middle of Arnhem, 'and it's only the second day...'

The discovery that General Urquhart was still alive came too late for Mackenzie to change the decisions he had already made. At nine o'clock that morning, conferring with the chief gunner, Colonel Loder-Symonds, he said: 'The only one with any chaps is Hicks. We can't order him to deflect part of his strength. But the time has perhaps come when he ought to come here and order himself to do it.' Swiftly he explained that this had been Urquhart's own decision just before they set out. Loder-Symonds concurred and together, the two colonels set out to find Brigadier Hicks. Fifteen minutes later the ageing officer had taken over command of what was left of the First Airborne Division on the ground. As ten o'clock approached and Wilson's men started laying out the markers on the dropping zone of the Fourth Parachute Brigade, which was expected at that hour under its commander Hackett, the Red Devils seemed to be in firm hands once again.

Back on the bridge, Frost had beaten off the first real organized German attack with armour.

The Germans had come in at eight o'clock precisely: sixteen half tracks, laden with SS Panzer Grenadiers, and armoured cars. Thereupon there had ensued what Frost called: 'the most lovely battle you have ever seen!'

Under the cover of a 20mm flak cannon, supported by two 88mms, firing directly along the bridge, they rattled forward confidently to carry out Harzer's order to 'sweep the Tommies off the bridge!' Again Frost ordered his men to hold their fire. Silently the paras waited, fingers crooked around their triggers, their lips moving soundlessly as they counted each new vehicle as it swung up onto the bridge itself. One … two … three … four…

Behind the six-pounder anti-tank guns, the layers pressed their right eyes to the rubber-ended sights while the loaders waited tensely, a long gleaming yellow round in their arms, ready to reload immediately.

Vicious red tracer was zipping across the bridge now towards the British positions. A mortar opened up with an obscene belch. Still the paras held their fire. Now the first German halftrack was rattling ever closer to the 'daisy chain' of Hawkins grenades laid across the road. The paras held their breath. In a minute the halftrack would hit one of them and then the fun would start.

But to their surprise the halftrack went over the line of mines without one of them exploding. One of the Panzer Grenadiers in the back even had the cheek to wave to the expectant paras. The second halftrack passed the barrier. A grenade exploded with a muffled crump. But it, too, rattled on, though as Major Hibbert reported, 'one of the Germans sitting on the back was catapulted into the air and landed in the road. When he hit the road, he clanged, he was so full of lead'.

That started it! The first heavy PIAT anti-tank bombs began to wobble their way through the morning air towards the Germans. The 6-pounders opened up with a vicious crack, followed an instant later by the dry hysterical rattle of the machine-guns. The first German halftrack came to a halt, stopped suddenly as if by a gigantic, invisible fist. Another slewed to a standstill, spilling men everywhere and burst into flames. A third ran right over the embankment and overturned with a rending crash. The battle was on.

Captain Mackay was alarmed by a cry from one of his sappers: 'Armoured car below!' He rushed to the window of the school-house to see a second go by, only about a dozen yards away. He was helpless. He had no anti-tank weapons. But the halftracks which followed were different. They had no roofs on them and they were 'dead meat' for his men.

The first rattled by in a rush, but a lucky grenade caught it and sent half a dozen grenadiers in their camouflaged smocks sprawling. The second came on with its machine-guns blazing. A para next to Captain Mackay fell dead. But the SS men did not escape. A volley of lead struck the two drivers. They sprawled dead over the wheel and the big clumsy vehicle came to a sudden halt. The sappers picked off the panic-stricken survivors one by one as they tried to escape.

'This caused the remaining halftracks to stop out of view,' Mackay remembers today, 'and gave me a breathing space to organize a system for their elimination.'

Ten minutes later two rushed his positions, letting him have everything they'd got. As they passed the first halftrack which the sappers had knocked out, the paras shot the driver and his assistant. Both fell, but only the assistant was killed. The driver, blood streaming from his wound, tried to reverse frantically. There was the booming sound of metal striking metal as he crashed into the other halftrack. Both came to a halt. Viciously the paras concentrated all their fire on the entangled vehicles. One shot up in flames. Thick black oily smoke began to pour from it. Mercilessly the paras mowed down the Panzer Grenadiers, as yet another halftrack tried to rush their position under the cover of the smoke. In Mackay's terse military prose: 'It was similarly dealt with and there were no survivors.'

Thereafter there was a momentary lull while both sides considered what to do next. Suddenly Mackay heard a clanking of tracks below. He looked out of the shattered window to find himself staring straight into a German officer's face only five feet away.

The German's reaction was quicker. 'With a dirty big grin' on his face, he loosed off three shots with his pistol. Only one shot hit

Mackay and smashed his binoculars. Mackay's boys rallied quickly. Lead crashed into the defenceless Germans. As the half-track slammed into the wall, hopelessly out of control, it was full of dying and dead SS men.

As the Germans began to step up the mortar bombardment of their positions, Frost knew he had beaten them off again. A long line of German vehicles were blazing fiercely along the bridge and would continue to smoke until the battle was over. But when he started interrogating the first of the prisoners to come, sullen-faced 17- and 18-year-olds with the gleaming SS runes on their collars, and he found out that they belonged to a reformed SS corps, his elation vanished. He knew the élite of the Germany Army would not sit on their thumbs until assistance arrived from the Second Army; they would attack again and again. He began to have his first serious doubts about the outcome of the action.

But in Mick Tucker's building, morale was still high, in spite of the door having been blown off and the persistent mortar shelling. 'Mousey' had just come back from another position, his eyes wide and staring with strain, yelling angrily: 'Some bastard has pinched my Luger!' The men tried to calm him, but the young officer would not be calmed. He walked over to the window boldly, as if there were no enemy outside. Instinctively, he loosed off a burst with his sten. At once he swung round and cried: 'Who fired that burst?' He looked at the men huddled against the wall accusingly. *'Who?'*

Mick Tucker realized that the young officer was 'shell happy' from the beating he had taken at A Company's position. He pointed to the bottle of white wine someone had found in the cellar and shouted above the roar, 'Give him a drop of that.'

One of the glider pilots knocked the head off the bottle and offered it to the shaken officer, while Tucker used the pause in the battle to dig into a glass of raw salted Dutch herring he had found.

A few minutes later 'Mousey' was shaking his head violently, as if he were coming out of a long sleep with great difficulty. 'Do you know,' he said in his normal voice, 'some bugger has pinched my Luger.' Calm had been restored in the machine-gunners' position. All seemed well on the bridge.

2

To Brigadier Hackett, 'the broken-down cavalryman' as Urquhart called him jokingly, all did not seem well as he hit the DZ at precisely two o'clock. The heather was on fire and he had just lost his favourite ashplant. The first, he thought, had been pinched by Urquhart, and now he had managed to lose its replacement.

While the men of the 4th floated down everywhere to the accompaniment of machine-gun fire from Bittrich's SS men, who knew about the landing, he searched the heather for the stick. Ten frightened Germans appeared. But Hackett had not time for them. *'Warten Sie hier,'* he told them severely in German, one of the several languages he had picked up in the course of degree-hunting. Finally he found it and collecting his prisoners, marched them towards the RZ.

On the perimeter the German SS snipers opened up as he did so. Wilson's pathfinders went into action to winkle them out. They flushed out a couple, who grovelled at their feet begging for mercy. They had to be kicked to their feet before they could be marched away. They were the lucky ones. Some time later German troops called on Wilson's men to surrender.

'We shouted back,' Wilson recalled later, 'that we were too frightened to do so and that they must come and get us. Sixty of them were fools enough to do so and were wiped out with twelve Bren guns at a range of a hundred and fifty yards. They died screaming!'

Hackett was met by a worried Mackenzie, who knew the ex-Hussar would not like the news he had brought about the change in command. Hackett did not. He protested.

Mackenzie shrugged: 'You'll only upset the works if you try to do anything about it.'

Hackett did not reply, but turned to watch the first of his men move off. As he did so, Mackenzie ventured hesitantly: 'The plan now is for the 11th Battalion to move in support of the drive for the bridge – immediately.'

Hackett reacted sharply. He felt it was his job to decide how his battalions should be placed. 'I don't like to be told that one of my battalions has already been nominated,' he snapped at an unhappy Mackenzie. 'As it happens, it is the right one to send.'

Angrily, the touchy little brigadier set about re-organizing his attack, telling anyone who cared to listen that this was 'a grossly untidy situation', while a worried Mackenzie set off back to Divisional HQ, telling himself that Hackett was obviously not pleased with the Hicks' appointment and wishing that the missing Urquhart would turn up again and sort the mess out.

But General Urquhart was in a mess himself, a decidedly sticky one. He, Lathbury, and Fitch's HQ were trapped in a Dutch house. Behind him on the balcony, which was piled high with a barricade of furniture, Lathbury was taking pot shots at German soldiers. Outside in the front young Major Waddy had just stopped a German Mark IV tank with a Gammon bomb before being killed by the blast from a mortar bomb.

He walked over to Lathbury: 'We must get on,' he said. 'We'll have to try and break out.'

'I agree,' the Brigadier agreed. 'Our best prospect seems to be to get out the back way and push on into the town where presumably the rest of the Brigade are now involved.'

The decision made, the two men hurried down the stairs while the paras of the 3rd covered their escape with smoke bombs. Mischievously Lathbury said: 'Would you like to throw a bomb, sir?'

'No, you're much better at it then I am.'

As the two of them attempted to climb a fence, Lathbury's sten went off. The 9mm slug hit the pavement just near the General's size ten boot. Urquhart told him off. 'It was bad enough,' he remarked, 'for a divisional commander to be jinking about in what was now hardly more than a company action, and it would have been too ironic for words to be laid low by a bullet fired "by one of my brigadiers".'

Lathbury regarded his sten with disgust. 'I'm awfully sorry. A temperamental weapon at the best.'

Then they were off, followed by their escort, made up of two young officers. They ran down a long street with intersections every twenty yards. As they dashed by the first of them, a spandau opened up. They ran on. The second loomed up. They increased their speed. But this time they were out of luck. Lathbury fell, badly wounded. Dodging the lead cutting the air all around them, the remaining three dragged the wounded Brigadier into a terrace house, while a stolid middle-aged Dutch couple watched them in open-mouthed amazement. Swiftly they laid him on the floor and tore open his blouse.

The Brigadier had been partially paralysed by a bullet which had nicked his spine. The deathly pale Lathbury could go no further. All three of them knew that soon the Germans would be coming looking for them. Almost as if he knew what they were thinking, Lathbury looked up at them and whispered: 'You must leave me. It's no use staying. You'll only get cut off!' Urquhart looked at Cleminson and Taylor, the two young officers: 'We must try to get some proper medical attention for him.' He stopped short.

A head in a German coal-scuttle helmet had appeared at the window. Urquhart did not hesitate. He pressed the trigger of his automatic. At that range he could not miss. The window shattered. The German yelled in agonized pain and fell back.

Now the Dutch couple stepped in. They offered to take care of the wounded Brigadier. Hurriedly they dragged him to the cover of a space under the stairs at the top of the cellar steps. They made a quick farewell, and slipped out of the back door into a maze of tiny, fenced suburban gardens, with the Monday washing still hanging in some.

They ran into the kitchen of a house in the Zwarteweg. A plump, solemn Dutchman tried to warn them in his own language that the enemy was already coming round the corner. They did not understand the words, but they understood the look of alarm on his round face. They clattered up the stairs of Herr Derksen's house. On the landing Urquhart flung a glance out of the tiny window. The street was full of field grey uniforms. Cleminson hissed: 'We can't get out this way. The place is crawling with 'em.'

Taylor, who had checked the back, nodded at the stairs. 'Can we be sure of these people?' he asked. 'There's an open attic over this room from which we might keep the entrance in view.'

While they were discussing their predicament, a self-propelled gun rattled up and parked just below their window. Hurriedly they climbed up to the attic shelf and pulled the detachable ladder up behind them. Hardly daring to breathe now, they checked over their resources and waited: three pistols and two hand-grenades each.

Time passed.

Urquhart who had a sweet tooth, passed out his bag of sweets and two bars of chocolate which he had swopped with his batman Hancock for his own cigarette ration. Down below, the firing had ceased, but they could still hear German voices. In the end Urquhart said: 'I think it's time we tried to get out. I don't how you chaps feel, but we are less than useless cooped up here.' As Urquhart wrote much later, 'I felt that as a divisional commander, I ought not to be indulging in such frolics of evasion.'

'I don't think it's going to be that easy yet,' Cleminson remarked doubtfully. 'But we can take a look.'

Taylor lowered the ladder and passing into a bedroom, checked the street. The two other officers followed. Taylor turned: 'They're down there still, the SP crew.'

Urquhart looked over his shoulder. The Germans were standing around their vehicles, smoking while others fiddled around tightening tracks. 'There's no future in this,' Urquhart announced abruptly. 'We're contributing nothing. We could lob a grenade on this thing and make a dash for it.'

But the big Scot could see that the two others were not impressed. He looked at Cleminson and said: 'All right, we'll have a

121

majority decision on this.'

'Even if we knock out the gun and its crew, which we could do quite easily,' Cleminson said, 'we would be killed or caught. I'd prefer to wait for an attack to catch up with us rather than go prowling around.'

Thus, as Urquhart was to say himself, he 'was outvoted'. As his élite Division commenced its bloody martyrdom, its commander hid in a provincial Dutch attic.

3

'The stable boys' – the politest name given to the Household Cavalry by the rest of the Guards Armoured Division – had moved out of Valkenswaard that morning. The day had been misty and the country wooded: therefore they had moved with caution, forgetting Montgomery's order to 'drive ahead with the utmost energy; any tendency to be sticky or cautious must be stamped out ruthlessly'.

But now the lead scout car of the troop commanded by Lieutenant Palmer had finally linked up with the 'Screaming Eagles' – the US 101st Airborne, at Woensel north of Eindhoven. The assistant divisional commander Brigadier-General Gerald Higgins had bad news, however, for Lieutenant Palmer: the northern end of Eindhoven was still in German hands and the road bridge at

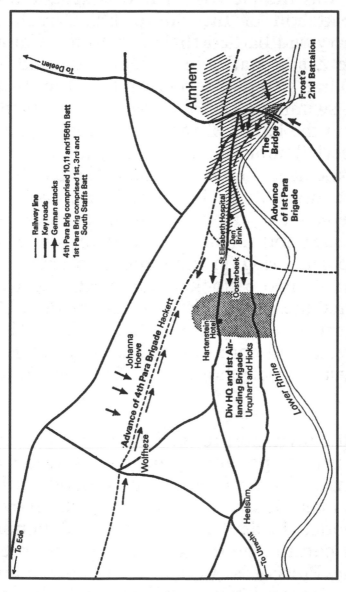

DAY TWO: 'I only hope the others don't think I'm letting them down.' – Dying Para on bridge to Father Egan

Map labels:

To Deelen

Arnhem

Frost's 2nd Battalion

The Bridge

Advance of 1st Para Brigade

St Elisabeth Hospital

Den Brink

Oosterbeek

Hartenstein Hotel

Div HQ and 1st Air-landing Brigade Urquhart and Hicks

'Advance of 4th Para Brigade Hackett'

Johanna Hoeve

Wolfheze

Lower Rhine

Heelsum

To Ede

To Utrecht

Legend:

—— Railway line

▬▬ Key roads

↑ German attacks

4th Para Brig comprised 10,11 and 156th Batt

1st Para Brig comprised 1st, 3rd and South Staffs Batt

Zon over Wilhelmina Canal had been blown by the enemy. The one bright spot in the affair was the fact that Major LaPrade and his battalion of the 506th US Parachute Infantry had battled their way to the Canal, where Major LaPrade, a lieutenant and an NCO had stripped and taken the other bank after swimming across. Now both banks were in the hands of the Screaming Eagles.

Eagerly Palmer began to relay the news to an expectant General Adair: 'Stable boys have contacted our Feathered Friends!'

Thereafter a stream of messages began to pass back and forth in clear, demanding, in particular, bridging equipment to span the Canal. At two o'clock, Guards HQ received the final message: 'For your information, US Airborne's telephone number is Zon 244!' Thereafter all communications were carried out via the telephone of a friendly Dutch doctor.

But the invitation to 'call Zon 244' was the only bright spot in a grim day. A troop of Shermans under Lieutenant Prescott of the Grenadier Guards managed to push on over a wooden bridge, but it collapsed behind them cutting them off. Thus by late afternoon, Prescott's tanks were across and Palmer's were blocked at Zon, while the rest of the Guards Division was still stalled at Eindhoven.

Lieutenant Wingfield recalls the long line of Shermans lining up, impatient to move on, when the tank commander nearest him called, 'Royal Tiger tanks a mile ahead. Get under cover. Tiffies have been called.'

The next instant the planes peeled off from the fighter 'cab-rank' and came zooming in at 450 mph. Just over the famous Eindhoven Philips works they let fly with their rockets. To Wingfield, cowering beside the Sherman, they looked like 'foreshortened lamp-posts with plumes of smoke bursting from the back'.

The next instant they struck their target. There was a thick throaty explosion. A plume of dark smoke jetted upwards. A black object sailed lazily through the smoke. It was the Tiger's turret, complete with gun. The tank commander swallowed hard. They moved on.

But Eindhoven still remained in German hands and Montgomery's great drive north was twenty-four hours behind schedule.

Meanwhile Brigadier Hackett's 4th Para Brigade had begun to move out from DZ. The original plan had been changed now. Hackett's 10th and 156th Battalions were to seize the high ground north of Arnhem, which Dobie's now decimated 1st Battalion had been unable to do, while his 11th Battalion, plus two companies of the South

Staffordshires, were to join what was left of Dobie's 1st and Fitch's 3rd near the Elizabeth Hospital and attempt to break through to the bridge.

Satisfied that his Brigade was moving efficiently and swiftly, Brigadier Hackett drove to the new Divisional HQ at the Hartenstein Hotel. And he was in a bad mood, which was not helped by seeing the ground floor dining-room laid out with maps and forms, as if the Division were in a training scheme back in England and not fighting for its life, sixty miles deep in enemy territory. Against the background of a blood-red sky, stitched by the white and green of tracer, he and Hicks had it out.

Hackett had got on very well with the elderly infantryman. Now he took him to task about his organization of the Divisions. Worried that in the confused street-fighting of Arnhem itself, the 1st Parachute Brigade men might fire on his own 11th Battalion by mistake, he asked who was in overall command near the bridge.

Hicks said that the battalions were working individually. 'I know it's clearly unsatisfactory from the point of view of a normal command set-up,' he admitted unhappily, but in his opinion, there was no other way to do the job. The main thing was to break through to the bridge.

Hackett said he understood, but he wanted

126

a 'tidier plan'. 'I must have an objective,' he snapped, his anger unconcealed. 'I think we should first take the high ground east of Johanna Hoeve. I will then see what I can undertake to assist the operations in a Arnhem – and I want a series of times so that I can relate my actions to anyone else's.'

He finished with an outright threat. Unless a plan was made on these lines, he would challenge Hicks' right to command of the Division.

For a moment there was a heavy silence in the room, broken only by the crackle of small arms fire outside. Then Colonel Preston, the Division's senior admin officer, came in.

Hicks, his face set and angry, swung round and said: 'Brigadier Hackett thinks he ought to be in command of the Division.'

The ex-cavalryman snapped an angry disclaimer; he had said no such thing.

Hastily Preston left the room, leaving the two brigadiers shouting at each other. He told the Duty Officer to get hold of Colonel MacKenzie immediately. The senior staff officer was fast asleep when the Duty Officer shook him awake with the excited words. 'Come down quickly... The two brigadiers are having a flaming row!'

On the bridge they were still fighting and dying. Both sides had set fire to wooden houses to illuminate the bridge. By this garish light, they sniped each other.

In Mick Tucker's house, the roof had gone by now and the defenders had to crawl across the floor unless they wanted to stop one of the stream of bullets which came through the windows and door. Undaunted, tough-looking Captain Panter had come in to distribute German cigarettes, which had been captured. They were received gratefully by the worn, unshaven paras in spite of the fact that Panter had just overheard a recipient say: 'The old bastard thinks he's Father Christmas!'

Now, however, Tucker's house was being subjected to a heavy and deadly accurate mortar 'stonk'; and just before every fresh round, Tucker could have sworn he heard the sound of a church bell. He cautiously surveyed the church tower nearby, already holed by a German shell. And then he spotted the German observer. 'Outside on the balcony he was, signalling to the mortars with the bell. I told the others and a couple of the glider pilot boys soon saw him off. They rigged up two Brens at maximum elevation and waited for him to ring his bloody bell again.'

As the German observer came out onto the balcony, the two Brens snapped into action. The sergeant pilots poured two whole magazines of tracer into the German.

He went down 'like a sack of bad potatoes', as Tucker recalls today. Thereafter the mortar fire on the machine gunners' house was decidedly less accurate.

But the Germans were very close now. Father Egan, the Catholic padre, was sheltering in one ruined house when a cheerful begrimed para said conversationally: 'Well Padre, they've thrown everything but the kitchen stove, haven't they?'

The next instant there was a terrible crash, followed by the ceiling falling in – complete with gas cooker! As the paras began to pick themselves up and dust off the bits of rubble, the soldier who had spoken turned to Egan and said: 'I knew the bastards were close, but I didn't think they could hear us talking!'

But the defenders' humour was beginning to run out. They had been on the bridge twenty-four hours now and there was no sign of relief from either their own Division or the Second Army. Time and time again Frost peered into the flames trying to spot the first of the relief, but he looked in vain.

At a conference held near the Elizabeth Hospital, the officers of the 1st Para Brigade and those who had joined them from Hackett's command had decided to wait till dawn the next morning, Tuesday, before they would attempt to break through to the bridge. As for Horrocks' men, they were still stalled at Eindhoven and already beginning to bed down for the night. As one of them recalls, 'every man had a bed in one of the nearby houses – complete with clean sheets and pillowcases. I daren't think how many of the good folk of Eindhoven spent that night in armchairs or on sofas, but every man in the regiment was accommodated like a king'.

Thus the great killing of Frost's young men began. As Monday, the 18th September, 1944 gave way to Tuesday, Father Egan knelt down at the side of a twenty-year-old boy who, according to Captain Logan, the medical officer, had only a quarter of an hour to live.

'If you'll bring a couple of stretcher-bearers along, Padre,' he said quietly, looking up at the priest from the rubble on which he lay, 'I can handle a rifle. Just let them put me in position.'

'I'm sorry,' Egan whispered, trying to placate the dying boy, 'but the stretcher-bearers are too busy just now.'

The para nodded his understanding. 'I only hope the others don't think I'm letting them down.' Ten minutes later he was dead.

DAY THREE

'We're getting short of ammo, so when you shoot, you shoot to kill'.
– Major Dickie Lonsdale to the survivors of 1st Para Brigade.

The 1st Para Brigade's attack began at dawn. Like grey ghosts the survivors of the 1st and 3rd Battalions, supported now by Hackett's men, started to filter through the houses towards the German positions.

At first all went well and they made good progress, with Dobie's 1st in the lead. But as the light increased, the German snipers firing at them from the high ground on the flank were joined by the guns on the other side of the Rhine. Multiple flak and 88 mms commenced slamming into the long strung out columns.

'It was tough,' Corporal Dukes of the 1st recalls, 'but not too tough, at least for my battalion. We bashed on regardless.'

But not for long. The 1st was trapped in a long unprotected strip of open ground, only some thirty yards wide, where they were subjected to all the Germans could offer. The 1st's after-battle report is eloquent in its stark simplicity about what happened next. 'R Coy six men left. S Coy fifteen men left (approx) … T Coy eight men left. Bn HQ about ten left.'

Dobie went forward to make a personal recce. He found that what was left of his T Company was cut off and could not break away from the German SS troops against whom they were battling. A vicious hand-to-hand struggle developed for the possession of a house. With their young CO at their head, the paras forced an entry. But they paid a high price for their temporary cover. Dobie was hit in the eye and arm and when the gasping attackers had finally taken up their new defensive positions, he found he had only six men left.

What happened next is best expressed by the after-battle report: 'Enemy in rear… Tanks outside our house. Many civilians in cellar with us. Nothing more to be done. Four wounded in our party … 07.30 SS entered house. Party taken.'

Four hours later Dobie, his wounds hastily dressed, his badges of rank removed, was on the run, a fugitive from the SS who were everywhere, or so it seemed. The First Parachute Battalion, the country's first real parachute formation formed by the renowned 'Dracula' himself, no longer existed.

Fitch's Battalion suffered the same fate.

Being nearest to the Rhine, it suffered the whole weight of the German barrage. Trying to cross the open strip, it was systematically mown down by the enemy. Fitch ordered the withdrawal. But now there was no chance of making an orderly one. It was *sauve qui peut*.

As they moved out in small groups, the German fire intensified, as if the enraged gunners were angry at losing their prey. Casualties were heavy and when the handful of survivors reassembled at the Rhine Pavilion, Colonel Fitch was not among them.

Now it was the turn of the 11th Battalion and the South Staffords. They had a strange advance. For minutes they were subjected to shattering small arms fire which would be followed by a loud echoing silence in which the advancing men could hear Frost holding out on the bridge less than a mile away. They pressed on and took Arnhem's museum in spite of heavy opposition. Then their attack stalled. Both the Battalion Commander and his Second-in-Command were captured. Assistance was demanded from the 11th Para.

Colonel Lea of the 11th hurriedly formed his men up. But he was under the mistaken impression he was still covered by the South Staffs. He was soon to learn his error.

Suddenly German Tigers loomed up out of the fog of war like great primeval monsters. The paras, out in the open and with few anti-tank weapons, fell back in disorder, taking severe casualties. Here and there men broke. Control began to go. Lieutenant Colonel Sheriff Thompson of the 1st Light Regiment, an artillery unit, swiftly went into action and stopped the stragglers. Briskly he got the shocked men, their eyes wide and staring with fear, under control.

As more and more fell back from the decimated, confused regiments, each of which had lost its commanding officer, he placed the couple of hundred of them under the command of Major Lonsdale, who had been wounded several times in the face. In the thin, bitter rain which had begun to fall now, what was left of the 1st Parachute Brigade started to trudge back the way it had come, its dead littering the road. The first attempt to relieve the bridge that day had failed abysmally.

The Canadian, Leo Heaps, in the company of a like-minded American para Lieutenant, had been 'swanning around' – to use his own words – in the hope of finding out how close the relief force was to the bridge when he bumped into those same survivors.

They were in the shell of a wrecked church, soaked to the skin and covered in blood and mud from crawling through ditches to escape. 'It was a terrible sight,' he thought. 'Each man was weary to his bones and miserable and most were wounded.'

Then he almost bumped into Major Lonsdale who had been wounded in the face, and was covered in blood. He asked him why he didn't go inside for treatment.

Lonsdale grinned through a blood-caked mouth and said: 'I've been hit three times, but I'm still good for several more.'

As he went inside to talk to the battered survivors, Heaps' eyes fell on the broken stained glass window through which it seemed as if the sun were 'a little red with blood'.

Inside, Lonsdale also faced the survivors of the 1st, 3rd, 11th and South Staffs, two hundred left out of over two thousand, standing in the splintered pulpit. 'You know as well as I do,' he said, 'there are a lot of bloody Germans coming at us. Well, all we can do is to stay here and hang on in the hope that somebody catches us up. We must fight for our lives and stick together.'

As if to emphasise his words, the German artillery started another 'hate' at that moment. But the roar did not break the hold the wounded Major had on the men.

'We've fought the Germans before,' he continued. 'In North Africa, Sicily, Italy. They weren't good enough for us then and they're bloody well not good enough for us now! They're up against the finest soldiers in the world. An hour from now you will take up defensive positions north of the road outside. Make certain you dig in well and that your weapons and ammo are in good order. We're getting short of ammo, so when you shoot, you shoot to kill. Good luck to you all.'

2

Just as the Germans had wiped out the 1st and 3rd Battalion, General Urquhart, thanks to their attack, found his way back to the new HQ at the Hartenstein Hotel. Realizing 'how much better it would have been for me to have stopped in the St Elizabeth Hospital area for a little time, in order to tie up the advance of the 1st and 3rd, the 11th Battalion and the South Staffords', he ordered: 'Someone will have to get down into the town right away to co-ordinate these attacks. It will have to be a senior officer.'

Colonel Hilary Barlow, Brigadier Hicks' second-in-command, was chosen for the task and set off immediately. He was never seen again. Quickly Urquhart turned his attention to the 4th Para Brigade's attack and realizing that pressure was building up rapidly on Hackett's front, decided to drive out and see the 'broken-down cavalryman' himself. They met at the edge of a thickly wooded copse near the railway embankment. Almost before they could begin their discussion, three Me 109s roared in at ground level and while the two brigadiers hugged the ground, proceeded to strafe the area.

When they had finally gone, they picked themselves up and dusted the earth from their uniforms.

'I'm delighted to see you're out of it, sir,' Hackett said, and Urquhart guessed that it was not only his health which was concerning the brigadier; now he would not have to take orders from Hicks. 'There were all sorts of ugly rumours.' He swung round and pointed to a ridge towards the east, where a fierce local engagement was going on. 'The Boche are shooting from the woods to the north and beyond to the east,' he said, and explained that he had tried to push on several times without any success; but had had no further troops available to outflank the Germans. 'Unless the enemy alters his plans in such a way to favour us, there's not much future for the brigade in its present line of advance.'

To the men of the 10th Para stalled at a crossroads, it seemed their future had already been decided. Signaller Burrows, a stocky regular from Sunderland, at that moment found himself in a strangely composed patrol, including the signals sergeant, Len Hunt, the MO and his medical orderly. The fact that the Battalion was already reduced to such measures, indicated to Burrows, who was a veteran of the desert, that 'things were pretty shaky'.

Cautiously, against the background of a German mortar 'stonk', they advanced along what looked like tennis courts, bordered by a six-foot high wire fence. Suddenly the MO who was armed with a revolver, hissed: 'Germans!'

They ducked instinctively. About three hundred yards off, three German soldiers were standing in the open quite unconcerned.

'They haven't seen us,' Sergeant Hunt said, 'come on, let's get them.'

They pushed forward swiftly until they got within range; then they opened fire. One went down, throwing up his hands dramatically. The second fell without a sound. But the third – obviously not hit – dropped behind a bush. Elated by their little victory, Sergeant Hunt said: 'I'm going to winkle the bastard out.'

He ran forward. The next instant the third German fired. Sergeant Hunt fell dead. Before they could react, the unseen enemy fired again. The MO dropped. 'All right,' the medical orderly cried, 'let's get the bastard.'

But he and Burrows hardly had moved out

of their cover when the German dropped the medic. 'Christ,' he groaned, 'I've been hit in the arse!' Burrows grabbed him and together they limped off the way they had come back to what was left of their HQ, dug in near a crossroads.

They arrived in time to hear that General Hackett had ordered the 10th to withdraw. Unless they grabbed the railway crossing at Wolfheze – the only exit from the embankment for the 4th Brigade's vehicles and anti-tank guns – there was a good chance of their being cut off from Hicks' Brigade. Now things really began to go wrong.

RSM 'Chalky' White, who had been knocked out at the drop and wounded in the neck, saw that they would have to cross a large open field, completely dominated by enemy fire, before they could reach the safety of some woods beyond. It was going to be a tough dirty business, he told himself grimly, especially in view of the fact that the Battalion was not holding together as it should have done. The 10th's lack of training as a cohesive unit back in the UK was now paying off badly.

But the 10th were going to be spared nothing. Just as they prepared to make their dash, the first section of the gliders from the Polish Brigade began their landings and added to the confusion.

As Polish war correspondent Marek Swiecicki recalls: 'At that moment (the cast off from the tugs) something happened which we had not expected. From the north other tiny dots ... grew and grew ... *Messerschmitts!*

'Their machine guns snapped and barked... Several gliders caught fire and ... dived in mad flight to the ground... One of the gliders broke up in mid-air like a child's toy, and a jeep, an anti-tank gun and people fell out of it... When they (the *Messerschmitts*) stopped, the forest opened up. Skirmishing Germans, looking in the distance like rabbits jumping, or field mice, moved forward. The German infantry fired at the gliders... The bullets tore through the gliders' wooden walls, over the jeeps and guns which had been brought out and then over the men, throwing more and more to the ground. The men who had escaped whole fled. Yes, they fled – for it could not be called a retreat or a defence.'

Some of the 10th broke ranks to help men they took to be Poles. A hail of Spandau fire mowed them down. The handful left scrambled back to safety frantically. Now the crossing began. 'But we didn't come all the way here to run away. Sar'nt Major!' Burrows protested.

Chalky White, the man who one day

would be a respected church verger, gave him an unprintable answer.

The German guns spotted their opportunity. As the paras broke cover, they opened up with everything they had. Man after man went down. The bullets cut great holes in the 10th's ranks. Now it was no longer an orderly withdrawal; it was a panic-stricken retreat. Burrows remembers pelting by the Polish gliders, bullets stitching deadly patterns at his heels.

RSM White made the other side before him. His chest gasping with the effort, his wounded head throbbing crazily, he snapped at the men manning a six-pounder gun to 'do something'.

The familiar bark of the touchy bantam-sized NCO had its effect. They snapped into action. A few Brens followed their example. Slowly some form of organized cover was laid down for the rest who were to follow. But by now the damage was done. The ploughed field was littered with the bodies of the 10th Battalion.

But the RSM had no time for the dead; he had to concern himself with the living. Moustache bristling with anger at the whole untidy business he doubled across to where a group of officers were shouting at each other in confusion.

'Will you stop that shouting gentlemen, *please!*' he barked.

His own CO, Colonel Smythe, who had only a couple more days to live, appeared from the centre of the excited throng: 'Don't bloody well shout at me like that, Sar'nt Major!' he cried angrily.

For the 10th Battalion the end was near.

Urquhart had just returned to his HQ at the Hartenstein Hotel when he was alarmed by the wild cry: 'The Germans are coming!' He looked out of the shattered window.

Small groups of soldiers were running across the lawn, their eyes wide with fear, obviously out of control. They were followed by twenty or more under a tall young officer.

Swiftly he called Mackenzie. Together they rushed out and tried to intercept them. Shouts were of no avail. In the end he had to use physical violence to get them to return to their positions. Their heads bent in shame, they did so, while Urquhart dressed down the tall officer who had led the panic-stricken rush to the rear.

But by now the rot had set in. A little later, Mackenzie inspecting the perimeter found a slit trench abandoned, with a loaded bren and a nest of grenades carelessly left to the enemy. General Urquhart called his commanders together and impressed upon them they must take the most severe measures to halt the growing 'unease and edginess' among their men.

Lieutenant Leo Heaps, wandering around the perimeter that afternoon, sniper-hunting with his American pal, the paratroop lieutenant Johnny Johnson, saw weary men with beards everywhere in the slit trenches who asked the same old tired question: 'When are the tanks coming up from the south?'

3

By now the Guards had reached the outskirts of Nijmegen. But Slim Jim's 'All Americans', the 82nd AB, had still failed to take the vital bridge from the SS battalion holding it, even after three frontal attacks. Colonel Breitmeyer, the Guards' Intelligence Officer, drove to meet Gavin and Browning in the 82nd CP, located in a wood south of Nijmegen, where a joint plan of attack was swiftly drawn up.

Their decision was a quick dash, with combined tanks and paras, for three objectives: the road bridge to the east, the railway bridge to the west and the post office located centrally between the two. The western bridge was to be assaulted by a mixed force of Grenadiers and paras from the 505 Para Infantry; the eastern bridge by paras and Irish Guardsmen.

At four o'clock that afternoon, roughly when the ill-fated 10th Para were facing up to their own terrible moment of truth, the eastern force set off towards their fourth bridge assault in three days. All went well until the lead tank, commanded by Lieutenant J. Moller, spotted the traffic roundabout, some three hundred yards away from the bridge.

An 88mm gun tore the still air apart violently. There was the great booming sound of metal striking metal. Moller's Sherman came to an abrupt halt with its commander slumped dead within the turret. As flames started to pour from the gleaming shell hole skewered in the tank's side, its surviving crew members made a frantic dash for safety.

Still the dusty Shermans came on, followed by Gavin's paratroopers, moving silently forward over the battle-littered cobbles in their rubber-soled jump-boots. One by one the 13th Squadron's tanks were brewed up by the German fire until in the end the paras were left without armour, one hundred yards short of the roundabout. Cursing angrily, their commander First Lieutenant James J. Smith gave his men the signal to withdraw. The 'All Americans' had failed once again.

In the centre, the Allied attack was more successful. The post office was captured by the Irish Guards, who found 'there was nothing in it but civilians in the cellars and dead Germans behind the counters'. But still the attackers were without a bridge. Now it was up to the Guards' party commanded by Captain J. Neville.

Neville's column moved off – led by a Dutch guide – with the tanks well-spaced out and the infantry in carriers. Neville himself directed the operation from his tank in the centre of the column. At first the advance was uneventful, thanks to their guide's knowledge of the terrain. Then they bumped into a machine gun nest which was speedily knocked out. But the fierce snap and crackle of the small arms fire attracted a German *Panther* to the scene.

In the confusion it missed the column and they were able to move within sight of the bridge without serious casualties. But as Neville surveyed the opposite bank, he could see he was in for trouble: the Germans were well dug in and armed with both heavy machine guns and anti-tank cannon. As he recalled much later:

'As the light was beginning to fade, we decided upon an immediate attack. The plan was simple, if unimaginative. Three tanks were to charge the opening in the embankment, while the other two gave covering fire. At the same time the Americans, aided by the infantry carriers, were to gain the embankment to the south and drive out the machine-gunners from the flanks.'

But Captain Neville's hopes were soon dashed. As soon as his three tanks rumbled forward, they came under heavy and accurate German fire. The lead Sherman was hit and 'brewed up' immediately. All but one of its crew was killed. The next was struck an instant later – and then the third one. The 'Yanks', as the Guards called their para allies, fared little better. They ran into heavy machine-gun fire. Two German self-propelled guns appeared from a tunnel in the embankment and joined in the slaughter. Swiftly the steam went out of the advance and Neville decided to call off the attack. 'Hell's Highway' was living up to its name.

As the depressed Guards bedded down for the night, the Germans set fire to houses near the vital bridge so that it would be illuminated during the hours of darkness; and cowering in his cellar, an outraged Dutchman wrote: 'The centre of the town is like a hell. A rustling sound like that of a waterfall, uncanny and terrifying, fills the air and seized with panic, thousands and thousands fly from this doomed Nijmegen. Those who live on the outskirts stare in terror at the whirling sea of fire from which huge columns of smoke emerge to write a fierce indictment on the night firmament.

While the fire is doing its destructive work, an incessant rain of shells come screeching and whistling over the burning town. There are no words to describe this holocaust.'

4

For his part, Frost, who had just managed to grab his first catnap in nearly three days, looking over his shoulder at the burning centre of Arnhem, thought: 'I never saw anything more beautiful than those burning buildings.'

But the Colonel had little time for admiring the brutal beauty of a burning Arnhem that evening. The Battalion had really begun taking casualties now, as the Germans stood off and commenced a systematic blasting of the few houses held by his worn, begrimed men. Now a Tiger tank rattled up rustily and joined in the slaughter. The tough CO of his A Company, Major Tatham-Warter was hit, as was Father Eagan. But although both were to remain on duty, Private Tucker, desperately trying to get his little 38 set to work in the machine-gunners' house, was soon to remark to the signals sergeant, Welshman 'Toc' Evans, 'Toc, if this goes on, you'll be the bloody CO soon!'

During a pause in the firing, Captain Briggs

of the 3rd thought he heard the relief troops advancing towards their positions. Hurriedly he organized his men to shout the 2nd's famous war-cry, known to everyone throughout the Division: *'Whoa Mahommed!'*

No answer came, so Briggs tore down wallpaper from the walls of the house held by his group and formed a primitive six-foot megaphone with it. Hoarsely he shouted the crudest British Army swearwords he could remember through it. But still to no avail.

Mick Tucker had more luck. Suddenly a faint voice began to crackle in his earphones and it was in English. Hastily he turned up the volume and listened. 'Close down network,' the faint voice ordered. 'Close down network now!'

Tucker was an experienced enough soldier to know that the Germans had learned the British Army's simple codewords – 'Large Sunray', 'Sunray One' 'Sunray Two' etc – but he could not take the risk of losing the first contact he had made in seventy odd hours of battle. 'Identify yourself … identify yourself,' he rapped urgently and clicked over. There was no reply.

He tried again. 'Identify yourself, please, identify yourself please!' he repeated desperately. But no further answer came save that grim command. 'Close down network now!'

And then as the German tanks started firing again, making all further conversation impossible, Tucker threw the set to one side in disgust and picked up the German 08 rifle he had been using all day – instead of the useless colt – and doubled back to his window. The attack had started once more.

Captain Simpson of the Engineers located in the school building spotted the Tiger first, as it rolled up to the north-west corner of the place, only twenty odd yards away. Horrified he watched as its great low-hanging 88 swung round slowly and stopped facing their position. The Germans seemed to have all the time in the world. And then the gun-layer fired. A great six-foot hole appeared in the west wall. Rubble and red-hot metal hissed through the air everywhere. A man howled, clapped his hand to his shoulder and sat down suddenly, a look of outrage in his eyes.

The Tiger's gun erupted once more. Another great chunk of the wall disappeared suddenly with a roar. But then for some reason or other unknown to the shocked, wide-eyed defenders, the great 60-ton monster backed away and disappeared from sight as abruptly as it had appeared. Hastily they rushed to their positions. But there were not so many of them left now – nineteen out of the original fifty. As Captain Simpson recalls:

'Our nerves began to show the tremendous strain. The men's faces in the flickering lights of the fires looked terrible – their eyes red from want of sleep, three days growth of beard, blackened by fire fighting and whitened again with thick plaster gave them the grimmest of appearance.'

Captain Wood, a platoon commander, had an even grimmer picture of the scene that terrible night. 'Row upon row of houses aflame. Jerry tanks everywhere, roaming at will, and being attacked by us with Piats, sticky bombs and 36 grenades. It had now been 72 hours of ceaseless fighting – no sleep, a day without any kind of food and some ten hours since the last water had gone. Every house was defended or taken by hand to hand, each floor told its story – shrapnel pock-marks, bullet marks, blood-spattered stairs, floors and walls, our own dead and those of the enemy everywhere, some still locked together as they died.'

But the tremendous will to resist of the 2nd Parachute Battalion was still there. That same evening a handful of scared, dirty young SS soldiers appeared suddenly at the windows of Tucker's house. They nearly died a sudden death until someone spotted they were unarmed.

'*Kamerad*,' their spokesman cried plaintively, '*Kamerad*.' Their intention was obvious. They wanted to surrender.

For a moment the paras considered. They could not take the *Waffen SS* men prisoner, that was for certain. But if they mowed them down without weapons and they were themselves taken prisoner later, they knew what their fate would be.

Finally someone shouted coarsely: 'Go on, bugger off – we can't use you here! Go back where you came from!'

For one long moment the young Germans looked at the paras incredulously. Then Tucker's menacing gesture with his rifle made their words quite clear. Ducking their heads against the fire coming from their own lines, they ran back the way they had come and began burrowing into the nearest ruins to wait for the morrow.

Wearily the paras settled down to await the next attack. Stepping over the wounded gunner, who lay face down in the rubble – he had been severely wounded in the buttocks – the young signaller began to make yet another soup for the old Dutch lady in the back bedroom.

5

The 10th was breaking up. Breaking off action during daylight hours was bad enough at the best of times even for experienced

151

soldiers, but the 10th was virtually pinned in on one side by the damned embankment. More and more men started to get cut off from the main body under Colonel Smythe. RSM 'Chalky' White was dug in near the embankment with nine other men when the word came up from the paras in the nearby position. 'Last man – last round! It's from the Colonel.' Grimly the battered men of the 10th faced the growing darkness, prepared for the slaughter which must come now. But 'Chalky' White and his men were not fated to die just then. Fifteen minutes later, the somewhat elderly adjutant crawled up to White and whispered, as if the Germans were only a matter of yards away.

'Sar'nt-Major, we're breaking out in small groups. You'll take yours that way.'

'But that's the way we've just come, sir,' he protested.

The Adjutant did not seem to hear. RSM White, being the good NCO he was, obeyed orders. With the men strung out in single file behind him, he set off in the direction ordered by the Adjutant. They had not gone far when a house loomed up in the dark wood, and by the sounds coming from it, White knew that it was occupied by Germans. He turned to warn the others and found he was completely alone.

Signaller Burrows of the 10th, dug in with a

larger group in the same wood, never even had a chance to break out. With the Germans covering every exit, the officers, it seemed, had no other choice left but to surrender. Dazed and bewildered by what had happened to them this terrible day, the weary group heard their officers command: 'We're going to give up. And remember you're all corporals when they ask you. In the prison camp you don't have to work if you are an NCO.'

A few minutes later the SS started to emerge from the woods, led by a young officer whose first words to the numbed paras was the classic phrase: 'Gentlemen, for *you* the war is over.'

Some of the 10th fought to the very last. Captain Queripel, a burly looking officer from the Channel Islands, had already rallied his scattered company once and led it into a counter-attack to recapture one of the Battalion's lost anti-tank guns, although he was badly wounded in the face. But as that miserable day grew closer to its end, he found himself cut off with a handful of men in a ditch. Now he had been wounded again, in both arms. Still he was full of fight. Twice he picked up German stick grenades and flung them back at the enemy. But he knew time was running out for his men; he knew, too, that they would never make it if they broke and ran without cover.

In spite of their protests, he ordered them to retreat while he covered them. Piling his few grenades on the top of the ditch and gripping his sten more firmly, he gave his last order. 'All right, go – *now!*' As they pelted away, he fired his final burst of 9mm slugs into the German positions. His men would never see him again. He was to win the first VC of that terrible day.

While Hackett tried to withdraw his shattered brigade, with the 7th KOSBs which had been fighting under his command already beginning to move back into the Divisional area, a worried Urquhart began to review his strength. His para battalions – 1st, 3rd and 11th – were down to three hundred men, each battalion without a commanding officer. The South Staffs had a hundred men left. As far as he could gather from Hackett, the 156th Para Battalion, which had lost its CO, Sir W.R. de B. des Voeux, had 270 under command while its neighbour, the 10th were down to 250. Now they were all attempting to crowd into the Divisional area.

Urquhart knew what that meant. With the weak force he had left, he 'could no more hope to reinforce Frost than reach Berlin'. As an eerie calm, broken only by occasional muffled explosions and the burst of small arms settled on the Divisional area, General

Roy Urquhart knew that Frost and his battered command could only survive a matter of hours now.

And far away at SHAEF's press headquarters the correspondents were busy scribbling away at the dispatches which would make the headlines in the morning papers in New York and London.

'Battle of the West nearing its last phase. Best news since D-Day. Great developments imminent. The outcome of the last battle in west is being decided. Field Marshal Montgomery's left hook has, with perfect timing, landed on the German chin, and it looks like a knockout blow. There is perfect co-ordination between the Airborne and Second Army armour. Their operations continue to be extremely successful and everything is going according to schedule...'

DAY FOUR

'Even after defeat, these men left the battlefield with morale unbroken'.

-SS General Bittrich.

At dawn, Mackay issued the last of his benzedrine tablets to his sappers in the school to face the attack that would soon come in. His men had had no sleep for over seventy-two hours now. Their last food had been twenty-four hours earlier; their last water twelve hours. They would need the pep pills.

The Tigers came as expected, the field-grey infantry stretched out behind their massive protection in the familiar 'grape', as they called the tactic.

Now the sappers were alone on the eastern side of the bridge. All round them the houses once held by Frost's paras were burning, save for the one at the crossroads held by the enemy. But the handful of unwounded sappers fought back like madmen, using their puny Piats and handful of sticky bombs against the lumbering metal monsters. It took them three terrible hours, but in the end the enemy had had enough. Withdraw-

156

ing in reverse, covering what was left of the SS Panzer Grenadiers with their twin machine-guns, the Tigers moved back across the battle-littered bridge the way they had come, leaving the house still in Mackay's hands.

Now he had time to take stock of his men as they crouched in the rubble on this grey drizzling Wednesday dawn. 'Splattered everywhere was blood,' he would write much later. 'It lay in pools in the rooms, it covered the smocks of the defenders and ran in small rivulets down the stairs. The men themselves were the grimmest sight of all: eyes red-rimmed for want of sleep, their faces, blackened by fire-fighting, wore three days' growth of beard. Many of them had minor wounds, and their clothes were cut away to expose roughly fixed, blood-soaked field dressings. They were huddled in twos and threes, each little group manning positions that required twice their number. The only clean things in the school were the weapons.'

Looking at the survivors that morning, Mackay realized that he would never have to give the last order: 'These positions will be held to the last round and the last man.' For his men 'were conscious of their superiority. Around them lay four times their number of enemy dead.'

At ten o'clock, as the sun started to come up through the fog of war, the enemy gave up their attack on the schoolhouse with the Engineers. Instead they concentrated on the 80 men left, out of the original 400, under the bridge's arches. Soon the 2nd's rallying-cry, 'Whoa Mahommed', shouted time and time again to those men by Mackay would remain unanswered and the young Engineer officer would know that 'it was only a matter of time before we succumbed…'

It was just about that time that Urquhart, who had just ordered Hackett to give up any further idea of advancing to the ridge, was called urgently to the phone.

'Hello, Sunray,' a cheerful voice called.

But Urquhart was suspicious. The speaker at the other end might be an English-speaking German. 'Can you give me an inkling who you are?' he asked.

'It's the man who goes in for funny weapons,' the unknown said at last. Urquhart realized that the other person was conscious that the Germans might be tapping the line as he racked his brains to discover who his caller was.

'The man who is always late for your "O" groups,' the other man added equally mysteriously.

Then Urquhart tumbled to it. It was Major Freddie Gough of the Airborne Recce Squadron. In what seemed now another world, as divorced from this as the Earth from the moon, he remembered how the dashing Major had even been late for the planning of Market Garden itself. 'My goodness,' he exclaimed, 'I thought you were dead.'

Swiftly, now that the identity problem had been solved, Gough briefed him on the situation at the bridge.

In his turn General Urquhart said that the Division was in 'poor shape.' 'I'm afraid,' he said, 'you can only hope for relief from the south. For the moment, we can only try to preserve what we have left.'

Gough did not answer for a moment. Urquhart imagined he could hear the sounds of renewed fighting at the ridge in the silence. 'It's pretty grim... But we'll do what we can.'

'Well, then, good luck!'

It was to be the last conversation the two officers would hold for many a long month. The Battle for the Bridge was entering its final phase.

2

Together Colonel Giles Vandeleur of the Irish Guards and General Horrocks walked along the banks of the river at Nijmegen, looking the troops over. The plan that afternoon was for the 3rd Battalion to lead the assault, heading for the high ground, a thousand yards north of the highway bridge. The 1st Battalion would fan out to the west, forming an arc – together with the 3rd – around the bridge's northern exit. Both formations would go in by power boat.

But Horrocks, who had seen his share of action in this war ever since he had commanded an infantry battalion in the great retreat from the Western Front to Dunkirk, could note no apprehension in the faces of the big Guardsmen. Pulling Vandeleur to one side, he said: 'Look, some of 'em are sleeping, others are joking with each other, others are dreaming of home, no doubt. Don't they realize they are to make a daylight river crossing in the face of a determined enemy and many will be dead or wounded in a couple of hours? I wonder if they can make it?'

Colonel Vandeleur was confident. 'Of course, we all wonder that, sir,' he answered, as the artillery bombardment started, heralding the new attempt to take the damned bridge, 'but my men are veterans.'

At five minutes to three, the Divisional guns started to put down smoke on the far bank before lifting to fire HE shells at targets further beyond. On the British-held bank, the Guards were given a quick course in how to manage the power-boats. Then at three o'clock precisely, they moved off, racing through a hail of fire towards the bank to launch their boats. The Germans brought their 88mms and flak to bear on them. Boat after boat took direct hits. Men were flung high in the air, splashing down dead into the water. Others slumped over the side, dyeing the water with their blood. A few – signallers and mortarmen – went right to the bottom, carried down by the weight of their equipment, and drowned helplessly. To an American observer, the shell fragments looked like a 'school of mackerel on the feed', as they burst everywhere in the water.

But they pushed on. General Browning, the former Guardsman who had helped to plan the great operation, watching them cried: 'Look at 'em, unbelievably wonderful men and certainly great soldiers!'

The first wave hit the far bank. The smoke screen had started to clear. But still the second and third waves braved the murderous German fire and followed them across. Then they were across too, and had begun advancing, suffering terrible casualties. The Guards had gained a toe-hold on the other side.

The news flashed back to the only reserves left: Number One Squadron, 2nd Grenadiers, commanded by Major Trotter with Captain Lord Peter Carrington as his second-in-command. Immediately Trotter

called an orders group in his hotel headquarters. His orders were simple. Number
One Troop was to make 'one mad rush over
the bridge' to link up with men on the other
bank, and was then to be followed by the
rest of the squadron.

Before the meeting broke up, Trotter shook
hands with the sergeant who would be in the
lead tank – Sergeant Robinson, an 'old
sweat' who had been with the Grenadiers
since 1934, and said: 'Don't worry, I'll let
your wife know if you don't come back.'

Robinson, who had been brought up in the
pre-war Guards tradition of asking, 'Permission to speak, sir,' before daring to address
such a lordly person as a second-lieutenant,
mumbled an embarrassed 'thanks'.

Lord Carrington, one day to be Minister
of Defence, was not so reticent. 'We thought
that someone must be round the bend to
order an assault on the bridges. They were
certain to be mined and would probably be
blown up under us as we crossed.'

They rattled off from the laager area at six
o'clock. Robinson was in the lead in a Sherman armed with a 17-pounder. Behind him
came Sergeant Billingham. His Sherman
had the smaller 75mm, as did the two
remaining tanks of Robinson's troop.

Carrington coming up in the rear thought
that the lack of enemy or anything else on

their side of the bridge was 'intimidating'. 'There was tension behind the emptiness of it. We knew there had been fighting for this place for a couple of days and that this assault was the culmination.'

And then it happened. Just as Robinson's tank had nosed its way on to the bridge, a 88mm shell careened off the cobbles just in front of him and shook it violently. Robinson fired his smoke discharges. A soft plop. Thick white smoke clouds began to spread along the bridge. Hurriedly the 88 switched targets. But Guardsman Johnson of Billingham's tank had spotted the 88's gun flash already. He let the gun have four quick rounds of AP. The gun stopped firing suddenly. Swiftly Robinson switched tanks. Over the radio Major Trotter ordered the attack had to go in 'at all costs'. Robinson pushed off again. Three German anti-tank guns opened up at them. A soldier armed with a *panzerfaust* fired at them. And missed. The projectile slammed into a nearby girder. But that was not all. Above them, German soldiers started dropping grenades on them. They were being bombed from the air.

Now the German AP shells were coming in so fast that they seemed like small arms fire as they bounced off the Sherman's steep glacis plates. Later Guardsman Johnson was to say: 'I swear to this day that Jesus Christ rode on the front of our tank!'

The troop of tanks hit a roadblock. The only way through meant the Shermans had to turn broadsides on. But an anti-tank gun covered the awkward opening. Undismayed Robinson went for it like a bull at a gate. Frantically the gun-layer on the 57mm swung the long barrel round. Johnson fired first. One – two – three shells went whizzing through the air. A cloud of brown smoke. Ugly, red flame and the gun lurched to one side, its crew sprawled out extravagantly all around it. Robinson did not hesitate. The next instant his Sherman rolled over them. Going at top speed, its tracks covered in blood, the tank rattled down the ramp from the bridge, Robinson yelling in his Guards' NCO voice for the rest of the troop to keep up.

But already two of them were blazing wrecks in the road behind him. Robinson's tank came to a wide, tree-lined avenue. A great cumbersome Ferdinand SP rumbled into view. Its gunner fired first. The white tracer shell hurtled towards them frighteningly – and missed. Johnson, acting now as Robinson's gunner, didn't give the German a second chance. He started pumping high explosive shells at it at top speed. From a church opposite, small arms fire erupted. Lead started to strike the turret like heavy summer rain on a tin roof. Johnson let the place have a burst of machine fire. Robinson

2nd Army's Advance (Sept. 17th – 25th 1944)

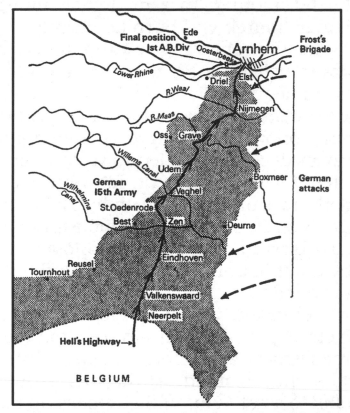

Final position
1st A.B. Div
Ede
Oosterbeek
Arnhem
Frost's
Brigade
Lower Rhine
Driel
Elst
R. Waal
Nijmegen
R. Maas
Oss
Grave
Willems Canal
Udem
Boxmeer
German
attacks
German
15th Army
Veghel
Wilhelmina Canal
St.Oedenrode
Best
Zen
Deurne
Eindhoven
Reusel
Tournhout
Valkenswaard
Neerpelt
Hell's Highway→
BELGIUM

'Don't worry, I'll let your wife know, if you don't come back.' –
Major Trotter to Sgt. Robinson 2nd Grenadier Guards

had no such scruples. 'Use the 75,' he bellowed, his face covered in sweat. Johnson pressed the electric turret device. It swung round smoothly. The next instant, he had smacked the church squarely with a 75mm shell. And another. In a matter of minutes the Dutch church was burning fiercely.

'If you see anything move, shoot it!' Robinson yelled in his stentorian voice as they rumbled forward again.

Three-quarters of a mile passed without serious opposition. Then they spotted the railway bridge. They rattled towards it, every man tense with excitement, Johnson sweeping both sides of the road with his Browning. Suddenly there were two terrific explosions. The hot blast hit Johnson like a blow from a flabby damp fist. For a moment he thought he was blinded.

But Robinson, who had closed his eyes instinctively, opened them to see a tall rangy figure in American uniform waving to them. 'A Yank,' he breathed, as the driver pulled the tank to a halt. Out of the ditches on both sides of the road, US paras scrambled up, broad grins on their dirty tired faces. One of them actually kissed the tank and their officer told Robinson that 'they were the sweetest guys he had seen in years!'

The Allies had their bridge over the Waal at last. As the crow flies, it was ten miles now to Arnhem.

3

On that same day, a worried Montgomery, made uneasy by the lack of real progress by the Second Army towards Arnhem, and Eisenhower's reaction to it, wrote the Supreme Commander a letter. It read:

'Dear Ike, I thank you very much for your letter of 20 September sent via Gale. I cannot agree that our concepts are the same and I am sure you would wish me to be quite frank and open in the matter. I have always said stop the right and go on with the left, but the right has been allowed to go on so far that it has outstripped its maintenance... I would say that the right flank of 12 Army Group should be given a very strict order to halt and if this order is not obeyed we shall get into greater difficulties. The net result of the matter in my opinion is that if you want to get the Ruhr you will have to put every single thing into the left hook and stop everything else. It is my opinion that if this is not done then you will not get the Ruhr. Your very great friend Monty.'

But the 'net result' of Montgomery's plans for further support for the Arnhem operation was very different from that which the worried British General had anticipated when he had written his strong letter condemning Eisenhower's strategy.

That damp Wednesday, as General Eisenhower settled down in his new HQ at the Petit Trianon, Versailles, soon to be surrounded there by a staff of 5,000 soldiers and civilians, he must have felt that he had made a mistake in giving the Englishman his head on the Arnhem operation. Then it seemed that he was still hoping to parley it into the great thrust for the Ruhr, excluding the Americans Bradley and Patton from any of the subsequent glory.

Eisenhower was indeed remote from the battlefield that September, cut off from the mud, blood and the misery of the front. Hesitant and indecisive, he was cushioned from the grim reality by his 'family': his orderly 'Micky', who wrote a weekly letter to 'Mamie' telling her how the 'boss' was getting on; 'Butch', the former radio executive, who acted as his PRI man and who was a good man to play bridge or poker with; 'Tex', another card-player; and above all 'Kay', his 'driver-secretary' who over these last two years had somehow been transformed from a British civilian-driver into a captain in the American WACs, complete with BEM, Cross of Orange-Nassau etc, etc.

But if he was cut off from the shooting war in the imperial surroundings of Versailles, he was acutely aware of and sensitive to public opinion, especially in the US press. Now, on this Thursday, he began to realize, not only that Montgomery had not realized his true place in the 'team' – as Eisenhower liked to call his front-rank generals – but that he had gotten himself bogged down in a costly adventure because of his pig-headed obstinacy.

When his Chief-of-Intelligence British General Ken Strong, a tall dark-haired Scot, had informed him that there was good reason to believe that the First Airborne could expect to meet an SS armoured Corps at Arnhem, he had sent him and Bedell Smith, the hot-tempered American Chief-of-Staff, to warn Monty. The British Commander had refused to meet Strong and two days before the drop, Strong had received a message from the 21st Army Group, stating that Montgomery would ask Eisenhower for his dismissal if he persisted in his warnings. Montgomery had known all the time the 2nd SS Panzer Corps was in the Arnhem area; still he had gone ahead with his bold, even foolhardy, plan because he had hoped it would develop into something more: the realization of his dream to lead the advance into the Ruhr.

At the beginning, when it had looked as if Montgomery might have a chance, he had silenced Bradley's angry objections that 'Monty would slip off on a tangent and leave us holding the bag'. Now he realized that Montgomery was failing badly at Arnhem. Already his own American generals were beginning to ask awkward questions about the wisdom of Market Garden and the fact that it was holding up the advance of the American armies. Soon these same awkward questions might be posed in the headlines of Stateside papers; and Dwight D. Eisenhower, America's 20th century Grant, whose sights were already perhaps set on the White House, could not risk that eventuality. That September afternoon, the Supreme Commander decided to call a conference of all his top commanders to settle once and for all the future of the Allied advance into Germany. The fate of Operation Market Garden was almost decided now.

4

The survivors of the 10th Para Battalion were filthy, exhausted and bleeding as they swung off the main road, following the line of shattered trees into the HQ area. But General Urquhart watching them come in thought 'their discipline was immaculate'.

Colonel Smythe, his right hand bandaged, saluted and reported breathlessly: 'We've been heavily taken on, sir. I have sixty men left.'

'What has happened to Hackett?' Urquhart asked, after absorbing the information.

'He'll be here as soon as they can disengage, sir,' Smythe replied. 'They were in rather a mess in the woods up there.'

'Mess' was the understatement of the day. As the 10th's sixty survivors trooped away to the cover of a few houses, Brigadier Hackett and his handful of paras from the 156th, 10th and his own HQ, were trapped in a thick wood. The SS had surrounded the place and every time they tried to emerge, they were met by a withering hail of spandau fire. Now the SS were standing openly at the ends of the fire-breaks and trails, utterly confident of their victory, crying: 'Come on Tommy – come on.'

Hackett, crouched in a thicket with his men, felt that they had had it. 'The men … made no secret of their conviction,' he wrote later, 'that the Division had been liquidated. They were none the less ready, even after the rough time they had had, to make an effort to rejoin it.' Grimly he sized up the situation and in the end decided that he would try to make a break-out as soon as it got a little darker.

All that long afternoon, the SS alternatively taunted the shattered remnants and tried to rush their positions. Time and again they were thrown back. Once Hackett, armed with a German rifle like most of his men now, led a bayonet charge on a spandau nest, thirty yards away, which was making life unbearable. He found himself alone in the machine-gun pit, with dead SS men sprawled around the still glowing machine-gun. He threw an excited glance into the nearby foxhole. A young SS trooper crouched there in terror, head pressed ostrich-like into the sandy soil. For a moment Hackett hesitated, bayonet raised. He saw how the poor field-grey cloth stretched tightly over the boy's skinny shoulder blades. Then he lowered the bayonet. He could not bring himself to drive the sharp point into such a bundle of helplessness. He aimed a kick at the boy's backside and fell back with the rest of the paras as other Germans opened fire on them. Ten minutes later the boy, whose life he had spared, was back at the gun, pouring a steady stream of tracer at them.

At 4.30 on that terrible afternoon, with the casualties filling the trenches and the tree-covered shelters all around, Hackett knew he would have to get out of the wood before his force was wiped out completely. He ordered the charge.

The paras broke cover. In a frenzy of rage, fear and crazy abandon, they charged the German positions. The very desperation of their attack took the enemy by surprise.

Here and there a man was hit and fell screaming. But the rest pressed on. Then they were in the German positions. Now it was the turn of their tormentors of that long bloody afternoon. But there was no time for them to wreak their full vengeance. With Hackett at their head, they ran on, chests heaving frantically, their breath coming in hectic, leaden-lunged gasps. Then suddenly they were through. Before them loomed up the positions of the Border Regiment. Seconds later they were in the perimeter. As Hackett recalled: 'It all seemed wonderfully peaceful by comparison with the day's performance in the woods.'

At ten to seven that night, a worn Hackett reported to Urquhart with his surviving seventy men. Urquhart complimented him and told him that he would take over command of one half of the perimeter the following day – Hicks would get the other one. But now he was to 'take a night's rest'.

When Hackett had trooped off with his weary men, Urquhart walked back to his own HQ to check the signals. Earlier that day, he had radioed Browning: 'Enemy attacking main bridge in strength. Situation serious for 1 Para Brigade. Enemy also attacking position east from Heelsum and west from Arnhem. Situation serious but am forming close perimeter defence round

173

Hartenstein with remainder of Div. Relief essential both areas earliest possible. Still retain ferry crossing Heveadorp.'

But there was no answer waiting for him at the hotel HQ. Unknown to him, Browning would not receive it till the following day. On that Thursday, he, Browning, would radio the commanding officer of the 52nd Division, who had offered to take in a glider-borne brigade to relieve the battered First Airborne: 'Thanks for your message, but offer NOT repeat not required as situation better than you think.'

Now extremely worried, Urquhart decided he must do something to help Frost on the bridge – and that 'something' would have to be in the hands of the cheerful Canadian Lieutenant, Leo Heaps, who seemed to belong to no one in particular. Heaps had just finished his first meal of the last 15 hours – sausages, ham, potatoes and stewed apricots – when the General called for him.

He found him in a smoke-filled room, the earphones still clamped to his ears. Heaps felt that 'everything he said and did was calm and confident. But (that) he didn't smile now quite as often as he did two days before'.

Wearily Urquhart took off the earphones. 'Would you like to try and get through tonight to the bridge at Arnhem?'

As always, Heaps was eager for any new

adventure which would get him away from the usual British Army 'bull'. He agreed to 'have a good go' immediately, asking for two jeeps for the supplies, a guide and an interpreter. The rest he would arrange himself. A tired Urquhart gave him *carte blanche*.

In the growing gloom the Canadian made hasty preparations. Martin Knottenbelt, an attached Dutch commando, volunteered to go with him as did a sleepy-eyed local, dressed in German jackboots and an old British uniform. Johnny, the American paratroop lieutenant, was also eager to go.

Thus the last attempt to get to the bridge set off. Their plan was simple. They would try to cross the Lower Rhine at the ferry, find the Guards' tanks and swing back to the bridge with them from the south. Using the cover of the tanks, they would attempt to run the German gauntlet and cross the bridge with the vital supplies. It was a bold plan, but young Lieutenant Heaps was not a man to be put off by danger. Indeed as they sneaked out of the Divisional perimeter and headed south to the river in their two jeeps, the Canadian thought it was all 'too easy'.

It was very dark when they reached the ferry after cutting through the German lines, but still they could see the ferryboat itself. It was twenty feet from the shore, secured to the bank by a heavy metal cable. A glider pilot whom they had taken with them reported to Heaps that the sappers who were supposed to be guarding the ferry had just beaten off a German attack with hand grenades, less than thirty minutes before.

Heaps absorbed the information. But his mind was on the problem of how to get to the ferry. In the end, as no one else seemed eager to brave the fast-running Lower Rhine, he decided that it was up to him. How he was going to do it, he did not know.

Swiftly ordering Martin and Johnny to stay with the jeeps, he ran to the cable. Against the flashes of German artillery fire from across the river, he saw that the cable was sufficiently high above the water for him to shin along it to the ferry. He hesitated no longer. With his bottom dangling in the icy water, he pulled himself to the boat hand over hand. He dropped on to it, and discovered after stumbling around in the dark boat, now being shrouded in the heavy wet mist rising from the Rhine, that it was moved by a big iron wheel. If one let it go, the cable would unwind itself and the ferry would slip into the stream again. By winding it in the reverse direction, however, he could get back to the bank. Hastily he removed the lever holding the wheel. Before he could stop it, the ferry had moved swiftly a further twenty feet into the middle of the Rhine.

Struggling desperately to get the lever in

position again, he called for Johnny to come and help him. In a few minutes the American had joined him. Together they tried to turn the wheel. It wouldn't budge. By the light of a sudden explosion, they finally saw why. The Germans had smashed the gears. They had no other choice but to return to the bank.

Soaked and depressed, they began their wild ride back to the Division HQ, making enough noise 'to resemble a tank regiment on the move' with Martin sounding the horn loudly. On all sides they heard frightened Germans scurrying for cover in the bushes. After reporting the failure of their mission to General Urquhart, Heaps and Johnny fell into a heavy sleep on the top floor of Divisional HQ. The last attempt to reach Frost from the First Airborne area had failed.

5

Cardale, the ex-student of theology, who had had to suffer a great many jokes on account of his piety since he had first joined the 2nd Battalion in Italy, had finally been blown out of the house he was holding by the bridge. Now, with thirty other survivors, he was 'mouse-holing' from one blazing house to another when he came across a dying para lying alone in the rubble. 'Are the medics on their way, Tony?' he asked, looking up at Cardale.

'Yes, they're not far behind,' Cardale lied and ran on. But not for long. Their lead man was shot down as he doubled to the next house. Suddenly Germans were everywhere. An SS man stuck a sub-machine gun through the shattered window of the house they were in and ordered them to surrender. Cardale realized there was no way out. Their hands began to go up slowly. Totally exhausted, they were herded away and placed between two light tanks, their guns directed on the paras. Then they were searched. Just before they were marched away, 'we flung away our helmets and put on our Red Berets – our last act of holding our heads high'.

It was about that time that Tucker and the machine-gun section finally abandoned their house. It was falling down about their heads, the roof and upper storey already ablaze.

'Outside and dig in in the garden,' an NCO barked.

They needed no urging. By the garish light of the flames, they began to dig in. Suddenly the young signaller remembered the 'little old lady'. 'What about the woman?' he yelled in alarm.

'Stop there, I'll get her,' Captain Panter cried.

He dashed forward towards the burning house. Suddenly he yelled with pain and dropped to one knee. He had been hit. But he got up again and ran inside the house. A few minutes later, he was out again, his uniform smouldering. 'She's dead,' he reported laconically. 'Now get yer heads down and when the house cools off – nip back in again before the Jerries!'

But they were fated never to get back. It was just about then that Major Gough asked for a truce in order to evacuate their wounded, which included Colonel Frost who had been forced to give up his command to Gough. The Recce Major saw the Germans were coming too close to their own positions under the cover of the white flag and moving towards the still intact jeeps. He ordered the enemy not to come any closer.

'We cannot remove your wounded unless we use your jeeps,' the Germans shouted back.

As Frost tugged off his badges, Gough waved for the Germans to come closer. A few minutes later when they had gone with their pathetic bloody burdens, the shooting started again and as Tucker's group started to move into the old woman's house, they were met by *schmeisser* fire. The Germans were in occupation.

179

'It was a terrible moment,' Tucker remembers today. 'We knew now that there was no hope. But there was no panic. As the order came, "move back to the school", the lads fell back in single file against the background of the burning houses everywhere, as if they didn't want to go!'

Dodging from house to house, running the gauntlet of the bullet-swept lanes, they reached the school to be told by an officer whom Tucker didn't recognize: 'We're going to break out in small parties.' Swiftly Tucker was assigned to a group of six men to be led out by Constable van Kruijk.

At the Brigade HQ, Major Christopher Hibbert crouched at a window saw the first of the para prisoners led off. Knowing that the cellars were filed with their wounded – some 250 of them – whom he couldn't sacrifice by any further resistance, he decided to break out too. Swiftly he checked his remaining men. There were about two platoons of them, divided into five sections, each one commanded by an officer. Each man had, on average, one magazine left plus a couple of grenades. Enough for them, Hibbert thought, to break through the German cordon. He ordered them to prepare to break out too.

Mackay and Simpson had fourteen men

180

capable of fighting left. With Simpson in the van and Mackay bringing up the rear, the fourteen would protect the breakout of the twenty-one wounded. But it was going to be a very 'dicey business'. Sixteen of them to cover twice that number of wounded with the Germans everywhere. Yet Mackay knew that if they didn't break out now, it would be either death in the cellar of the blazing school building, or surrender; and he was determined not to surrender now. Thus they, too, got ready to move.

As Private Tucker finally flung away the useless field telephone which he had carried with him throughout the battle and prepared to move out, he recalled suddenly that confident briefing so many light years before. 'You'll be on the bridge exactly twenty-four hours. Then Second Army will link up with us. From Arnhem, we'll turn left for the advance on Amsterdam!' How utterly easy and light-hearted it had all seemed.

Within minutes of moving schoolhouse, the Engineers' party bumped into trouble. Simpson and six men up front were wounded; another killed in the first vicious bursts of spandau fire. The party split up in disorder. Together with the remaining six unwounded men of the original fifty, Mackay doubled back the way they had come. Desperately, they tried to break through the ring of SS men. But everywhere Harzer's troopers of the 9th SS Panzer were waiting for them in the blazing maze of houses.

Suddenly they bumped into a group of fifty young Germans grouped around two yellow-painted training tanks, smoking and chatting, as if the battle were already over. Mackay did not even give them a chance to draw their weapons. The seven desperate paras emptied their stens into the SS men. They went down as if scythed by a gigantic mower. Throwing away their now useless machine pistols – they had no more ammunition – Mackay ran on with the remaining four men, leaving two of their number dead and wounded behind. They split up. The Germans were everywhere now in the confused, burning wilderness of Arnhem. Mackay dropped over a wall into a garden, and as the SS, combing the area for survivors, came closer and closer, he played dead. An NCO kicked him in the ribs to check. Mackay accepted the blow without a murmur. The NCO passed on. But a man following him was not so trusting. He thrust his bayonet into the 'dead' Engineer. He came to life suddenly with an angry shout of protest. The next instant he was up against the wall, hands over his head, being roughly searched by his captors.

There were not many men left in the bridge

area now. As their ammunition started to run out, the paras held their fire for longer and longer periods. The SS moved in for the kill. Open-mouthed with awe, they saw how two dirty, unshaven young paras emerged suddenly from a cellar. While the first one tried to draw the Germans' fire, the other one went for them, armed only with a trench knife. Both were felled by a rapid burst from a machine-gun and taken prisoner. But their last desperate attempt to fight back was something, according to an SS officer, 'which impressed the battle-hardened German troops because it was not spontaneous but obviously thought out'. It was the last act of armed resistance on the bridge.

Now they were running for their lives. Major Gough of the Reconnaissance Corps, the last commander of the bridge, had just ordered a wounded RASC officer, David Clark, to surrender with the rest of the casualties as soon as the Germans closed in on their house. He refused. 'You're a pretty strong chap,' he said looking up at Gough. 'You could carry me pick-a-back.'

But there was no time for that now. The Germans were lobbing stick grenades through the shattered windows to hasten the process of surrender. Gough dived under a pile of logs. There was the heavy crunch of jackboots over the debris. Gough tensed, hardly daring to breathe. Among a shower of timber, he was dragged out into a group of young teenaged Germans, staring down at him wide-eyed.

In spite of the fact that he was now a POW, Freddie Gough could not help laughing at their 'impossibly young faces'.

Private Tucker and Sergeant Cloves were hiding in some rubble. The German patrol was coming nearer. Tucker, hardly able to keep his eyes open now, prepared to fire. 'Don't fire yet!' Cloves hissed.

Seconds later he was fast asleep and Cloves had to clap his big dirty hand over the Ulsterman's mouth to prevent the Germans hearing his snores. 'Can't you bloody well pick a better place for a kip!' he whispered angrily.

They split up. 'I was completely lost,' Tucker recalls. 'I knew the rest of the Div was somewhere to the west, but Arnhem was a maze as far as I was concerned. And I didn't know the exit.'

He found himself in a ruined, burning church. Everywhere in the smoke-filled interior there were men – German and British. Tucker heard furtive noises in the next room. The SS!

He pulled out his last grenade and tossed it through a hole in the wall. A muffled crump. A high-pitched scream. The noises stopped suddenly. Three para officers and a private were crouched in the rubble next to a line of toilets. He dropped down beside them. 'There's a Jerry with a machine-pistol covering the exit!' someone hissed. One of the officers crawled forward carefully and took aim with his Colt. He pressed the trigger. Nothing happened. Like Tucker's, his 45 was on the blink too.

'I'll draw their fire first,' the private volunteered.

He rose and attempted to dash across the corridor. But his reactions, after nearly four days without sleep, were too slow. A burst cut him down before he had gone a yard. Tucker and an officer reached out and pulled him back into cover across the floor.

'I'm getting bloody cold,' he whispered hoarsely. Then his head lolled to one side. He was dead.

Tucker made off. He would do it alone. Suddenly he saw a group of men wearing red berets through a hole in the wall. His face lit up. Without checking, he burst into the group, shouting a greeting. Too late, he saw that they were prisoners, covered by machine-guns posted at each end of the alley. A young SS man frisked him for weapons and handed him a peppermint drop. The soldier spoke some English and Tucker, defiant like they all were, said: 'The Russians'll give you some stick for the way

185

you've treated them, after the war.'

'We treat them the way you treat the Irish,' the SS trooper explained. Tucker grinned. 'Is that so? Well, listen I'm Irish – so what do you say to that?'

The SS man wouldn't believe him.

Some time later their party was put in an ancient truck for transportation to the nearest cage at Zutphen. It was a mixed group, containing Major Hibbert and the soldier-writer Anthony Cotterill, who had been captured after hiding in a coal bin. Christopher Hibbert had been depressed by the first sight of the 20 officers and 20 unwounded other ranks, who were the sole survivors of the fighting on the bridge, but now he was determined to escape again. Tucker, crowded in next to cockney 'Soapy' Hudson and Private McCracken, was planning the same action.

McCracken, who had just been informed before the drop that his wife had given birth to a child, was not so keen. 'I've not seen my nipper yet,' he said wearily. 'Besides the war'll be over in six months. It's not worth it.'

Two middle-aged German soldiers took up their positions on the tailboard, eyeing their prisoners warily. Unknown to the men inside, a young SS man armed with a machine-pistol was hanging on to the truck's running board. The Germans were taking no chances.

Suddenly Hibbert pushed forward, followed by Major Mumford. The guards were taken completely by surprise. In an instant the two Majors had dropped over the side and were running hard for cover. The two Germans started shouting. The remaining paras pushed forward and started grappling with them to prevent their raising the alarm. But a German truck coming from the opposite direction had already spotted the escape and done that. Their truck squealed to a halt. The enraged SS man ran round to the back. Without thinking he fired a full burst into the truck. At that range he couldn't miss. It was a massacre. Hibbert's ill-considered escape resulted in eight men's deaths. Cotterill would never write another novel and Private McCracken would never see his 'nipper'. But the tragedy wasn't finished yet.

Red-faced, furious young SS men ordered the paras out of the truck. Tucker and Soapy Hudson, both wounded, attempted to lift a dying young para from the bloody mess on the truck's floor. He refused their aid. 'I'll do it myself,' he said thickly.

When he staggered to his feet, they saw that the back of his head looked as if someone had thrown a handful of strawberry jam at it. He tottered over to the pavement and collapsed there. A Dutch doctor appeared from nowhere and tried to help. Angrily the SS yelled at him to go away. As he did so, he whispered, 'Courage ... courage'. On the pavement, the young para from Liverpool died, his most precious possession, a tin of looted tomatoes, rolling from the top of his smock.

Pushing and kicking them, the SS men forced the paras against the wall. They thought the paras had slaughtered the two middle-aged *Wehrmacht*. Now the Tommies were going to pay for their murder. Tucker knew this was the end. With his hands above his head, he lined up beside Soapy and a fellow Irishman Private Fitzpatrick, who had been badly hit in the shoulder.

Suddenly Major Gough burst into the throng of SS men and began arguing with their senior NCO. The conversation seemed to go on for ever, while Private Tucker waited for the bullet which must come. In his twenty-three years he had experienced a lot of war – Palestine in '38, the retreat to Dunkirk in '40, Crete fighting Student's paras in 1941, Africa, the Sicily drop, and Italy in '43 and now Arnhem – but he had never thought it would all end like this: shot against a wall in cold blood.

It was at the very last moment, that a Volkswagen jeep, containing a German Intelligence officer drove up. He spoke English too. 'These are British soldiers,' he told the SS NCO, 'not Russians!'

Sullenly the NCO ordered the survivors to

get back in the trucks again, ordering, 'Everybody on the floor. Anybody who puts his head above the tail-board gets shot.' Thus they began their long odyssey into Germany. Behind them, the bodies of the dead started to stiffen slowly on the bloody pavement.

Even their enemies were impressed by them. In his official report to Himmler *Sturmbannfuhrer Krafft* wrote: 'About twenty-five years of age on the average and the best type, mentally and physically. They all had some five or six years' service and most of them were veterans of North Africa, Sicily, Italy and Normandy. They were well trained, particularly for independent fighting and of good combat value. The officers, graded up in rank according to age, were the finest in the whole British Army. Very well schooled, personally hard, persevering and brave, they made an outstanding impression.'

Bittrich, the man who had planned the German counter-attack which had beaten them, felt: 'They were typical of the extremely tough and highly trained British soldiers who had fought against us since the beginning of the invasion. A classic example of the indomitable fighting spirit of these troops was the performance of the British forces at the bridge in Arnhem; even after defeat these men left the battlefield with morale unbroken.'

189

Now, as the dawn began to break, silence descended on the bridge. The SS men pressed on to begin the attack on the paras grouped round the Hartenstein Hotel, and the bridge was left to the dead. They had come a long way for this final date with death. Some of them had still been schoolboys or working in factories when Lieutenant, acting Captain, acting Major Frost had carried out the first real para attack on Bruneval; others had already fought their models, the German *Fallschirmjaeger*, at Crete by then.

But together they had fought in Sicily, whored in Italy, gone Yank-bashing in Grantham, covered mile after mile with the 'airborne gallop' on the murderous training schemes in Yorkshire until they had formed a unique tightly-knit team which felt it could never be beaten.

It had been beaten, but only after the 2nd Parachute Battalion had ceased to exist. But the sacrifice of those young men, scattered dead and staring at the new day with sightless eyes along that silent bridge, would not be forgotten as long as people remembered the name Arnhem. They had lost, yet they had won too.

The battle of the bridge at Arnhem was over. The battle for the cauldron had still to begin.

TWO:
THE CAULDRON

DAY FIVE

'Why on earth am I still alive!'
–Lieutenant Peter Stainforth,
1st Para Battalion.

At nine o'clock on the morning of 21st
September, General Urquhart held a
Divisional conference in the ground floor
room of the Hartenstein Hotel. Outside,
German artillery was firing with depressing
regularity and there was the usual snap and
crackle of the defenders' lighter weapons. A
jeep had driven up carrying new casualties
and they were being rushed to the casualty
clearing station. Somewhere a mortar
howled and the first of the six bombs fired
by the German 'moaning minnie' started to
tear the morning air apart.

Swiftly Urquhart passed out his orders.
Hicks would have under command the
Border Regiment, the KOSBs and a mix-
ture of Poles, glider pilots, Engineers and
Wilson's Independent Company. Hackett
would get the 10th and 156th, the Lonsdale
Force (the remnants of the 1st, 3rd and
11th Paras), the South Staffs and Colonel
Sheriff Thompson's Light Regiment of

artillery. In all they would have some three thousand troops under command, holding a horseshoe-shaped perimeter, with woods and fields to the west and centre and the trim suburb of Oosterbeek to the north and east.

In essence it was a bad position to defend. The Hotel HQ had been picked by chance and it was too good a target for the German gunners; in addition it was a mile from the river and the vital ferry. As for Sheriff Thompson's artillery position, it was not the best. It, too, had been regarded at first as provisional. For it, too, was dominated by the Westerbouwing, still in British hands, but only just. Once the Germans drove off the single platoon of the Border Regiment holding it, they would be able to command Urquhart's whole position. Later some of Urquhart's staff officers were to argue that he should have made the Westerbouwing hill, a hundred-foot high, just off the ferry, the centre of his defensive position.

Now, as the Germans started to line up their forces for the attack, Urquhart was satisfied that his position was the best available and while his brigadiers hurried off to get on with their jobs, he drove to the 1st Battery's CP.

He was greeted by good news. Captain Macmillan of the airborne artillery announced that he had just contacted Second

Army artillery by radio. Urquhart's head gunner, Colonel Loder-Symonds, immediately requested help from the 64th Medium Artillery Regiment. The Second Army agreed to fire missions along the First Division's perimeter from eleven miles away. It was going to be a tricky manoeuvre, but soon the medium guns were placing their shells at distances of no more than one hundred yards from the paras' front.

Cheered somewhat by the response Urquhart drove back to the POW cage located on a former tennis court. With the aid of an interpreter he addressed the two hundred odd prisoners who were protesting they were being unduly exposed to the mounting mortar barrage from their own lines. 'We expect you to behave in the way that British soldiers have to behave in such conditions as these,' he told them severely. 'We will do everything possible to enable you to dig in. As for food, I know how you are feeling. But we have none ourselves and you will get what is due to you as it becomes available.'

Urquhart's guess that 'once it is suggested to a German that he is not as good as someone else, he damn soon tries hard to prove that he is' proved correct. As he turned to leave, the POWs started to use their mess tins to scoop away dirt and gravel.

But the General was not quite right about the Division's lack of rations. At least Boy Wilson's pathfinders were not going hungry. While some of the Division went four days without food, they had their tame rabbits, some scraggy chickens which went on pecking and scratching quite calmly despite the bombardment, which provided them with two meals a day. Once a kid ran across their front. It did not survive long and went into the company's cooking pot very rapidly.

But on that particular morning, Wilson's hundred surviving paras dug in under Hicks had begun to spot all the signs of a German pre-attack build-up. A tiger Tank, handfuls of infantry crouched at the ready, heaving machine-gunners taking up their positions to cover the attackers' flanks. It looked as if Brigadier Hicks' command would bear the first brunt of Bittrich's attack on the 'cauldron', as the enemy would soon call it.

Hackett was inspecting his new command. He met his staff captain, a cool young officer named Jasper Booty, who sat on the edge of his foxhole twirling his bullet-holed red beret round his forefinger. 'You know, sir,' he told an amused Hackett, 'the trouble with these bloody Germans is that they don't know what to do!'

Hackett hoped he was right. He moved on to visit Lonsdale and Major Cain of the

South Staffs, who was commanding the Glider Pilots, and were destined to win the Division's fourth Victoria Cross within the next twenty-four hours. From there he visited the dressing station, located in a big white house next to Oosterbeek Church, which belonged to Mrs Kate Ter Horst who was helping the doctor 'Morph' Martin to tend to the wounded.

He had just stepped outside again when a mortar shell exploded close by. His companion, Major Maddon, was killed outright. Colonel Sheriff Thompson was badly wounded. Hackett himself was hit about the face and hands. Swiftly 'Morph' Martin cleaned him up and the Brigadier took refuge in the 1st Light's HQ. It was obvious that it wasn't only Hicks' command that was in for trouble.

But it was the 7th KOSBs, grouped around the shattered Dreyeroord Private Hotel at the northern extremity of the perimeter, which took the first attack on that gloomy Thursday.

For two days now the Scots had been suffering from constant shelling and pin-prick attacks; now, under their CO Colonel Payton-Reid, the 'stolid patience with which we had endured his constant pin-pricks gave way to a ferocious lust for revenge' (thus their CO). As the mortar stonk stopped suddenly, leaving behind a loud, echoing silence, the KOSBs grouped around the hotel stood by in their fox-holes. They knew what that silence heralded – a German attack.

They weren't wrong. The enemy began infiltrating their positions from the woods, sidling from tree to tree like so many grey timber wolves. But the KOSBs were waiting for them. Cursing angrily, they opened up with everything they had, using their three-inch mortars almost like cannon at the shortest possible range. It was a bloody slaughter. The Germans dropped by the score. But they didn't break. Instead the survivors flopped to the ground and began to return the Scots' fire. But now the Scots' blood was really roused. The order went from foxhole to foxhole: 'Fix bayonets!'

Everywhere there was a frenzy of fumbling. The little skewerlike blades were fixed to the ends of their rifles. Those who were armed with stens swiftly changed magazines. They were ready. 'Charge!' an officer yelled.

In a crazy rush they were out of their holes like their fathers before them in the mud of Flanders and running screaming at the Germans, carried away by the wild excitement of it all. The SS broke. Throwing away their weapons, the survivors fled the way they had gone, leaving a hundred dead behind them. The first real attack of the day had been well and truly stopped.

Wossowski's Training Battalion and their instructors from the Hermann Goering Division rode to battle on bicycles – after all they were in Holland. Leaving the road from Wolfhezen to Oosterbeek they turned into a narrow track running through a wood. There was no sign of the enemy. They pedalled on 'at ease', four hundred young men, going into their first battle as airily as if they were heading for a 'May Day' outing, so beloved by German men.

Ahead was the Westerbouwing Hill, surmounted by an observation tower, belonging to the café on its summit. It was just visible above the pines. It seemed unoccupied. They cycled towards it. And then they ran into the Borderers' ambush. It was sheer slaughter. One who was there on the German side remembers: 'We were attacked by murderous machine-gun fire. Some were hit before they had time even to throw themselves to the ground, let alone take cover.'

But the young recruits were the best the Hitler Youth had to offer, all potential NCOs, and when the order came 'Company – Company charge!' they did not hesitate. They scrambled over the dead and dying, inextricably mixed up with the fallen bicycles and started to attack the height. Doggedly the Border men resisted. But they were hopelessly outnumbered. Bit by bit they were pushed back by the Germans, who were experiencing their first taste of combat and taking tremendous casualties because of their inexperience. The Luftwaffe men took the base of the wood, pushed on into the shattered café itself. The first prisoners were sent back. To the novices they seemed 'elite troops, fellows tall as trees, well fed and excellently equipped'. The café was theirs. They began to descend the hill in the direction of Oosterbeek, driving the paras in front of them.

By the time they reached the Borderer's main positions, the Wossowski Battalion had lost all its officers, save one lieutenant, and half its other ranks; but it had gained the vital position. Now the whole of the one mile long and half a mile broad cauldron was under German domination. More import-ant, the Germans could now survey the ferry, Urquhart's last link with the other side of the Rhine. Soon the Polish Para Brigade would be landing there at the Driel DZ. How would they get across the fast-moving river now to help their British comrades?

2

Captain R. Langton of the Irish Guards, the leading squadron, was given his orders at Nijmegen Bridge at 10.40. They were very

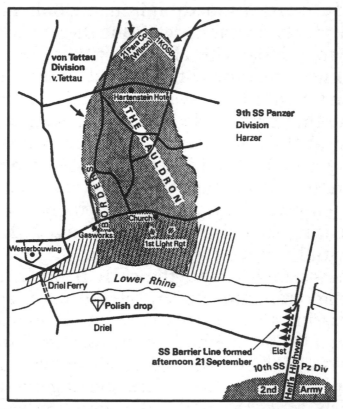

'A collection of individuals holding on.' – Gen. Urquhart

simple: 'The situation at Arnhem was desperate' and he was to 'go hell for leather up the road and get to Arnhem bridge... H hour would be eleven hundred hours precisely'.

Captain Langton organized his force swiftly. It was a squadron in name only now, having only six tanks left. But there was no time to quibble with HQ about that. Besides the other squadrons of his Battalion were not much better off. He was ready just in time.

The first tank rattled away, followed at an interval by the next. Langton himself brought up the middle. They passed a bend where they had heard two 88s were sited. It was empty. They rolled on, their speed increasing steadily, as Langton urged them on with his cries of *'faster, faster!'*

They swung round the next bend in the road and ran into concentrated fire. In rapid succession three of his tanks were shot off the road. The 88s had withdrawn to a strip of wood, where with the assistance of a troop of Tigers, they were picking off the British tanks at will. The great advance came to an abrupt halt once again. It was only a matter of hours now before the great Polish drop at Driel – right into the hands of the Germans.

The stalled Irish Guards saw the first Dakotas at quarter past four. Half a mile ahead close to the river, the whole weight of the German flak swung into action. Suddenly the grey sky before them was peppered with ugly black spots. Still the pilots came on. Slow, steady, purposeful. Then the great formation of 110 Dakotas was over the dropping zone. The first black shape hurtled out of a plane. And another. Yet another. Suddenly the grey sky was full of hundreds of parachutes like so many falling mushrooms. A parachute failed to open. The Pole went plummeting to the ground beyond the Lower Rhine.

For a few moments, both Germans and British seemed to have stopped the ground battle to watch this dramatic airborne interruption of the bitter fight for the road to Elst. But as the first of the Poles in their grey airborne berets started to hit the ground, the battle of Arnhem erupted again. As the 88s opened up again and the first Irish Guards' Sherman was struck, the Poles began to spread out. General Stanislav Sosabowski had joined the fight.

Although an enraged Sosabowski realized that afternoon that his men had been dropped too late and in the wrong place, especially as the Driel ferry now seemed to be about to fall into German hands, he did not know that his drop had caused a crisis in General Wilhelm Bittrich's Second SS Panzer Corps HQ. Already Himmler was pressing for his recall on no less a charge than treason, though Field Marshal Model was refusing to release him. Now the Poles had appeared from nowhere on the wrong side of the Rhine. The problem was – what would they do next? Would they try to cross into the First Airborne's lines, where Harzer's 9th Panzer could deal with them in due course? Or would they push towards the Nijmegen–Arnhem road and cut off the 10th SS Panzer from its base?

Bittrich, worried as he was, acted decisively, as always. He withdrew Major Knaust's SS Battalion from the attack on the perimeter and ordered it to rush across the Arnhem Bridge in order to defend the Elst–Arnhem road. Together with a company of Panther tanks and artillery from the 10th SS Panzer, Knaust was to prevent any attempt to cut the vital road link or capture Elst.

Harzer, the acting commander of the 9th Panzer, was also contacted. He was informed that he must destroy the Poles immediately. But for a change, luck was on the side of the Poles, enraged as they were at what they now thought was a completely bungled operation. They had dropped in the polder country, criss-crossed by ditches, where the country roads were narrow and easily defended and the fields too soft and marshy for tanks. Harzer, the man who had boasted he would 'scatter or destroy this

Polish parachute brigade before nightfall', found he could not use his tanks. The Poles would have to be driven out by infantry – and infantry was in short supply. Suddenly it appeared that there might be a chance of rescuing the trapped paras after all. If only the 2nd Army could link up with the Poles!

3

Harzer's reaction to the Polish landing was violent. Within the hour his SS men were attacking the whole eastern side of the perimeter with tanks, SPs and infantry. The KOSBs, the Independent Para, Lonsdale's Force, they all came in for their share of the Germany fury.

Lieutenant Peter Stainforth in Lonsdale's Force was moving through a wood with a line of survivors when they hit the German positions. At twenty yards' range an SS man let him have a burst with a machine-pistol. The German missed and fled. Stainforth fired a long burst instinctively. He heard the German gasp with pain. But he didn't drop. He plunged on through the undergrowth. Stainforth's blood was up. Shouting to the rest to swing to left and right, he went in after the wounded SS man. He doubled through a clearing, across a country road and spotted his man, lying on the ground next to a tree. Two other SS men in camou-flaged smocks were bending over him.

Stainforth yelled: *'Hande hoch!'* The Germans' reaction was to swing round their rifles. Stainforth let them have a couple of eight bullet bursts. Without a sound they dropped to the ground and lay still.

Suddenly the whole wood came to life. Germans were everywhere, jumping from half-finished foxholes, throwing away spades, grabbing frantically for their weapons. He had bumped into a whole SS company.

Two Germans swung a spandau machine-gun round on him. They were only thirty yards away and he had no time to aim properly. He felled them with a burst. Two others died a moment later. A couple of others scrambled into a ditch, his slugs kicking up the dust at their feet. One didn't make it. A single boot flopped over the edge of the bridge and stayed there motionlessly, its owner dead. As Stainforth retreated out of the hornet's nest he had stirred up so un-wittingly, he kept asking himself: 'Why haven't I been killed yet? Another second perhaps … why on earth am I still alive…?'

The casualty clearing stations were begin-ning to fill up rapidly with wounded now. The tall blue-eyed Dutch blond Mevrouw Ter Horst, whose big house was now being used as one of them, wandered through the long corridor, filled with seriously wounded men, their bodies covered in glass splinters from the windows so that they looked as if they had been sprinkled with icing sugar. Medical orderlies were giving those in severe pain shots of their precious supply of morphia and writing the dosage on the man's forehead with a copying pencil. The wounded were everywhere – even in the lavatory. There one of the chaplains, a little, curly-haired, bespectacled captain was actually trying to clean out the stinking mess next to the wounded soldier. Mevrouw Ter Horst was astonished to see him doing such work. 'A captain and even a chaplain doing such work,' she told herself. 'You should have had five years of German discipline!'

But even the wounded managed to retain their sense of humour in the hell of the cauldron. Led by the MO and the KOSB's second-in-command, Major Coke, who had been wounded, a group of wounded Scots set off to walk to their casualty clearing stations. They didn't get far. At a crossroads they bumped into a German patrol, ready to fire on them until they spotted the MO's Red Cross flag.

Coke, who spoke some German, went forward with the MO to meet the stiff young German lieutenant in charge of the patrol. 'We're just going out to our RAP,' Coke said, as if this were the most understandable thing in the world.

'All I know is that you are in our territory,' the German snapped. 'You are our prisoners therefore.'

'Oh you can't do that,' Coke protested. 'We're under the Red Cross flag. You can't touch us.'

The young German's brow creased in thought. He was obviously undecided and Coke pressed home his advantage. 'Run away home,' he said. 'We're going to our house.'

In the end the German took him to see 'my major'.

The German Major thought his subordinate's story was one of the best jokes he had heard in a long time. He soon corrected the lieutenant and Coke and the rest found themselves German prisoners-of-war. On the road to the cage, they came across two enemy tanks. On the spur of the moment Coke stopped them, hand upraised like a peace-time traffic policeman, and conferred with the officer in the lead tank. A few minutes later he came back to the KOSB's waiting wounded.

'Climb aboard,' he said grandly.

'Bloody hell,' one of the Scots breathed, 'he's commandeered the bloody thing.' He had. Thus the wounded rode into captivity in style.

By evening the attacks on the perimeter had started to die down. In the Recce lines, Sergeant Quinn went sniper hunting. Using a dummy made of a pillow, a broomstick and para helmet, he lured the Germans to fire and disclose their positions. By the time light gave out that day, the 'Recce boys' had accounted for ten German snipers.

Major Boy Wilson of the 21st Independent Company, who had had a hard day, returned to his slit trench, lit his pipe and stared contemplatively at an apple tree growing nearby, heavy with plump red apples, until the stars came out and he could see the apples no longer.

Hancock, Urquhart's batman, crawled out with a Dutchman to get water for the wounded lying packed in the Hartenstein's cellars from a well close to a burning haystack. Just as Hancock said to the Dutchman in an urgent whisper: 'Mind the bucket doesn't rattle against the side', the civilian lost his grip of the handle. The bucket clattered to the bottom of the well with a hellish row. German fire erupted on all sides. It would take Hancock three hours to get back with the precious water.

Back in the Hartenstein's cellars into which he had been forced to move his HQ that day, Urquhart pondered his situation. The vital ferry had been lost now and as the Poles had no boats, there seemed little hope of their being able to get across to reinforce his hard-pressed garrison. During the day his casualties had mounted rapidly too. What was he to do?

Lieutenant Leo Heaps, the irrepressible Canadian, who had spent the afternoon listening to German propaganda and a record of Glenn Miller playing 'In the Mood' over and over again, knew what he was going to do. Together with the American Johnny he decided to cross the Rhine that night and contact Second Army off his own bat.

That night they crept into the Borderers' position near the river, their trenches filled with dead men. After sizing up the situation, they said goodbye to the paras and scurried to the river bank. Swiftly they inflated their life preservers and were about to enter the icy, swift-flowing water when they heard the soft splashing of paddles. The two young men tensed, weapons gripped at the ready. The boats came nearer. They caught snatches of men speaking in a tongue unknown to them. At least it wasn't German. Then they saw them, outlined against the ruddy light of a sudden explosion. They were in British uniform, grey floppy berets on their heads, paddling towards them in small rubber dinghies. It was the first of the Poles.

Five minutes later Leo Heaps and his American companion had persuaded a couple of them to paddle them back the way they had come. Then began the tough job of tugging the dinghy up over an embankment, across fields, through trees until both the paras were gasping for breath.

But their Polish companions seemed tireless. They urged the other two on until finally one of them stopped and grunted. It was answered by a grunt from behind a knoll.

The reply seemed to satisfy the Poles. They beckoned the two escapees from the cauldron forward. Behind the knoll there was a group of some one hundred Poles in position, congregated around Lieutenant-Colonel Meyers, the First Airborne's engineer officer, who had gone over earlier in an attempt to organize the Polish crossing. Swiftly they shook hands and explained they were going to push on to try to contact the Second Army at dawn. Meyers wished them the best of luck and returned to the task of trying to get the Poles across before it was too late.

Heaps and Johnny, soaking wet and exhausted, tramped off into the darkness towards the sound of the guns.

Back at Hartenstein, General Urquhart made up his mind just about then. He knew Market had failed. Montgomery's bold plan had not come off. All that was left now was

211

to save the battered remnants of his once fine Division. As RSM Lord, formerly of the Guards, handed him his ration of two boiled sweets for the evening, he ordered the following message to be sent to Browning at Corps.

'No knowledge elements of Div in Arnhem for 24 hours. Balance of Div in very tight perimeter. Heavy mortaring and machine-gun fire followed by local attacks. Main nuisance SP guns. Our casualties heavy. Resources stretched to utmost. *Relief within 24 hours vital...*'

DAY SIX

'When all this is over, I'd like to see these men flown back to England and marched through London, just as they are – with six days' dirt on 'em!'

– *Anonymous para sergeant.*

In England Friday the 22nd September dawned cold and grey, with a definite hint of rain in the air for most of the country. For the undernourished middle-aged war workers, finishing their dried egg on toast, of if they were lucky or careful, their once-a-week 'real' egg allowed on the ration, it promised to be a typical, depressing late September day.

But if the weather were depressing the news was not. According to the *Daily Express* and *Daily Mail,* MPs were flocking back to Westminster after the summer recess, 'hoping that before the next holiday – at Christmas – the war will be over... There will be a jubilant end-in-sight atmosphere.' And the war workers sitting in their kitchens, finishing their food, with the lights on and the blackout curtains drawn back for the first time in five years could believe it. In most towns now they had been switching on the street lights in the centres all week for curious crowds of little children, who had never seen such wonders, to stand and gawp at. It was also confidently forecast by the papers that there would be big cuts in Civil Defence before the month was out. Indeed some of the more prominent trade union leaders were preparing to ask the coalition government under Mr Churchill, not known to be a particularly good friend of organized labour, to ensure that a massive housing programme was speedily put into action and some form of minimum wage guaranteed for the workers.

The news from the front was good too. Uncle Joe's Red Army boys were on the outskirts of Warsaw and on the Yugoslav border. In Italy the progress was slower, but the Yankee Fifth Army and the good old Eighth Army were pushing the Jerries back ever further north. As for the British Liberation Army in North West Europe, it seemed only a matter of days now before they broke through the last German defensive line.

There seemed only one fly in the ointment. Nothing had been heard of the paras at Arnhem for over twenty-four hours. The SHAEF correspondents reports had been vague now for over a day and this morning's was not much better. It read: 'Every step of the British thrust ... is being contested by strong German forces and the fighting is the heaviest that General Dempsey's men have encountered.' Nothing at all about the paratroopers though. A couple of local paras filled in the gap with the account of a meeting between the Queen and a para just before they had taken off for Arnhem. According to the story, she had noticed that the man had a dart board with him. This had surprised her and she had asked: 'Whatever are you taking that for?'

'Well, you never can tell, your Majesty,' he said replied respectfully. 'A dart game always helps to pass away dull evenings.'

'Tears came to her eyes.'

For those who rose an hour later and had their 'reconstituted eggs' served to them in a silver warming dish, *The Times* could add a little bit more about the Arnhem mystery, in the form of the official German com-muniqué. It was brutal in its simplicity and severely to the point: 'Apart from a number of hedgehog positions west of Arnhem, organized resistance north of the Lower Rhine has ceased...'

Across the Channel, in Paris, the cor-respondents were finishing a late breakfast at their mess in the Scribe Hotel – bacon and eggs and as much real coffee as they could drink for ten cents, 'the best bargain in Paris', they were both heard to boast. Now they were waiting in the shabby lobby for the requisitioned Parisian buses and drab olive staff cars which would take them out to Ver-sailles for the great conference to be attended by the top brass from all over the command.

By this time, Eisenhower, settled in his new quarters at St Germain, a comfortable house which had been Field Marshal Gerd von Rundsted's billet until the month before, had already finished his tenth cigarette. Tclck and Caacie, his pet dogs, were doing fine, he had been informed, but one of his cows, which supplied his house with milk, was unfortunately going dry. He dismissed the disturbing piece of news and prepared to drive to his office.

Now the brass had started arriving at Eisenhower's office situated in a small white stone annex behind the stately Trianon Palace Hotel, where a bronze bust of Goering had been turned with its face to the glass-walled foyer. Devers was there with his staff, having flown in from the Vosges Mountains.

Now Bradley arrived with his advisers. Like their bespectacled chief they were angry and out for blood. Patton was being attacked along all his front, and was screaming for supplies and aid. But due to Montgomery's 'pencil-like thrust' which was hogging all the transport, or so it seemed to them, no supplies were forthcoming. Indeed Old Blood and Guts had flown to Paris the day before to protest to Eisenhower personally. To no avail. Now Patton was really squawking. In Paris he had learned that Devers was going to take numerous troops from his own Third Army.

Eisenhower appeared and shook the hands of his two Army Group Commanders. 'Brad' made a comment about 'Ike's' new office and the general who had been with him in the same West Point class of 15 – 'the Generals' Class', they would call it later – commented ruthfully: 'It's too elegant. I'll rattle around the place and get lost.'

The brass prepared to enter the conference room. It was just then that Major Hansen, Bradley's aide, informed his chief that SHAEF staff were betting that the 'Field Marshal' – he meant Montgomery – would not turn up. Thus, as Bradley spotted Montgomery's Chief-of-Staff, big, jolly, red-faced General 'Freddie' de Guingand in the high echoing room, he was not surprised. Montgomery had ducked the meeting, and he could guess why. De Guingand, who was well liked by the American generals, did his best. He explained that Montgomery was still confident his troops would secure a bridgehead over the Rhine at Arnhem, from which he would then thrust into the Ruhr.

According to de Guingand, his chief felt that 'to take quick advantage of the favourable situation in the Nijmegen area, it is essential that the right corps of Second Army – the Eighth – should develop at once a strong thrust on the axis Gennep–Cleve–Emmerich', from which it would be later directed onto the north west corner of the Ruhr. To do this, Montgomery expected Eisenhower to direct the 12th Army Group to take over the existing Eighth Corps sector at once.

An enraged Bradley, listening in silence to the big Britisher's exposé, knew what that meant: Monty would take over his First Army again to do the job. He flashed a glance at Ike. But if the bold suggestion had irritated the Supreme Commander Bradley thought he 'restrained his irritation with uncommon self-control'.

Montgomery's messenger was not yet

finished, however. His chief, it appeared, wanted more. He felt that affairs on the Allied front were in a sorry state and that there should be an overall ground commander under Eisenhower to control the fighting. And there should be one candidate only for that office – Field Marshal Montgomery.

At the end of the great conference de Guingand was to signal his chief: 'Excellent conference. Ike supported your plan one hundred per cent. Your thrust is the main effort and gets full support.' How deluded the Chief-of-Staff was.

In the end, the Supreme Commander decided that the envelopment of the Ruhr from the north by the 21st Army Group, supported by the US 1st Army 'is the main effort' of the 'present phase of operations'. To do this, Bradley's 12th Army Group was to undertake no further aggressive action. But there was no talk of appointing Montgomery the ground commander for the whole of the Allied armies; and the words 'present phase of operations' held a menace, which de Guingand did not perceive when he sent his triumphant signal to his chief. Unless Montgomery could realize some of his grandiose promises, in particular the capture of the Arnhem bridge, essential for the drive forward, the green light which he had now been given temporarily would quickly turn to red again.

The next few days would be critical, not only for the trapped First Airborne, but also for Montgomery's career. If he did not relieve the paras soon, Eisenhower would withdraw his temporary priority and that would be the end of his great dream of leading his victorious armies into Berlin, as the Western Allied General who had played the greatest part in defeating the German foe. Now everything would depend upon the speed with which General Horrocks got his men moving out of Nijmegen.

2

On that foggy Friday morning in Holland, 'Jorrocks' went to see Brigadier Essame, commander of the 43rd Division's 214th Infantry Brigade. The Guards Division had been fought now almost to a standstill. This morning it would be up to Essame's infantrymen to attempt to swing round the German defences behind the Waal and barrel their way to the Polish positions at Driel. And 'Jorrocks', who so far had not received one visit from the man who had planned the whole bold operation – from Montgomery or his Allied Commander Dempsey – knew how vital it was that the breakthrough should be achieved this day. Although he had no concrete information about what was going on in the Airborne's positions, he could guess. After six days of combat against two SS Panzer divisions, they would be obviously near the end of their tether. They would break soon and he could not let that happen. Thus, as the mist began to clear over the village of Osterhout (Essame's first objective) 'Jorrocks', who commanded 100,000 men, prepared to help direct the activities of a mere 3,000, the 214th Brigade. The dash for Driel was under way.

While Colonel George Taylor's Duke of Cornwall's Light Infantry waited in their carriers to begin the dash, the Somersets went over the embankment into the attack on the little huddle of red-brick houses which was Osterhout.

The artillery bombardment which had been pounding the German positions for the last forty minutes stopped abruptly. There was no sound now save the steady crunch of the infantrymen's boots over the boggy meadows, the mist still wreathed around their legs. One hundred yards. Two. Still no enemy reaction. And then it came. The spandaus opened up with a vehement, high-pitched hiss. Here and there a man fell heavily and disappeared into the mist. Their pace quickened. Officers shouted orders. Red-faced NCOs cursed angrily and the heavy-set Somerset farm boys broke into a clumsy run, the inevitable white enamel tea mug tied to the back of their packs jumping up and down as they did so.

The small arms battle rose in intensity. Along the line of carriers, Colonel Taylor's Cornishmen puffed their cigarettes anxiously and the reinforcements kept going to the ditches to urinate. The 43rd had an unlucky reputation. By the end of the war it would have suffered the most casualties of any division of the British Liberation Army. The old sweats in the battalion maintained boastfully, almost as if they were proud of the fact: 'three weeks they give you in this lot before you catch a packet.'

But on this day the old sweats were apparently going to be proved wrong. Soon the first German prisoners started streaming in, prodded along by jubilant sweating Somersets. 'It's ours,' they yelled to the waiting Cornishmen. 'We've got her.'

Colonel Taylor did not wait any longer. As the firing started to die down in the shattered smoking village, he gave the order to mount up. The carriers burst into noisy life. Blue smoke clouded the road everywhere. The infantrymen flipped their cigarettes over the sides and they were off. B Company in the lead swerved off the road into some boggy orchards. 'German tanks ahead,' they radioed the CO.

'Push on, change plan, seize D Company's objective,' Taylor radioed back urgently. He was not going to tolerate any stickiness on the part of his lead company.

B rolled out of the orchard onto the road again. Before them now lay the exit from the village and the route to Valburg, the next objective. Behind them a tense Colonel Taylor wondered if their luck would hold good. Might they stay lucky and capture it too?

B radioed: 'Two enemy tanks spotted a thousand yards ahead.'

Taylor didn't hesitate. 'Ignore them,' he ordered, 'mount your tanks and carriers.' He knew speed was essential if he was to break through before the SS recovered. Tearing off his equipment, he ran up the road. Shouting and threatening, he got the slow plodding lead platoon moving fast.

Now the Cornish column – armoured vehicles and anti-tank guns in the lead, soft-skinned vehicles in the rear – started to barrel forward. Ignoring the danger of ambush or mines, they tore up the road towards Valburg. Thirty minutes later they had taken it. Everywhere surprised Dutch farmers and their wives burst out of their houses, 'wild with joy, shouting and cheering till their lungs almost burst', as Colonel Taylor recalled just after the war. But the Cornish Colonel had no time to play the role of liberator. He had to get to Driel before the

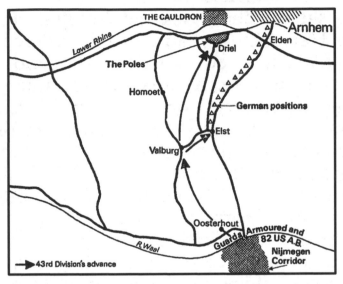

'The 9th SS Panzer Division is to attack the remains of the 1st British Airborne Division from all sides and destroy them as speedily as possible.' – SS Gen. Bittrich to Col. Harzer. CO 9th SS.

SS woke up finally to the fact that he had slipped through their front. Now he was only a matter of a couple of miles away from the Polish positions and the ferry.

Earlier that day, a tired Urquhart, who had just found his RSM Lord trying to coax some of his men out of the cellars back to their slit trenches, received his first signal from Horrocks. It read: '43 Div ordered to take all risk to effect relief today and are directed on ferry. If situation warrants you should withdraw to or cross ferry.' Despite the fact that the ferry was no longer in British hands, the message cheered Urquhart considerably. He signalled back: 'We shall be glad to see you.' Nevertheless, he thought that neither Horrocks nor Browning really understood the tough situation he was in. He decided, therefore, to send his surviving senior staff officer on the adventurous route taken the night before by Heaps across the Lower Rhine to contact Horrocks and 'put him in the picture'.

Mackenzie, a small, solemn-faced Scot, revealed no emotion when Urquhart told him he had been chosen for the highly dangerous mission. He listened attentively without protest as Urquhart explained: 'It's necessary that they should know that the Division no longer exists as such and that we are now merely a collection of individuals holding on... Make clear to them, Charles, that we're terribly short of men, ammunition, food and medical supplies and that we need some DUKWs to ferry the Poles across.' He paused and added significantly. 'If supplies don't arrive tonight, Charles, it may be too late!'

All around the perimeter now, the weary survivors were under constant attack. 'That day I had a couple of raw potatoes picked up in a garden and a drink of rainwater from my helmet which I collected during the night,' Private Dukes of the 1st Para Battalion, dug in near the ruined Oosterbeek Church, recalls. 'Now the Jerries really started to belt us.'

The SS, who had been ordered to finish off the First Airborne that day, were dug in less than a hundred yards from the Church position, commanded by a 3rd Battalion Major named Bush. Now with the aid of an SP gun, they started to 'take out' the paras' slit trenches systematically. Soon wounded were lying everywhere, moaning piteously.

'All the same, morale was terrific,' Dukes remembers. 'Even when the only water they had for the wounded was out of lavatory cisterns in the ruined houses.' Staff Sergeant Callaghan of the same force helped to keep it that way too, by casually wandering among the wounded wearing a very tall and ancient Dutch top hat he had 'liberated' somewhere or other, telling them airily: 'It doesn't matter at all. Nothin' could hit me under this.'

But the SPs and the Tigers were getting bolder and bolder, knowing the paras had pathetically few anti-tank weapons left. In Major Cain's command, he had a Piat and a Polish-manned 6-pounder anti-tank gun left, and the Poles were dying rapidly. Whenever a German tank appeared, they ran to their exposed gun, fired off a shell, losing men all the time and then charged the bemused Germans hell-for-leather. Now the whole road was littered with their grey-berreted bodies.

They had just discovered that there was hardly anyone left to man the six-pounder, when a SP started to nose its way aggressively into the paras' positions. Major Cain knew that if he did not stop it, they wouldn't last much longer. He quickly organized a stalk with an artillery officer named Ian Meikle.

Meikle shinned up the wall of a ruined house and took up his position crouched behind a chimney stack, concealed from the SP which lay directly below. Then he began to shout his fire orders to Cain armed with the clumsy Piat. His first shot missed. So did his second, as it whizzed its way over the house and dropped harmlessly into the road beyond the hidden SP. Just as Meikle was about to shout his third command to the sweating, black-faced Cain, his chimney stack erupted in a burst of flame. The mass of bricks crashed into Cain's slit trench together with the artilleryman's dead body. The para next to Cain fought his way out and fled, screaming. Cain shouted angrily for him to come back. He continued running. In that same instant, another tank started to work its way down the road. The remaining paras shouted to Cain for help. He doubled forward to the corner. The steel monster was only a hundred yards. Swiftly he loaded the pear-shaped bomb. Pressing the padded shoulder rest against his body, he yanked the trigger. The Piat exploded. He felt a terrific kick in the shoulder. The German tank stopped suddenly and Cain thought he had hit a track. But the enemy's gun was undamaged. It cracked into action.

The first German shell missed, but it raised a huge cloud of dust and smoke at such short range. His head singing wildly, Cain fired again. This time the bomb struck home. The tank started to smoke thickly. Hurriedly its black-bereted crew began to bail out, firing their machine pistols as they raced across the road. They didn't get far. Cain's Bren-gunners opened up swiftly. The Germans crumpled to the battle-littered

227

road dead.

The Major had no time to rejoice at his victory. Another steel monster had rumbled into view. He took a hurried aim with the Piat. But this time luck was not on his side. The bomb exploded within the clumsy anti-tank weapon. Cain went reeling backwards, his face bleeding from countless little wounds where the metal had struck him, blinded and with two black eyes. 'I was shouting like a hooligan,' he recalled much later, 'shouting to someone to get on the Piat because there was another tank behind. I blubbered and yelled and swore.' His men dragged him off to the Regimental Aid Post.

Half an hour later he was back at his post again, his nerve recovered. That day he won the Victoria Cross. Of the five who won it during those terrible ten days he was the only one who survived to receive the coveted honour from his King.

But all the men who fought at Arnhem that day were not heroes. Sergeant-Pilot Louis Hagen, the German Jew, who exactly ten years before had been clearing out the slopbins at Torgau concentration camp, found a strange bunch of shirkers in the cellars of the Divisional HQ when he went there to report to General Urquhart on a patrol he had carried out.

They were men of all ranks and from all

228

regiments. 'They looked like people who had been seasick for days,' he recalled just after the war. 'Nothing in the world could coax them up. Down there they vegetated: ate, slept and relieved themselves in a world where only their fear was reality.' Some of them he recognized from his own Glider Pilot Wing. 'There was Sergeant A, quite a close friend of mine back at the station. He was a good-looking chap of twenty-eight, always neatly turned out, a good pilot... He knew what the war was about and like all of us, had volunteered to be a Glider Pilot...' Hagen tried to persuade him to come out of his cellar for his own good, 'because he was obviously going through hell.' But the Sergeant simply would not budge and Hagen did not want to use force, as RSM Lord was having to do with the shirkers now. So he left him cowering in the twilight world of the cellar.

In the cellar of the gardener's house, he found another former comrade for whom he did not feel so much pity. 'Staff Sergeant G was the tough guy of our flight ... always getting into scrapes with the chaps of other units and calling me "la-di-da" and "Miss Hagen" because I wore pyjamas and did not swear. He used to brag about what he would do once he met the Germans. He would take the first German child by the legs and tear it in two ... as the only good German was a dead German.' Now he had been reduced to a trembling wreck, hiding in the dark.

Morale was high in another such mixed unit, however: Boy Wilson's Pathfinders. CSM James Stewart, a regular soldier, had found them a strange bunch when he had first joined them, but now he was realising it was a 'privilege to serve with them'. For the Pathfinders were not just defending their positions near the crossroads at Oosterbeek, they were actually going over to the offensive.

Sneaking out of the position held by Lieutenant David Eastwood and Sergeant 'Sonny' Binick MM, one day to be – of all things – compere of 'Come Dancing' and World Ballroom Dancing champion, the pathfinders were picking off enemy snipers and kidnapping their sentries.

This day they had nabbed three of them. Now a German voice broke into their radio communications telling them that: 'You must let our boys go. Otherwise we'll come and take your Sunray.'

Wilson was not impressed by the German's threat to capture 'Sunray,' who was in fact Urquhart. He took the mike and cried laughingly: 'Come and get him – if you can!'

But as that terrible afternoon started to draw to a welcome close, Mevrouw Ter Horst's house next to the Oosterbeek was so crowded with badly wounded men that they lay under tables and were propped up within the open fireplace. Helping out the best she could, the tall blonde heard a group of shaken paras talk in awed tones about the accuracy of the enemy snipers.

'They shoot you in the back,' one of them commented.

The Dutch woman turned on the speaker: 'Each of you is a better shot than those snipers,' she proclaimed. 'Any one of you can beat them!'

She passed on her way majestically to help a wounded artilleryman who has taking suicidal risks to bolt across the garden to fetch water from a pump, actually running across dead paras bodies to do so. Now she almost bumped into him as he raced through the shattered, bullet-pocked door, his chest heaving. She gasped when she saw the colour of the water. It was the bright red of blood.

3

Taylor and his leading company of Cornishmen had finally reached the Poles. Swiftly he listened to Mackenzie's story of the Airborne's plight and helped him to signal it to Horrocks, who replied immediately, 'Everything will be done to get the essentials through.'

But already a hitch had occurred of which Taylor was as yet unaware. As he planned to help the Poles to cross the Lower Rhine, his own tail was being threatened by a column of the 10th SS Panzer Division.

CSM Philp was rattling towards the Rhine in a Bren gun carrier when he saw a column of tanks advancing towards him at a fair speed. When he was within a hundred yards of them he noted with a sense of shock that they all bore crosses, and the crosses were black. Philp could do nothing but continue towards them. Two of the German tanks pulled out of the way, not recognizing the tracked vehicle as British. The third didn't. Philp actually bumped into it. The commander's head popped over the edge of the turret. He began to remove his goggles. The CSM didn't give him a chance. He fired. The German slumped down dead. The two tank gunners opened fire furiously. The one gun was too low, however, the other too high. Both missed, though Philp could feel the heat of the tracer hissing by him. Hastily the CSM prepared to abandon the carrier. His head crashed into the 88 and he fell out into a ditch, followed by his men. Hurriedly they crawled further into the reed-covered, muddy ditch while five Tigers, supported by a dozen infantrymen, rumbled into view. That was enough for the CSM. He and his men beat a rapid retreat, but did save the rest of the 'soft' vehicles from running into the German armour.

It was obvious, though, that the Duke of Cornwall's could not allow the Germans to dominate the vital country road. Guessing that the armour would move back on Elst now it was getting dark, and leaving the road to the infantry, they set an ambush for the five Tigers.

It worked like a dream. A German dispatch-rider on a motor-cycle headed the column. He hit one of the mines and disappeared in a flash of blinding red light. Still the Tigers came rumbling on, firing Verey lights every few seconds to illuminate the road.

The infantrymen crouching in the ditches on both sides of the road, their faces greasy and unreal in the red light of the flares, told each other that the Jerries were windy, despite the massive protection of their sixty-ton monsters.

As the first Tiger rumbled into their chain of 75 type mines, Major Parker, in charge of the ambush, yelled *'Fire!'*

Six Piats cracked into action. There was a tremendous rending explosion and the Tiger slewed to a stop. The second tank went up on a mine. Desperately the driver of the third tried to reverse and ran into a string of mines that had been put out behind it. Young

Private Brown of the Cornwalls, who was going into action for the very first time, doubled forward with his Piat. He ran until he was only a matter of yards away from the stricken Tiger, then he fired. The bomb rocked the Tiger from side to side as if it were on the high sea. But the blast knocked out young Brown's eyes and blinded him.

As CSM Philp began dropping grenades down the remaining tanks' open turrets, British fire called down by someone unknown started to fall on the Cornwalls. The Sergeant-Major dropped wounded, too. The cry of 'stretcher-bearer!' went up everywhere. As they doubled forward to pick up the blinded youngster, his face covered with blood, he said: 'I don't care. I knocked the bugger out!' Then he passed out. The dash for Driel was making its demands in blood and human life. And there was more to come...

At first, Colonel Taylor of the Cornwalls had thought he might attempt to retake Arnhem Bridge, but Mackenzie and the rest convinced him that would be impossible. He concentrated then on getting men and supplies across the Lower Rhine into Urquhart's perimeter. Unfortunately everything went wrong.

The cable with which they were going to draw the Poles' boats across the river broke.

Then the two DUKWs, which would ferry the urgently needed supplies across simply could not cope with the terrain in the darkness. They ended up in a ditch within sight of the river, hopelessly bogged down.

Now it was up to the Poles to try to get across in rubber dinghies, with the Airborne engineers ferrying them back and forth. In spite of enemy fire, the current and the darkness, they braved the crossing, watched by their helpless commander General Sosabowski, sad and angry at seeing his fine men being thrown away in such a manner. Only 35 men made it, and Sosabowski used an armoured car radio to signal Horrocks: 'All we can do now is trust in God. We have no food or ammunition. God bless you all!'

But on this black Friday, Horrocks was being confronted with still more problems. Back at his HQ he had just had time to ponder Mackenzie's information that the First Airborne Division probably would not last another twenty-four hours if the 43rd didn't reach them soon, when a staff officer bustled in to inform him that the HQ was now cut off. The Germans had launched an armoured attack on the Screaming Eagles' positions and broken them between Veghel and St Odenrode. Hell's Highway was now in enemy hands for a stretch of a couple of miles.

Horrocks could have groaned aloud. The news placed him in a terrible predicament. Should he ignore the threat to his rear? Should he use his reserve, north of the German breakthrough, the 32nd Guards Brigade, to support the Driel bridgehead? Or should he counter-attack to retake the enemy-occupied part of Hell's Highway?

At last he made his decision. The Guards would turn about and attack the Germans, supported by the Screaming Eagles and his own 50th Division coming up from the south. General Thomas's 43rd Division, already stalled virtually everywhere around Elst, would have to break through to the trapped paras. It would be twenty-five precious hours before Hell's Highway were opened again.

That night, 30th Corps' official communiqué recorded that the 'situation is grave'. For Horrocks, the good-humoured, always smiling commander, that night was 'about the blackest moment of my life'. He tossed and turned and could not get to sleep, plagued by the mental picture 'of the airborne troops fighting their desperate battle on the other side of the river'. It was a long time, until with an effort of will, he forced himself to go to sleep just before midnight.

It was just about then that General Urquhart was wakened to be informed that thirty-five Poles had landed and had been assigned to Pip Hicks' section of the perimeter. At the same time, his aide informed him that Major Breese of the Border Regiment was waiting to see him. Urquhart said he would see the officer who was to lead the dawn attack on the German-held height at Westerbouwing.

Breese was plainly pessimistic about his battalion's chances.

'The men are pretty exhausted,' the officer, who had been commanding the 1st Borderers ever since their CO had been captured on the first day, told the tousled-haired General. 'And even if we're able to establish ourselves on the high ground we will very likely be pushed off again for the lack of men in support.'

Urquhart absorbed the information. In the end he agreed that a failure at this stage 'would be fatal' and the Borderers should stay where they were instead of risking a withdrawal after a brief occupation of the dominating height. Major Breese mumbled his thanks, saluted and went out, leaving the General with his thoughts.

Whatever they may have been, we do not know. All we know is that the last two words of the 'sitrep' the Scottish General dictated that night were still brave and bold: 'Morale high'.

DAY SEVEN

'Portsmouth 1, West Ham 3;
Lecds 7, Barrow 9'.
—Football scores, 23rd Sept, 1944.

On the seventh day, the 7th Battalion the King's Own Scottish Borderers shaved in hot water. It was the first time most of them had shaved since the morning of the great drop. Then there had been nearly seven hundred of them. Now they were down to two hundred. The rest were dead, wounded or missing. But the King's Own Scottish Borderers shaved before the last battle as their forefathers had done before them on the Veldt and in the mud of Flanders. Morale was further heightened by a hot breakfast.

'It was as well that we started off in this spirit,' their CO Colonel Payton-Reid recollected much later, 'because there was no peace during the rest of that day nor the night which followed.'

Almost immediately the Germans started their attack. SPs, followed by infantry, began to worm their way towards the KOSBs' positions, confident that this time they would crush the stubborn Scots' resistance. But they were in for a surprise that morning.

Payton-Reid now had 30 Corps' artillery at his command, and although the KOSBs were not trained in directing long distance shots, they had set up a human observation chain in the shattered house which they used as an HQ. From his post on the roof an officer passed his message along this human chain to the wireless operator located in the basement who relayed the observer's instructions to the 30 Corps' gunners some nine miles away. Awkward, amateurish and slow as it was, the system worked. As the Germans attempted their first rush of that grey morning, shells descended upon them from nowhere and an excited radio operator relayed the great news to the senior officer listening at the other end with a great shout of triumph: 'Marvellous, you're right among then! We can hear the buggers screaming!'

In the glider pilots' position, there was some talk of washing and shaving, but as Louis Hagen records 'that was going a bit too far'. Thus the pilots spent the early hours of that day cleaning up their positions by fishing grenade fuses from bottles of cherries, preserved by the careful Dutch housewife who had once owned their shattered house, and disentangling ammunition and small arms from her vegetable store. Then they sat down and tucked into their usual 'slop-pail stew', made by a resentful former-batman turned cook, Private Buckley, who threw in everything and anything he could find and kept the bucket boiling all day long. It was regarded as 'not done' to ask the only private in the Glider Pilots' section what the stew contained; Buckley was touchy about his new found skill as a cook.

Soon after he had finished, Sergeant Hagen set off with an officer to get through to Brigadier Hackett's HQ, where he had been asked to report on a patrol he had carried out the previous day. He found Hackett walking about his positions, completely oblivious to the mortar bombs dropping all around. Together they went inside and the ex-cavalryman asked Hagen to draw in the German armoured positions, he had noted the day before.

Hagen did so, using his dirty fingers, until Hackett stopped him with an angry: 'For crying out loud, take your filthy hands away! You're covering the whole bloody map… Why don't you get yourself a stick and point it out properly?' He controlled himself. 'They all use their hands. I've had to tell them a hundred times.'

A red-faced Hagen breathed 'Yessir', and the interview continued normally; but although the Sergeant-Pilot was impressed by Hackett's man-to-man attitude, he felt that Hackett 'must have known better than

I did that there was nothing he could do about it'. The First Airborne had finally ceased taking offensive action. Now it had to sit tight in its defensive positions and take everything the enemy cared to throw at it. The Germans had begun to dictate the battle for the cauldron.

At Divisional Headquarters that morning, tempers were short as the German 'hate' started right on time and there was a hurried rush for the cellars. Urquhart's senior admin officer, Colonel Preston, stayed above ground and began shaving on the ops table. Urquhart gave him a quick order to get rid of his shaving gear and the chastened staff officer beat a hasty retreat.

As the mortar barrage began to mount in fury, Urquhart glanced around the faces of the men under his command. He could recognize the 'cumulative wear of lack of sleep and food and exposure. Dirt-caked and with heavy-lidded, reddened eyes, they had not an unlimited endurance before them'.

Although he felt their fighting spirit was still tremendous, he knew they couldn't hold out much longer under these terrible conditions. Thus in a slack period after the first 'hate' he made his first report of the day:

'Spasmodic shelling and mortaring during night. Otherwise little change in perimeter. Several attacks by infantry and SP guns or tanks supported by extremely heavy mortaring and shelling are in progress on north east of perimeter. 50 Poles ferried across river during night. Leading infantry 43 Div have arrived south bank. Hope they will be able to cross under mist. Sup situation serious. Majority no rations last 24 hours. Amn short – latter may be accompanying party from south.'

The big Scottish infantryman knew that the fate of his shattered Division now lay in the hands of General Thomas, commander of the 43rd, and somehow, Urquhart had a suspicion that Thomas would not be rushed under any circumstances, unless Horrocks at Corps forced him. As the snipers started their deadly work from the trees around the Hartenstein, Urquhart prayed that Mackenzie had survived the Rhine crossing and dash to the Polish lines so that he could impress upon the brass just how desperate the position was for the men in the cauldron.

2

Roughly when Urquhart was sending his signal, Colonel Mackenzie and Lieutenant-Colonel Myers were rolling along through the mist in two armoured cars of the Household Cavalry, taking the back country road to Nijmegen. A couple of hundred yards ahead of them, a two-man scout car (a Dingo) kept a tense watch for German armour reported to be about somewhere.

Suddenly the little convoy started to slow down. One of the sixty-ton Tigers, which CSM Philp and Private Brown had put out of action the previous night, was blocking the crossroads. As the two armoured cars came to a halt, the Dingo crawled forward to test the clearance. Just as the Dingo came parallel with the abandoned Tiger, a big cumbersome German halftrack appeared from behind a ruined church only a hundred yards away. The Dingo's driver put his foot down hard. The little vehicle shot forward, followed by an angry stream of tracer fire. Mackenzie's gunner snapped into action. The Daimler's six-pounder erupted. Swiftly the German halftrack backed behind a tree and the shell went wide. The armoured car driver did not wait for their response. He reversed frantically and landed in a ditch. Slowly but inevitably the Daimler toppled over on its turret, its gun buried in mud and wet leaves. Further down the road, Myers' armoured car turned rapidly and went to look for help.

With only one sten gun between them, Mackenzie and the two Life Guards scrambled to the cover of another ditch and burrowed under a heap of prunings. Now the SS men had bailed out of their halftrack and

spreading out, had begun beating the orchard looking for the three of them. One of
them was getting closer and closer. Dry-
mouthed and tense, the little Scot Mackenzie
whispered to the Life Guard with the sten:
'Any nearer and you must shoot! Then we'll
bolt for it.'

The young trooper nodded his understanding, his face pale and strained. As the
German in his camouflaged cape came ever
nearer so that they could see every detail of
his young face quite clearly, he started to
raise his sten. It seemed as if Colonel Mackenzie would never reach 30 Corps Headquarters now.

But on that day Horrocks' greatest concern,
it seemed, was to break the German barrier
line across Hell's Highway. American paras,
coming in as reinforcements, were thrown
in immediately, even when their planes had
been shot down and they had been forced to
make an emergency landing.

One Guards officer waiting to go into
action remembers a small group of such
Americans appearing suddenly in their
midst, slacks perfectly creased, laden down
with equipment, including brand new frying
pans, ready for a scrap. The Guardsman
asked them how England looked and one of
them replied, 'As sweet as a green pea.' But
the American paras had no time for small

talk now. 'Say, boys,' an NCO asked, 'which way is the battle?' The Guards officer pointed in the direction of a line of German 88s which they had been reconnoitring and suggested the Yanks should be careful. The paras, who had tried twice before to get to Holland and failed, pulled scornful faces. 'Say buddy,' a big NCO said, 'we came here to fight and that's what we're going to do.' The next instant the whole lot of them were off in their brand new jeeps, heading straight for the waiting 88s. They disappeared round a bend in the road. But not for long.

There was the familiar flat, rending crack of the German gun. An angry crackle of small arms fire. Much shouting. Then silence. Some time later the survivors came streaming back, their confidence somewhat impaired.

But the American paras were not alone in their careless disregard for the strength of the German opposition on Hell's Highway that morning. A little later a truck convoy of Coldstream Guards and tanks rolled up and prepared to tackle the German 88s. They too ignored the warning to take care.

Within five minutes of starting their attack, the three lead tanks had been knocked out in rapid succession. Their advance came to a quick halt. Swiftly an infantry attack under the cover of a mortar barrage was planned.

Meanwhile the Guardsmen grabbed a quick meal; after all it might be their last.

As they moved into the attack, the watchers who had warned them of what was waiting for them up the road, caught a glimpse of the Guards' CO, a thin, frail-looking man, being fed yet another enormous cheese sandwich by a huge Guardsman bodyguard, armed with a sniper's rifle. Then they too disappeared round the bend to face their own particular date with destiny. As one of the eye witnesses was to describe it later: 'The German mortars replied, wounded Guards began to trickle back, and then an outburst of noise, bangs, shouts and explosions, followed by silence...'

Mackenzie, saved by a force of tanks summoned by Colonel Myers, reached 30 Corps HQ, shivering with cold and wet. Boy Browning, the elegant Airborne Corps Commander whose HQ was located near Horrocks, thought they looked 'putty coloured like men who had come through a Somme winter'.

But Browning, the former Grenadier Guardsman, who set such great store by immaculate turnout and good form, did not seem greatly affected by their plight and the tale they had to tell. He listened to what the two colonels had to say with little comment then passed them on to Horrocks' HQ where their reception was equally frosty. To Mackenzie and Myers, it seemed that both corps commanders were too concerned with the German breakthrough of Hell's Highway between Veghel and Uden; they did not appear to be able to understand the full seriousness of the position within the cauldron.

A little later they were passed on yet again to General Thomas's 43rd Divisional HQ. The General affected breeches and brilliantly polished riding boots and he was a stickler for order. Nothing was ever to disturb one of his briefings (even when, in May 1945, his brigade major tried to interrupt a briefing to tell him the war had ended, the unfortunate Major was ordered out of the General's caravan until the briefing was over). He did not take kindly to the appearance of the two scruffy paras at his HQ.

His first reaction was to decide that Major General Sosabowski should be placed under the command of the much junior Brigadier Essame for the rest of the action, a move, which Mackenzie could not help thinking was bound to produce unnecessary friction. But General Thomas did not give him a chance to register his protest. He was told to go back to the Poles and get ready for the next stage of the 43rd's deliberate, in Mackenzie's opinion far too deliberate, plan of operations. Glumly the little Scot returned the way he had come, already beginning to realize that he had failed in his mission.

3

At midday, Boy Wilson's Pathfinders located at Oosterbeek crossroads were surprised as the hail of fire which had been slapping into their positions all morning stopped abruptly as if in response to a command. For a few minutes the weary Pathfinders stared at each other in red-eyed bewilderment. What was going on?

The answer to that unspoken question came a few moments later. A German officer, carrying a white flag, appeared hesitantly from the nearest enemy position and stood there waving it. Next to him there was a para medical officer with the Red Cross armband clearly visible around his camouflaged smock. CSM James Stewart, the regular sergeant major of the 21st Independent Para Company, was the first to react. The German and the MO were obviously from the dressing station at Schonard. Only a few minutes before he had sneaked out of their own positions to visit an old pal of his from the 11th Para, George Gatland, who had been lying on the floor there 'in his own gore' (as he would express it later). Just as the Germans had come in through the front door, he had slipped out of the back.

Perhaps, he told himself, the Jerry wanted to talk about evacuating the wounded.

But the German officer wanted more. He demanded from Stewart that his guns should be removed from the crossroads 'or accept the consequences in respect of our wounded in the Aid Posts set up in the hotels Schonard and Vrewik opposite'.

CSM Stewart listened in silence, his brow creased in a worried frown. He knew the Jerries had the Pathfinders by the 'short and curlies'. If they did not comply with the German's wishes, their own pals such as George Gatland would undoubtedly suffer. If they did, the abandonment of the vital position might well lead to the collapse of the whole perimeter. Hurriedly he passed on the German's message to Boy Wilson.

The grey-haired, normally good-humoured Major saw the problem immediately. He realized that it was too big for him to solve. He informed his superior Hackett. The latter knew he would have to stall the German somehow or other; time was of the essence. If he could put off the enemy long enough, the 43rd might well have launched their relief attack in the meantime. Thus it was that he went to meet the German officer personally.

After an exchange of salutes, as if they were enemies in some 18th century battle picture, instead of a paratrooper and a tank officer, representatives of the 20th century's most advanced formations, the German said: 'We are about to deliver an attack on this side of the perimeter. I intend to put down a mortar and artillery concentration on your forward positions.' Swinging round he pointed to the paras' casualty clearing station further down the road. 'We know that you have wounded there and we do not wish to put down a barrage that will hit them.'

Hackett nodded his approval of this noble assertion and wondered what the German was leading up to. 'I am asking you,' the enemy officer said, 'to move your forward positions six hundred yards further back!' Hackett almost laughed in the German's face. If he accorded with the German's request, Urquhart's Divisional HQ would be exactly two hundred yards behind the enemy lines. But he played for time. 'I must talk it over with my commander first,' he said, his face suitably solemn. Reluctantly the German emissary agreed and said he would meet Hackett at three o'clock.

Hackett hurried to Urquhart's HQ. The big Scot laughed when the Brigadier pointed out that he would find himself behind enemy lines if he concurred with the German's demands, but he said seriously: 'You will have to do as you think best. I'm not going to influence you.'

Hackett thought for a second and an-

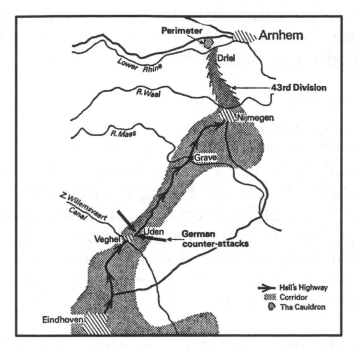

Perimeter **Arnhem**

Driel

Lower Rhine

R. Waal

43rd Division

Nijmegen

R. Maas

Grave

Z Willemsvaart Canal

Uden

Veghel

German counter-attacks

Eindhoven

→ Hell's Highway
▦ Corridor
◉ The Cauldron

'We shall hold on, but at the same time hope for a brighter 24 hours ahead.' – Gen. Urquhart swered: 'I'm afraid that the casualty clearing station will have to take its chance.'

Urquhart nodded wearily. 'That is the conclusion I would have come to,' he agreed.

At three o'clock precisely, Hackett met his German again. 'With great regret,' he told the enemy officer in his own language, 'we cannot agree to any move.' The German turned on his heel without another word.

One hour later the last attempt to re-supply the trapped Division by air came in. The men on the ground, starved of ammunition as well as food, did not know it, but this would be the last RAF supply operation. Air Vice-Marshal Hollinghurst, in charge of the drops, had suffered too many losses. At his HQ at Eastcote near Ruislip he had decided he would not take any more. The 123 planes now approaching Arnhem were to be the last.

They flew into the flak barrage in perfect formation at exactly 1,500 feet, searching for the airborne positions in the confused shattered suburb below: four-engined converted Lancasters and unarmed two-engined Dakotas sailing into the concentrated German fire, as if it didn't even exist. But as the supply planes circled, holding back their drop until they were certain they were over the trapped men, they started to take grievous losses. Plane exploded in mid-air and literally vanished. Another, its wing shot off, sailed down like a leaf snapped from a tree. A third, thick white glycol fumes pouring from its engines, dived for the ground at an impossible speed, huge chunks of metal being stripped off its crippled engines at every instant.

To the awed, angry men below, both German and British, there was nothing they could do but stare upwards, the battle on the ground temporarily forgotten in the face of such courage.

But in spite of their losses, the survivors came in for the drop. Hundreds of bright yellow, red, blue parachutes snapped open and began to drift down, looking to glider pilot Louis Hagen 'like an overcrowded and crazy illustration to a child's book'. Yet as the survivors of that last attempt to supply the cauldron started to fly away, the damaged planes straggling behind, his mood changed from awe to fear. Suddenly he felt 'terribly small, frightened and insignificant: something like an ant menaced by a steam roller'.

Slowly the gaily-coloured parachutes, bearing the precious supplies, began to drift towards the German lines. Like all the previous drops, the last one was a failure too.

The fight continued. At the glider pilots' position, 'Fearless Frank', who had won his name and a decoration in Sicily, collected ten sergeants to go with him on an offensive patrol. Fearless Frank had tried to make up for his lack of inches with a tremendous Guardsman's moustache. But there was nothing absurd about his offensive spirit, as he planned a night attack on a German-held house which was giving the glider pilots' position a lot of trouble.

Shortly afterwards as it began to grow dark, the NCO patrol slipped out of their own house and into the wood behind it. They doubled forward quickly and unseen, making sure as they advanced they had a safe line of retreat, by chalking guide marks on the trees and cutting the barbed wire and fences on the route. In a matter of minutes they had swung round behind the German house and prepared their attack, while the Germans in the front, poured rapid machine-gun fire into their now empty position.

Fearless Frank knew that his attack would have to be short, sharp – and for the Germans – not very sweet. If the enemy had time to turn their spandaus on his men, they wouldn't have a chance. Accordingly he ordered the patrol's Brens into a position some twenty yards away from the house while the rest of the NCOs crawled forward armed with grenades. Fearless Frank gave a quick look to see if everyone was in position, then he raised his hand and yelled in his funny, clipped way: 'All right – *now!*'

The Brens burst into frantic chattering life. In that same instant the NCOs lobbed their grenades through the shattered windows. The spandaus stopped abruptly. As Fearless Frank gave the signal to retreat, knowing he wouldn't be able to hold the house with his handful of men, located as it was in the middle of 'Jerryland', a heavy silence fell over the place. They had wiped out the German garrison. Yet as the glider pilots reached their own position once more without casualties, they felt no sense of triumph at their minor victory, only one of vague ill-defined frustration. As one of their number recorded: 'It wasn't really satisfying'.

It was not much different in Boy Wilson's position. Angered by the Pathfinders' ability to pick off individual German infantrymen, the enemy brought up an SP and then broke into Wilson's radio network to deliver an ultimatum: 'Withdraw your men or we will blast the dressing station to bits.'

Wilson had nothing left now but bluff. 'We've got a lot of Piats here,' he answered. 'If you don't clear off, we'll blast the lot of you.' The lumbering German SP scuttled to the rear. But Wilson's victory, like that of the glider pilots, was little more than a means of gaining a few more hours of respite before the final assault which would break into the cauldron and destroy it for good.

As the steady drizzle of most of that miserable Saturday gave way to a clear starry night, Urquhart sat down to discuss the fact that the survivors of the shattered First Airborne were serving little purpose now save as targets for German gunners, with his remaining senior officers, Hackett and Higgs. He did not want to give the impression that he was 'for hooking it', he told them, but he did want 'Jorrocks' to understand his real position. Sadly the two Brigadiers read through his draft and agreed with his assessment of the position on this seventh day of the battle. Thus at 8.15, the Divisional signallers relayed the message to 30 Corps HQ. It read: 'Many attacks during day by small parties inf. SP guns and tanks including flame-throwers. Each attack accompanied by very heavy mortaring and shelling within Div perimeter. After many alarms and excursions the latter remains substantially unchanged. Although very thinly held. Physical contact not yet made with those on south bank of river. Resup a flop, small quantities amn only gathered in. Still no food and all ranks extremely dirty owing to shortage of water. Morale still adequate, but continued heavy mortaring and shelling having obvious effects. We shall hold but at the same time hope for a brighter 24 hours ahead.'

Two hours later Mackenzie reappeared.

He crouched in the overcrowded cellar, swamped with wounded men tossing and turning in their sleep, sitting on Urquhart's chair near the wine-rack and told the Scottish commander what he had seen and heard that day; his meeting with Browning and Horrocks, and Thomas's plan to attack across the Lower Rhine with the Poles under command. As they huddled there in the gloom, the single naked bulb rocking wildly from side to side and casting great shadows every time another German shell landed, Urquhart and the rest of the staff officers hung on his words. They could mean the realization of a 'brighter 24 hours'. But even as Mackenzie said them in his careful precise soldier's way, he knew they were half truths. The way Horrocks and Thomas were setting about the operation, it must end in failure. The fate of the First British Airborne Division had already been sealed.

4

In England they were leaving the cinemas now. In the provincial Odeons throughout the country they had been showing 'by special request the picture that will live in your memory for all time, *Dangerous Moonlight*, with A. Walbrook and S. Gray and introducing the "Warsaw Concerto".' But most of the 'picturegoers' had seen it long before; their choice lay with the '$1,000,000 legs' of Betty Grable in *Pin-Up Girl* or the debonair charm of Jack Buchanan as Bulldog Drummond in *Bulldog Sees It Through*.

The pubs were crowded as the Yanks, the good-time girls, the war workers jostled each other to get a last pint before the landlord called time. That afternoon 'outsiders' had won both main races at Ascot and Pontefract and they were flush with money; and even if they hadn't bet on the races, most of them had plenty. At home their wives and mothers listened to 'Saturday Night Theatre' and completed the woollen scarves and jerseys on which they would sew the proud motto: 'Knitted in Great Britain for liberated Europe'. As soon as Holland was freed from the Germans, something which would happen in a few days now, the thousands of woollen products would be flown out there to be distributed among the newly liberated populace ready for the harsh winter that must come. That Saturday night there was a lot of talk about the new football season. After all it wasn't every day that Leeds lost to Barrow seven goals to nine.

As the pubs began to empty and the giggling girls with their new found boyfriends headed for the fish shops – 'no fish sorry, we've only got scallops' – the Poles started to move up into their start positions. That morning Horrocks and Thomas had decided that they should be moved across the Lower Rhine in the darkness. At first they had wanted to put two battalions of the 43rd's infantry across with them, but they had realized that that would be too difficult an operation with the Germans holding the opposite bank, so it had been decided that the Poles would have to 'go it alone'.

Just before midnight they started to draw their boats out of the orchards in which their positions lay and haul them up the high dyke that bordered the river. Beyond lay some twenty feet of grassy, muddy slope and then the dark, sullen river.

But it was not dark for long. Hardly had they breasted the rise with the aid of the Canadian engineers and Dorsets who were to ferry them across, when the Germans waiting for them on the opposite bank opened fire. Red tracer hissed flatly across the river like angry hornets. From behind the machine-gun positions, the 'moaning minnies' howled terrifyingly and seconds later the mortar shells commenced landing in the Polish positions. But the men in the grey berets pushed on under the covering fire of Brigadier Essame's artillery. Boat after boat of the sixteen available was launched into the water.

Now the river was as bright as day. A

fantastic pattern made by a myriad stabs and flashes of orange flame was reflected in its water. Here and there a shell fell short and hitting the soft mud bank hissed straight upwards like a Roman candle. Spurts of water were flung up all around the assault boats. The men cowered behind the low gunwales, thankful for any protection. Here and there a Pole, a little slower than his comrades, slumped forward dead, but unable to fall because they were so tightly packed. The first boat was hit. A mad frantic fumbling as the heavily laden survivors tried to divert themselves of their equipment, then they were striking out for the shore, the tracer hissing above their heads.

Another was hit and went down like a stone taking all its passengers with it. In a third, a lucky burst missed the Canadian pilot, but ripped the length of his passengers, killing most of them. He went on to deliver a boatload of dead men to the other side.

The first boat struck the mud bank. Desperately the Poles clambered up the embankment and ran for cover. Further on in the darkness, frantic voices yelled to them in Polish and English, 'Over here – over here, for Christ sake!' And each shout would be followed by triumphant bursts of German machine-gun fire. Still the Poles kept coming throughout that terrible night. The Germans lobbed stick grenades down upon them from their commanding positions. They wreaked terrible vengeance on the Polish ranks. But the 'stout-hearted Poles', as Brigadier Essame, who watched that night crossing, was to call them later, were not deterred. Their numbers mounted. Fifty – then one hundred. One hundred and fifty ... two hundred of them.

Hackett rushed them into his perimeter defence in person, his face contorted with anger, as time and time again they were shot even before the Brigadier could hurry them to the protection of a slit trench. And then his turn came.

There was the obscene howl of a multiple mortar. A shell landed only a matter of yards away with an ugly plop. Fist-sized fragments of red-hot steel hissed through the air. The Recce soldier with him fell to the ground with a muffled scream. Hackett himself felt a harsh blow in the pit of his stomach and thigh. He toppled over but caught himself in time. Biting back the pain he looked at the Recce man. His leg was badly broken, his khaki slacks full of blood. Forgetting his own injuries, he staggered to the Hartenstein and collected two stretcher-bearers. Finally he allowed himself to be attended to by the Division's chief medic Colonel Graeme Warrack. Ever since Hackett had known the well-built, prematurely bald 31-year-old MO, he had been jokingly suggesting that

Warrack should open the brandy which he knew they were issued with for such cases. 'You can produce those medical comforts now,' he said, as Warrack bent over him to begin his examination. 'The brandy's run out,' the medic said sorrowfully.

'And this is the moment we've waited eighteen months for,' Hackett cracked with a last attempt at humour as Warrack pumped the morphia into his bared arm.

Some time later Urquhart was notified. He went over to look at Hackett. The 'broken-down cavalryman's' face was grey and he looked to the worried Divisional Commander, as if he were in some sort of coma. At that moment he felt sure that Hackett would die. There were not many of them left now.

DAY EIGHT

'There was no ruddy place to run to now!'
    —Private Dukes, 1st Para Battalion.

Sunday 24th September.

The wind had changed and the young men of Harzer's 9th SS to the east of the cauldron tied rags around their faces on account of the stench: a compound of multiple faeces, gunsmoke and death.

But Colonel Harzer had no time for the sensitivities of his teenagers. As sixty Tigers from the 506 Tank Battalion, the first of his reinforcements, started to rumble into Arnhem, he ordered that the cauldron should be cut off from the river. Von Tettau's grenadiers from the *Hermann Goering* and his own 9th SS would push along the river bank and link up. Once they had done that, the fate of the 2,500 Tommies still capable of fighting within the cauldron would be settled once and for all. There would be no more attempts like that of the previous evening to link up with the British paras.

As the drizzle gave way to a thin, watery sunshine, the German artillery began to pound the cauldron and infantry started to move into their start positions.

To a weary Urquhart it took an effort of imagination to realize that it was just one Sunday ago that the Division had taken off so bravely from England and made a 'textbook drop'. Now that some élite Division, of which he had been so proud despite its criticisms of his appointment as Commanding Officer the previous January, lay in ruins. The ones who were still unwounded were beaten and hungry, with the daily ration in some units down to one sardine and a couple of hardtack biscuits per man. With an effort of will he set about his first task of the day: visit to the wounded now overflowing the cellars of the Hartenstein Hotel. Colonel Warrack took him round.

Most of the wounded lay on stone floors in their bloody uniforms, covered by filthy blankets – in most cases one blanket for two men. All supplies were low, including bandages. For bed pans they were using old Dutch bottling jars, and Urquhart wrinkled his nose at the overpowering stench. Even the ebullient Warrack was depressed by the sight of the terrible condition the wounded were in. 'Well, what's on your mind, Graeme?' Urquhart asked finally, when he had finished the inspection.

'If you don't mind,' the young medic said, 'I'd like to go and see the German commander and arrange for the evacuation of our wounded to his hospitals in Arnhem.'

Urquhart considered for a moment or two, while a seriously wounded soldier in the corner moaned piteously. He did not want the enemy to believe that the Division was ready to surrender; but he had to give the wounded at least a chance. 'All right,' he said at length. 'You may make the attempt on condition that the Germans understand that you are a doctor representing your patients and not an official emissary from the Division.'

Warrack nodded his understanding and

went to find someone to assist him in his unpleasant task of surrendering the wounded to the Germans. It was just then that Urquhart was called to the radio urgently. 'General Thomas, sir,' the staff officer explained.

Hurriedly Urquhart detailed his position to the commander of the 43rd Division. To emphasize the seriousness of it, he said: 'We are being very heavily shelled and mortared *now* from areas very close to our positions'. Thomas snapped impatiently: 'Well, why don't you counter-mortar them?... Or shell them?'

Thomas's reply confirmed Urquhart's suspicion that the men on the other side of the river had no inkling of the kind of hell the cauldron had become. 'How the hell can we?' he cried angrily. 'We're in holes in the ground. We can't see more than a few yards. And we haven't the ammunition!' And that was the end of the conversation. Within the cauldron tempers were getting short. The end could not be far off now.

Across the river that morning, the brass assembled on the roof of Driel's little church. Horrocks, Thomas, and Sosabowski surveyed the smoke-covered cauldron with their field glasses. The three commanders could see that the cauldron had no military value left. The high ground at Westerbouwing was in German hands and the cauldron's sole link with the Lower Rhine was a flat string of open ground stretching several hundred yards inland until it finally merged into some high wooded ground that could afford cover for anyone trying to relieve the trapped Airborne.

Thomas remained undecided as to what they should do next. The highly intelligent and volatile Pole, who had seen his men cut to pieces in two abortive attempts to cross, was against any further attempt to continue the Arnhem operation. Horrocks could see for himself how serious the position across the river was. But by nature, the man who had been both a German and Russian POW, would call his autobiography – with some justification – *A Full Life,* was an optimist; he knew how easily the man on the spot was blinded to reality by his own suffering and anger.

Besides there was Monty's great plan – the war-winning forty division thrust to Berlin – to be considered. Like the man who had made him, Horrocks knew that Britain's resources were stretched to the limit. The country needed an early end to the war so that she could face the uncertain future, which might well involve a confrontation with the massive Soviet power, from a position of strength. If he called off the Arnhem operation, Horrocks realized that there would be no hope of winning the war in

1944. It would drag on into an uncertain 1945 and he knew that his chief, the man who had given him the opportunity to rise from an obscure colonel of infantry to the commander of Britain's biggest corps in four short years, would not tolerate that. He had to have another go.

Just before he left, he made up his mind. That night Thomas's infantry and what was left of Sosabowski's Poles would make another attempt to fight their way across the river into the cauldron. The battle would go on. As Horrocks got in his Humber staff car and began the long and dangerous journey southwards to St Oedenrode behind his infantry escort, tense and trigger-happy as they drew closer to the menace of Hell's Highway, Thomas and a reluctant Sosabowski began to plan yet another attempt to cross the Lower Rhine.

But there were others that Sunday morning who had not given up on the First Airborne. At the office at Ascot, British Colonel Bill Campbell, air liaison officer with the 1st Allied Airborne Army, had just told his chief Brigadier General Ralph Stearley that the RAF had announced that there would be no more attempts to resupply the trapped paras. Air Vice Marshal Hollinghurst had had enough. He had lost the commander of operation, Wing Commander Davis, had one of his officers recommended for the VC posthumously for his daring bravery during the re-supply and suffered twenty per cent casualties on the 21st. Now yesterday's attempt had been a complete flop. The RAF was not going in again.

The downright energetic American General exploded. 'Goddammit, we'll dive-bomb the stuff to them with fighter-bombers.'

With typical get-up-and-go, he did not waste any time that Sunday morning. Picking up the phone he called the HQ of the US Eighth Air Force. 'Can you load up supplies for Arnhem?' he barked.

'Yes,' came the answer.

Stearley beamed at Campbell. Later he informed the British officer that USAAF Mustangs were having their belly tanks loaded with rations and ammunition. They would be ready to fly at noon, as soon as they had received a clearance from the 2nd Tactical Air Force.

Excitedly Campbell contacted Browning in Holland to tell him the good news.

Campbell and Stearley were not alone in their attempts to help. That morning Major-General Hakewill Smith, commanding officer of Britain's largest and best-trained division, the 52nd (Mountain) Division volunteered to fly his formation into Grave airfield to support the 43rd's attack. The 52nd, which had been trained in an air landing role, had not seen action since 1940. It had a high proportion of skilled NCOs and men who had been together since that time and was expensively equipped, being not only the largest but most costly division in the British Army.

Unfortunately Hakewill Smith knew that Montgomery did not like him personally. Earlier that year, Montgomery had visited the Divisional HQ in Scotland and interviewed Smith. 'You weren't one of my students were you Hakewill?' he asked the taller man. When Smith replied in the negative Montgomery lost interest completely and for months now, Hakewill Smith had despaired of ever getting his division into action. Now he saw his chance. Browning, who now knew just how badly infantry was needed on the Rhine, forwarded his request to Montgomery.

Now, for the first time since he had set the 17th as the start of the great operation, we get a glimpse of the man who had planned Market Garden. Around midday, at about the same time as 2nd Tactical Air Force had failed to give the 8th US Air Force Mustangs their clearance, Field Marshal Montgomery personally vetoed any attempt to fly in the 52nd (Mountain) Division.

2

Unlike Eisenhower, Bradley or Patton, Montgomery surrounded his conduct of the war in secrecy. He did not hold open house in a huge headquarters for 'visiting firemen', as did the American generals. He preferred a handful of caravans and radio vehicles, which he called home, from which he conducted the war with the aid of a handful of selected staff officers, 'my eyes and ears'.

There he lived, secluded with his picked young men, who sat at the 'master's feet' at the close of the day as he distilled his pearls of military wisdom before retiring to bed promptly at ten o'clock to finish off another day's battle with a glass of hot milk. (On VE Day, the 'master' did allow himself the self-indulgent luxury of a single glass of champagne.)

Thus we have no record of his activities in that crucial week which changed the character of the war in Europe and signalled the end of Montgomery's bid to become second-in-command to Eisenhower himself and, as Commander-in-Chief of all ground forces, the most powerful military commander in Western Europe. But we do know he was there on that day, repeatedly signalling Dempsey, the Commander-in-Chief of the British Second Army, about his management of the battle for Arnhem, and that he was slowly coming to the momentous decision, which that terrible September 24th had made inevitable.

By now he was nearly at the end of his tether. The month-long argument about strategy and about who should command had taken its toll. A month ago he had felt he had had victory in his grasp. He had known the answer to the great problem which was obsessing the Allied military leaders: the problem of how to finish the war by Christmas 1944. And despite the opposition of men like Bradley and the weakness (as he saw it) of the Supreme Commander, he had forced his argument through – even without the aid of Churchill and Alanbrooke, his two champions, now in Quebec.

Throughout that third week of September when he had seen his hopes slowly sliding downhill because of the inability of the First Airborne to capture the one single bridge at Arnhem (such a trifling objective and yet such a vital one) he had kept his nerve. In spite of the opposition which had been built up against him prior to the Friday conference, de Guingand had won the day and his bold dash for the Ruhr had been saved. De Guingand's jubilant signal: 'Excellent conference. Ike supported your plan one hundred per cent. Your thrust is main effort and gets full support' had given him new hope. Now, thirty-six hours later, he knew that the one, bold stroke, which would silence all the criticism of his being 'defensively-minded' and his inability to do anything but 'fight the Second Battle of Alamein over and over again', was failing rapidly. On this Sunday, now that the morning service was over, Field Marshal Sir Bernard Law Montgomery, would have to make a decision which was ethical as well as military. If he continued the battle of Arnhem, he would sacrifice the lives of another 2,500 paras for no further advantage. If he called it off, it would mean the end of his great dream of personal and national glory...

3

Together with the senior medical officer of the 9th SS, Skalka, Warrack rode in a jeep towards the St Elisabeth Hospital which Harzer was using both for his own and captured British wounded. The Germans knew the paras were nearly finished now, and they made no attempt to blindfold Warrack. Thus Warrack was able to see the dead lying everywhere among the rubble of the shattered houses and between the burned-out tanks and other vehicles.

He was shown into a room full of elegant German staff officers, so clean and well-dressed that they might have come from another world. The German Chief-of-Staff appeared with a map and Warrack pointed out the positions of the 1st's dressing stations. The German took the information in and remarked: 'I am extremely sorry that there should be this fight between our two countries.'

Warrack, dazed and weary and not a little bewildered by this contrast between his own and the 9th SS's headquarters, put forward his request, which was immediately accepted by the German. Thereafter he was given a drink, some sandwiches and allowed to have a glance at the British wounded in German hands. They appeared to be in better shape than those in the cauldron; their beds had sheets and they were being cared for by Dutch nuns and nursing sisters. The evacuation of the wounded went on most of the afternoon with some four hundred and fifty being collected under German escort. For a while the Poles, who did not recognize the Red Cross, continued sniping at the German medics and guards, but finally Colonel Marrable, a senior doctor, managed to stop them. The evacuation went on without further incident. At about four o'clock, Hackett and his chief clerk Sergeant Pearson, both seriously wounded, were placed on the stone floor of the big hospital's entrance hall. Captain Redman, passing through the hundreds of wounded to check the more serious cases, stopped at Hackett's stretcher and asked the Brigadier what was wrong.

'I've got a hole through the leg and I feel sick,' Hackett said thinly. Redman frowned down at Hackett's grey face and pinched blue lips; then he bent and had a look at the wound in the Brigadier's stomach, which the latter had believed at first been caused by something striking his equipment. 'When did this happen?' he asked.

'Probably the same time I was hit in the leg. I thought a shell cap hit my equipment over the solar plexus. I've been feeling it all day.'

Redman looked worried. 'Where does it come out?'

Hackett looked up at him. 'Blimey, don't ask me!' he exclaimed.

Carefully Redman turned him over. 'There is no exit,' he announced glumly.

A little while later, an unconscious Hackett was examined again by Captain Lipmann Kessel, an airborne surgeon, accompanied by an SS doctor. In every case so far the German had snapped: 'That one's no good, and I wouldn't waste time on this'.

Together the Jewish surgeon and the SS man examined the Brigadier, who was wearing no badges of rank. After a brief examination, the German straightened up and said: 'We always say – a head wound or a stomach wound, euthanasia's best.'

As casually as he could, Lipmann Kessell said: 'Oh, I don't know. I think I'll have a go at this one.'

They passed on, and the 'broken-down cavalryman' lived to become Commander-in-Chief of the British Army.

With the wounded evacuated, the battle for the cauldron continued. But by now the men were completely punch-drunk. Glider-pilot Louis Hagen who had been conducting a lone battle with some German dug in by a group of shattered pines, fell back close to the house next door which had been evacuated recently to strengthen the perimeter. Suddenly only three yards away a window was pushed open. He swung round. No one was in sight. But he could definitely hear voices.

He lobbed a grenade through the open window. It exploded with a satisfying crump. He followed it with another. But still the voices continued. He threw his final grenade and prepared to run for more in order the clear the Germans out of the vital position so close to his own when a quiet, controlled voice said: 'What do you think you're dong? Trying to kill us all?'

Hagen's heart missed a beat. Then he realized the full impact of what he had just done: he had thrown grenades at his own comrades. As he was to write after the war, 'It was the worst moment of the whole seven days and I wished I were dead myself.'

He ran into the house expecting to find a scene of bloody mayhem. But there were no dead sprawled out dramatically in their own gore. Everything seemed normal – if anything could be normal at Arnhem. He told the others he'd thrown the grenades.

'Oh, it was you, was it? Thank God, you didn't know your job! At such short distance, you should have waited four seconds until you threw. That gives another three seconds until the grenade explodes. As it was, we lobbed them out of the window as fast as you threw them. They all exploded just outside, and you're a fool not to have noticed it.'

But Hagen was not alone in not noticing the obvious. By now the survivors' resistance was completely automatic, a reaction trained throughout the years in the Army. Some broke down completely and wandered around the cauldron, weaponless, eyes wild, staring unseeingly, not even flinching when the mortar shells landed all around them. If they survived the would go behind the walls of special hospitals for good. But most fought on, battling not only against the enemy but also against exhaustion.

'We didn't talk much now,' Private Dukes

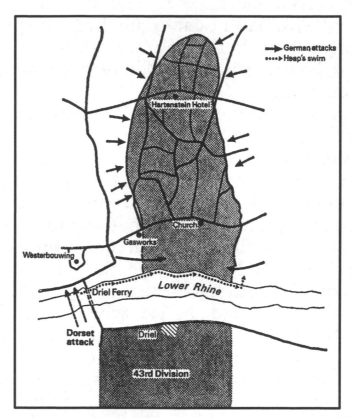

'I rather think it's our fault. We have been too slow.' – Col. D. Meynell, Chief-of-Staff 43rd Division

of the 1st Battalion dug in by the ruined church, remembers, 'even in the breaks between the shelling. We were too worn out. We slumped in our holes mindlessly. There wasn't even the need to clamber out and "squat". We hadn't eaten anything to speak of for days so there was no need. We stayed in our holes, waiting for the next bashing – like animals.'

A great numbness overcame them as the afternoon gave way to the evening. It was a numbness that would take weeks for many of them to overcome: one that Urquhart himself, not an imaginative man, would describe as 'an incredible lassitude that was to persist for weeks so that it required a conscious effort to attend to routine matters which normally I would have taken in my stride.'

In the shattered house which was the KOSBs' HQ, a 'battalion conference' was being held at this time by four men – the CO, Payton-Reid, a gunner named Walker who had become the Scottish battalion's second-in-command and Sergeant Tilley, a glider pilot who had appointed himself the stocky CO's bodyguard. Payton-Reid had begun the talking. But his voice seemed to come from further and further away. Then it stopped altogether. Minutes – hours – later he awoke to find the others slumped, heads resting on the kitchen table, snoring heartily.

It was with good reason that a clerk completed the Division's diary for that day in the stench of the Hartenstein's cellar with the words: 'Never was darkness more eagerly awaited...'

<h1 style="text-align:center">4</h1>

That afternoon Horrocks expounded his plan to force a crossing to 'Boy' Browning. But now the imperturbable ex-Guardsman could no longer be convinced by 'Jorrocks' theatrical talents. He left Horrocks' HQ and dictated a letter to his clerk, which would eventually reach Urquhart, revealing his lack of faith in the new plan.

Before he had a chance to dispatch it by courier, General Dempsey came into the Airborne Corps HQ. Browning explained to 'Bimbo' Dempsey what Horrocks intended to do that night. Dempsey, who had warned Montgomery of the dangers inherent in the Arnhem operation even before it had begun, nodded his agreement as Browning said that, in his opinion, Horrocks was being too optimistic. The 2nd Army Commander, who led over half a million soldiers throughout the 1944–1945 campaign in Europe and remained completely unknown, dominated as he was by Montgomery, knew what had to be done, now that his chief seemed unable to make a decision about the fate of the First

Airborne. 'I think,' he said to Browning, 'the time has come to withdraw the First Division.'

Horrocks, who understood Montgomery and his complex motivation much better than the retiring Dempsey, protested. He was still in favour of 'having a go'. He explained in detail his plan for that evening, using all his talent and ability to convince. Dempsey listened in silence, occasionally stroking his trim moustache as was his habit. Then he said softly: 'No. Get them out.' Considerate as always of the feelings of subordinates, he turned to Browning: 'Is that all right with you?' Browning nodded his assent.

A few minutes later Dempsey ordered the signallers to contact the Field Marshal. Montgomery's hand had been forced. Now he would have to make a decision. The soldier's great dream to drive into the heart of Germany and from thence into Berlin was dead. The war would last another nine months and another two million were fated to die before it finally came to its close in the summer of 1945.

5

The 43rd Division's crossing to relieve the

First Airborne was Heaps' swan song. The easy-going Canadian Lieutenant, always eager for a scrap, had been back and forth across the Lower Rhine a couple of times in the last few days ever since he had bumped into the van of the Second Army. Now he was on the Wessex's side once more, with a mission given to him by Colonel Myers himself. He was to go across in the first infantry assault boat in the general direction of the airborne positions. On an agreed signal, Myers would dispatch the amphibious ducks, laden with troops, a place indicated by Heaps with a flashlight.

For once, Heaps, who in the last week had tackled anything and everything without an apparent care, was worried. As he explained after the battle: 'I envisaged trouble. The place the infantry assault boats were to touch down at was at the ferry landings where we had tried to take our jeeps across three nights ago. The area was too far west of our positions. The infantry would have much additional work to reinforce us.'

But General Thomas had not bothered to consult Heaps when he had drawn up the crossing plan with General Sosabowski. In essence, the 4th Battalion the Dorsets under the command of Lieutenant Colonel Tilly was to cross at ten o'clock that night to seize the northern end of the Driel ferry, slightly west of the cauldron, while the Poles were to

281

go over on the Dorsets' right flank. A very simple plan, dependent on two things: little German reaction and a prompt start to the crossings, for after midnight the Lower Rhine would start to flow at a very fast rate. Once a heavily laden infantryman went overboard into the dark cold water, Colonel Myers knew he stood little chance of surviving. Punctuality and speed – they were going to be the two bases of a successful river crossing that night.

A cold bitter drizzle was falling as the first wave of the Dorsets assembled behind the dyke overlooking the Lower Rhine. Behind them the assault boats lay among the apple trees. There was no sound save the crunch of the occasional mortar on the other side of the river and the soft nervous coughs of some of the teenage Dorsets.

Heaps looked at the luminous dial of his watch. It was nearly midnight and they were already late. Two of the trucks bringing up their boats had taken the wrong road in the dark and driven into the 10th SS lines near Elst. Two others had skidded off the road into the ditch, and when the convoy had finally reached the Dorsets, they discovered that most of the boats were without paddles. They would have to row them across with the aid of shovels and entrenching tools.

A tense voice broke the brooding silence:

'Midnight... Let's go!'

Heaps grabbed the side of an assault boat together with some men of Major Whittle's B Company. Grunting hard, they shoved and pulled it up the slippy grassy slope of the dyke. It slid easily down the other side and plopped into the water. Hastily the twelve of them clambered in, and, bodies crouched as low as possible, they began to row across. The current seized them at once and within seconds they were sweating hard trying to keep the boat on course. The Rhine had already begun flowing at its maximum speed.

Heaps' group was lucky. They reached the other shore within a few minutes. They flopped down in the mud and lay still, assessing their situation while four of their number rowed back to fetch more of the Dorsets.

Now the Germans started to react. Spandau fire started to sweep the river with multi-coloured tracer. Major Whittle tumbled to the fact that the Germans were firing on fixed lines. He ordered his boats to swing a few yards to the left. But still the current was too much for them. It carried them closer and closer to the blazing factory some 400 yards downstream and threw their silhouettes into bold relief. Desperately the men dug their shovels into the fast-running water, now glowing red, and tried to steer away from the certain death awaiting them.

Crouched on the shore with eight survivors, Heaps could see the operation was failing. Fires on both sides lit the sky and cast a yellow-red glow over the men struggling in the water. He could see the old ferry now. It was in almost the same position that he and Johnny had left it so long ago, except now it had been sunk, and its gashed prow jutted out of the water.

Now the enemy was trying to seal off the river. The machine-gun fire never stopped and the ugly belch, plop and crunch of the mortar bombs was growing every second. More and more boats were going down. An assault boat made it. Unknown to Heaps, it would be the last he would see that night. An officer of the Dorsets crawled rapidly towards him. Heaps did not even give him time to ask his question. He pointed in the direction of the cauldron. With what Heaps thought was 'a weird shout', he got up and ran in the direction indicated, followed by his handful of heavily laden infantrymen.

Crouched in the glowing darkness beyond the burning factory, Major Whittle made a quick check of his numbers. Out of his two hundred strong company, he found he had just two officers and less than thirty men left. And before him loomed the Westerbouwing height manned by what was left of the NCO training battalion of the *Hermann*

Goering. He did not hesitate. He blew his whistle and drew his revolver. What was left of B Company began their assault of the key feature.

On the other bank, Colonel Myers, in charge of the twenty DUKWs bringing the vital supplies to his trapped Division, watched the slaughter, his face grim. But he knew that there was little he could do about it. Again Thomas of the 43rd had under-estimated the opposition waiting on the other bank. Now it would be up to his infantry to do their best. He must get across with the supplies and, more importantly, with two all important letters for Urquhart from Browning and Thomas.

Now, as the slower chatter of small arms fire on the other side indicated that British Brens were in operation, he ordered his clumsy-looking amphibians to prepare to cross behind the Dorsets' second wave. He could see that the opposite bank was still in enemy hands, but he was still hoping the Dorsets would be able to clear it. One – two – three – the first and only three of the awkward vehicles plumped into the Rhine. The rest would never make it. Myers made his decision. He sprang into the third one. It was a fortunate decision. It would be the last boat to get across that terrible night.

On the other side, Heaps listening to the

Germans shouting in the bushes all around, found himself trapped with a handful of survivors on a five yard square of gravel road, being continually swept by German tracer. Inch by inch, he and the Dorsets were easing their bodies deeper and deeper into the Rhine, as if the water would offer some protection against the lead flying everywhere.

Next to him an officer of the Dorsets cried frantically over and over again for artillery support. Finally the voice of the Artillery Major on the other side drifted lazily across. 'It's all right, old boy,' the artilleryman called in what the Canadian Heaps thought was an exaggerated British accent. 'Take it easy. We can't afford to waste any ammunition. But I'll see what we can do.' A little later one lone shell crashed into the German positions pinning them down. That was all. As Heaps recalled later: 'We were too desperate to become annoyed.'

As they crashed forward through the glowing darkness, Major Whittle could see that the Germans were well dug in at the top of the steep hundred-foot height. Now the Grenadiers of the *Hermann Goering* were rolling grenades down at them and the Dorsets were springing over them in order to let them roll on, as if they were playing some child's street game. But if they managed to dodge the grenades, they were not always so fortunate with the steady stream of machine-gun fire coming their way as they toiled their way up the wooded height. Man after man fell, but still the Dorsets pushed home their attack. Finally they made it and the Grenadiers pelted down the other side into the darkness. Swiftly a panting Major Whittle checked his numbers, as they dropped into the abandoned German trenches and prepared to meet the inevitable counter-attack. As he wrote himself much later, 'we were reduced to about fifteen'.

Myers' DUKW reached the opposite bank. It jolted against the mud flat and came to an abrupt stop. Myers did not need an invitation to scramble out of the obvious target. He could see that the Dorsets were getting nowhere. The handful of them which had managed to reach the opposite bank were obviously pinned down. Myers made a decision: 'I decided that I must go on to my own Divisional Headquarters in view of the importance of the message which I carried.' Then he had already assessed the mess on the other bank. 'I knew ... that the attack would not relieve the situation in the perimeter.' Clutching the vital message, which might mean the difference between life and death for the First Airborne underneath his smock, Myers bent double and began to splash his way cautiously through the shallows.

By now Heaps had also realized that the crossing had been a complete failure. Fokes, a survivor of the 2nd Battalion who had swum the river to escape the massacre of the bridge, said he would have another go. Heaps told him to report to Colonel Myers if he made it. But as the para dived into the deep water and struck out strongly for the other side, Heaps decided to stay behind; he did not relish the idea of a swim that night.

Now dawn was not far off and he realized it would be suicidal to be caught in the open. Heaps stripped off his excessive clothing, threw away his tommy-gun but kept his revolver and slipped into the river. He floated easily into mid-stream. Clear of the murderous fire of the shore he began to swim. Soon he struck out for the southern bank. But when he reached it, he found he was behind German lines. Close by he could hear the enemy whispering to each other nervously.

Once more he went into the water and struck out for the Airborne side, telling himself he would be safer there once the Dorsets had expanded their bridgehead. He caught hold of a log and rested himself on it. It was a bad mistake. The log carried him swiftly downstream. He passed the raging fires on the northern bank where Harzer's SS were trying to seal off the river from the cauldron position. He floated by a huge barge. Then he let go of the log and swam with his remaining strength to a stone jetty which lay silent and menacing in the darkness. He was three miles west of the ferry, deep in the heart of German territory. But Heaps was exhausted now, soaked and shivering with cold. He could not risk the river again. Gasping for breath he staggered along the jetty to a grassy slope where he flopped down gratefully.

Time passed. He forced himself to look at his watch. It was only two o'clock, though it seemed an eternity since they had first rushed the river. He lay there observing the terrible scene. 'To the east great fires were raging in Oosterbeek and Arnhem. The fires and the moon combined to form a myriad of fantastic forms, which shifted about on the changing black river. Sometimes I saw assault boats, sometimes I saw many men swimming and once I saw a great raft filled with Germans descending upon the infantry on the far bank.'

Now he was shivering badly. Dressed as he was in a pair of underpants and a battledress blouse, he knew he would contract pneumonia if he did not make a move soon. He began to trot up and down the bank to keep warm, forgetting all about the Germans. Now a strange, brooding silence fell over the scene of the river crossing.

Colonel Myers was completely alone now, as he waded cautiously through the shallows, trying to find a gap in the enemy defences on the bank so that he could slip through into the cauldron. Now and again he crouched, breath bated, as Germans passed close before slipping away quickly before he was discovered. Once he was fired upon. But the vicious burst of machine-gun fire which zipped through the darkness missed him. Soon, he told himself, he had to find a gap in the German line; he could not carry on much longer.

On top of the Westerbouwing height, Major Whittle's fifteen men stood to, shivering with cold. A voice cut through the darkness, speaking perfect English, 'I wonder,' it asked with extreme politeness, 'if you would care to surrender?'

Whittle's men were too exhausted for profanity. Despite the fact that they knew their refusal would mean a German counter-attack as soon as it was dawn, they replied with equal politeness to the unseen enemy: 'No, I'm afraid we wouldn't.'

A shivering Heaps had just completed another round of his lonely jetty when a voice with a slight accent challenged: 'Who is that?' Heaps guessed his interlocutor was a

German, but he was too cold and exhausted now to care much. He walked to the dark figure standing up to greet him, a machine pistol at the ready.

The English-speaking German's eighteen-year-old companion was very nervous. Every now and again he insisted on firing his *schmeisser* into the night sky to keep up his confidence. In fact, the two of them were very nervous, Heaps thought, as miserable as he was. They insisted on shaking hands with him and giving him chocolate – captured Rowntrees from the air re-supply containers. As he recalled later: 'They said they did not want to fight me and were really my brothers. They complied with my every wish. They were very scared.'

It was the same at the German HQ to which they took him. The Germans' battalion commander even gave up his own bed and blankets for the shivering Canadian in his soaked underwear. Heaps could see that the Germans were exhausted too. That night the battalion's intelligence officer, who was 'very solicitous and fatherly' actually tucked the Canadian into the CO's warm bed.

It was just about then that Colonel Myers finally stumbled into the paras' lines, soaked and absolutely worn out, but with the message safely tucked away within his smock. At last General Urquhart would have the authority to make his own decision about the fate of the remaining men trapped within the cauldron, reduced now to the size of four normal football pitches. Finally the ball was in his court.

DAY NINE

'The 25th was a day of crisis'.
— *Diary of 1st AB Light Rgt. RA*

Myers staggered into Divisional HQ at six o'clock on Monday morning, dripping water everywhere and was guided through the lines of wounded lying on the stone floors into the cellar, where Urquhart already alerted of his arrival, was rubbing his reddened eyes as he waited for him in the flickering, yellow light. Eagerly he grabbed the two letters Myers offered him, while the latter slumped down gratefully in the corner in a pool of water. The first was from Browning, and read:

'Dear Roy,
Sosabowski will be bringing you this, I hope tonight.
I will not labour your present position and it may be little consolation to you and the

292

1st Division when I tell you that the opinion held this side of the river is that the action of the 1st Division has (apart from the killing of the many Boche it has undoubtedly achieved) enabled 30 Corps and the Airborne Corps between them to capture the Nijmegen bridges and to break clean through the main German defence line of the Waal.'

Urquart breathed out hard and read on.

'From the information at our disposal, the German undoubtedly moved back the bulk of his forces from Nijmegen to Arnhem just before our airborne attack took place and instead of the Nijmegen crossings being an acutely difficult problem, the Arnhem crossings have become most acute in consequence.

You can rest assured that 30 Corps are doing their maximum under the most appalling difficulties to relieve you. As you know, I am responsible for from inclusive Nijmegen down the narrow corridor back for approximately 40 miles, and the road has been cut between us and the main body for 24 hours, which does not help matters much. It is now through again and the Army is pouring to your assistance but, as you will appreciate better than I do, very late in the day.

I naturally feel not so tired and frustrated as you do, but probably almost worse about the whole thing than you do.

I enclose a copy of a letter from Field Marshal Monty.'

Urquhart looked in the envelope again, but there was no letter. Till the very end of the 21st Army Group Commander was to remain absent from the paras' affairs although he had been the father of the scheme which would cause so many of their deaths. Hurriedly he read on:

'I hope to see you in a day or two.

It may amuse you to know that my front faces in all directions, but I am only in close contact with the enemy for about 8,000 yards to the south east, which is quite enough in present circumstances.

Yours ever
F.A.M. Browning.'

Urquhart was not amused. There was nothing in the letter which would enable him to make the decision he had to make save the hint that it was 'very late in the day'. Did that mean Browning did not believe the 43rd would be able to pull him out?

Eagerly he turned to Thomas' letter, written later than Browning's. Now the situation on the other side of the river began to grow clearer. Thomas wrote that the Second Army did not intend to form a bridgehead west of Arnhem and that his own division was finding it difficult to hold its positions on the Lower Rhine. He stated that he and Urquhart could arrange a withdrawal on a 'date to be arranged'. The withdrawal would have the code-name Operation Berlin.

Urquhart placed the letters down and turned to the shivering Myers. Swiftly he interrogated the Engineer on the Dorsets' crossing. Myers was gloomy. In his opinion, the crossing had been a total failure and he reiterated his belief that 'the attack would not relieve the situation in the perimeter'.

Urquhart nodded his thanks and wearily climbed the battle-littered stairs of the cellar. Outside, the battle had begun again. Unburied soldiers and fresh wounded lay everywhere, and the morning dew combined with a light wind had not removed the permanent stench of faeces and death. He stood there, bareheaded and alone, staring at the little Airborne pennant which he had planted so proudly in front of his HQ when it had still seemed that his elite Division would achieve its bold objective. Its blue-winged horse – the Pegasus – rode as confidently as ever in the wind; but the Division of that Tuesday no longer existed. Now the couple of thousand of starving, hunted survivors were weary automatons, hanging on from hour to hour until the enemy finally did them the favour of putting a sudden and violent end to their misery. He knew, as he turned to go inside again, that 'I could not expect much more of those who were still on their feet'. Filing carefully between the lines of wounded men, some of whom had only hours left to live, he called a signaller to him. Wearily he ordered him to raise General Thomas.

Just after eight, as the German 'hate' started to rise to a crescendo, he raised the commander of the 43rd Division. 'Yes?' he queried.

With no trace of emotion, Urquhart answered: 'Operation Berlin must be tonight...'

THREE:
THE ESCAPE

ONE

It was ten o'clock on Monday morning. General Urquhart glanced round the faces of what was left of his staff – Hicks, Colonel Murray, who had taken over Hackett's brigade, Mackenzie and Myers, plus his chief gunner Colonel Loder-Symonds. He could see just how tired they were. He felt more than ever that his decision to evacuate the cauldron was right: they could not take much more. 'Gentlemen,' he said without any attempt at drama, 'we are to clear out tonight!'

Swiftly he explained that the survivors would move by two routes, following a strict time schedule. 'In general, those farthest from the river will start first. I don't expect that either of the routes will be free from enemy interference, but they are the best available to us.'

The big Scot, who had once studied the classic withdrawal from Gallipoli in the First World War for a promotion examination, said that he would use it as the basis for their own retreat to the Lower Rhine. He visualized pulling back slowly from the northern face of the perimeter and moving systematically down each flank until it came to the turn of those men dug in closest to the river. As guides he would use the officers and NCOs of the Glider Pilot Wing. In difficult spots they would mark the escape route with the luminous tapes normally employed to designate minefields. He nodded to Colonel Myers. His sappers would be responsible for the last stage of the operation, once the paras had reached the river. All ranks would muffle boots and equipment. He paused and stated emphatically that there would be no attempt to engage the Germans; they would stand and fight only if there was no other way out.

Urquhart turned to Colonel Loder-Symonds and asked him if the retreating Division could expect much artillery support from the 30 Corps artillery.

'I'm sure we'll get all we want,' the gunner officer replied confidently.

'Good,' Urquhart said equally confidently, though he did not feel so sure about the outcome of the operation. After all, he would be trying to move some two thousand men out through a riverside bottleneck only six hundred yards wide. If the Germans spotted them before they got into the boats, he knew that the cost 'might be high – very high' as he admitted much later. Before he dismissed his senior officers, he emphasized that they must maintain the strictest security. The Division had a long day of fighting ahead and he did not want any prisoners babbling to the

Germans. Besides, once the tired, ragged men in the slit trenches started 'to look over their shoulders their effectiveness is reduced'.

As he dismissed them to their tasks, General Urquhart looked at his watch. It would be nearly nine long hours before he could start to move his paras; he could only hope they would survive that long.

At roughly the same time, Colonel Harzer, commander of the Ninth SS Panzer, met the bemonocled chief of Army Group B, Model. Field Marshal Model pulled no punches. He insisted on rapid liquidation of the cauldron in order that the Ninth SS could be released to meet the threat posed by the British in the Nijmegen area.

Harzer protested he was doing his best, but now, after over a week in Oosterbeek, a process of natural elimination had taken place among the Tommies. The ones who had been unable to learn how one fought in city streets were dead; the survivors were now experts who made his tankers pay a heavy price for every house they captured. Besides his Ninth SS was not up to full strength. Model, who was a realist above all else, nodded his understanding. Taking out his monocle and polishing it, he suggested that in order to cut down his losses, Harzer should use the full weight of his artillery to blast them out of their positions once and for all.

Harzer smiled grimly and informed his superior that this day he was going to use the largest cannon in not only the Wehrmacht, but on the entire Western front, to shatter the enemy defences.

Thirty minutes later the full weight of the German artillery started to descend on the British lines. As the first ragged, exhausted Tommy prisoners began to come into his HQ for interrogation, Colonel Harzer noted with satisfaction that their 'morale was sagging rapidly!'

All around the perimeter, those officers with inside information started to make their preparations for the retreat to the river, while the fighting went on around them. The luminous marking tape was laid out. The glider pilot officers, who were to act as guides, paced off the two escape routes as best they could. The seven chaplains who were to remain behind with the wounded, began putting their houses in order. Unnecessary equipment was smashed secretly or buried in shell-holes. The Divisional diary, obviously a key source for any inquiry into the First Airborne's conduct, was copied and passed out for two officers to smuggle out. Classified documents were burned.

At the Hartenstein, now buzzing with activity, Lieutenant Hardy, the surviving signals officer, released the signal carrier pigeons, of which one would reach Sir Richard O'Connor's Eighth Corps bearing the information that:

1.Have to release birds owing to shortage of food and water.

2.About eight tanks lying about in subunit areas, very untidy but not otherwise causing us any trouble.

3.Now using as many German weapons as we have British. MGS most effective when aiming towards Germany.

4.Dutch people grand but Dutch tobacco rather stringy.

5.Great beard-growing competition on in our unit, but no time to check up on the winner.

But there was little humour left among the dead and dying at the Taffelberg Hotel dressing station. It was hit twice that morning by gunfire. Three of the surviving orderlies were killed. Colonel Warrack, the hard pressed chief doctor, found the place a blazing ruin. He ordered it evacuated. Exhausted orderlies started to wheel out the seriously wounded on Dutch wheelbarrows, handcarts, ladders, doors – anything. And still the artillery came crashing down until finally the place was rushed by a company of SS men and the Reverend Harlow, the First Airborne's senior chaplain, was captured.

Not far away at another threatened dressing station within the shattered Oosterbeek Church, The First Light Regiment's chaplain, the Reverend Thorne, was running to and fro trying to succour the mounting number of seriously wounded men who were being brought in from the slit trenches outside, when an orderly staggered in shouting: 'There's a Jerry SP outside, Padre!'

Thorne's heart missed a beat. If the German opened fire, it would mean absolute slaughter within the church where the stretchers were so tightly packed that he had to walk over stretcher handles to get from one end to the other. Almost beside himself with fear for the wounded, he grabbed a Red Cross flag. He rushed outside with the orderly, not really knowing what he was going to do. But somehow he did it. Five minutes later the German driver put his big Ferdinand into reverse and drew off without firing a single shot. The wounded had been temporarily saved.

Now Harzer's SS men were pressing home their attack along the river in order to cut off the Tommies from the bank and seize the Division's surviving 75mms, the only guns left, apart from a few six-pounders.

At the Hartenstein, Urquhart stopped in his preparations when an excited aide brought him the news. He realized immediately that the German attack threatened his whole plan. Before he could react, even worse news followed. One of the Light Regiment's batteries had been overrun and a large group of SS men had penetrated the perimeter. One of the escape routes was cut off. Urquhart snapped out a series of orders. A platoon of weary paras armed with Piats were hurriedly sent to the gunners' aid. The gunners themselves were commanded to hold out to the last.

They did even more than that. At fifty yards' range they fired into the massed German tanks. Even the fanatical young teenagers of Harzer's Ninth SS could not stand up to such terrible fire. As great holes appeared in their ranks, they commenced to fall back. Frantic with rage at the British, hardened and brutalized in the long years of fighting in Russia, their officers kicked and punched them into the advance once more.

Again the gunners' 75mms cracked into action, firing over open sights, no longer caring that their supply of shells was running down rapidly. Their gun barrels glowed. Great piles of smoking yellow shell cases mounted around their feet. Then the Germans broke for good. As the paras began their attack, the infiltrators fell back, pushing aside those behind in their panic-stricken attempt to escape that terrible fire. For the time being the threat to the perimeter had been warded off.

2

Across the river, Colonel Henniker of the 43rd Division made his plans for the evacuation. Once, the big engineer, clad in a soldier's cape and with a steel helmet placed squarely across his forehead, had been a member of the First Airborne. He knew the men hidden by the smoke of war some couple of hundred yards away over the Rhine and he was determined to get as many of them out as possible. But he knew that the river crossing at night was fraught with danger. The Dorsets' crossing the previous evening, which had been such a tragic failure, proved that. Not only had he to compete with the darkness and the fast-racing waters of the Rhine, but also with the full weight of two German divisions' artillery fire.

But Henniker had an ace up his sleeve. Earlier that morning he had discussed the crossing with General Thomas and gained the latter's permission to attempt a ruse to divert the Germans' attention. And for once, Thomas had agreed. Under the command of Major Thixton of the RASC, a column was to drive up to the river from the west, complete with pontoons and bridging lorries, making a great deal of noise so that the

306

Germans would think a crossing was about to be made there. Thomas's instructions to Thixton were blunt and simple. 'I want you to be seen and shot at, Thixton – that's all!'

If the feint came off, Henniker would set up two ferrying points: one downstream opposite Westerbouwing, now in British hands; the other upstream opposite Oosterbeek. Both points would be serviced by mixed British and Canadian engineer companies, equipped with assault boats, powered by paddles or outboard motors. The 5th Dorsets, which had been cut to pieces two days before trying to take Elst, would provide cover from infantry attacks at these spots, while the whole weight of the 30 Corps artillery would drench the perimeter in order to prevent an attack on the cauldron.

However, Colonel Henniker's difficulties started even before the operation got underway. As soon as the code-word *Berlin* had been received at Thomas's HQ, he had sprung into action. Unfortunately there had been no time to recce the area. Now his engineers were in trouble everywhere as they tried to bring up the clumsy boats along narrow, twisting country roads with soft shoulders on both sides and deep ditches. Truck after truck slipped off the road and landed in the ditches. Everywhere the REME were in action, sweating and swearing as they tried to winch the clumsy three-tonners out of the ditches, their efforts interrupted every five minutes by the harsh, rending sound of yet another 88mm shell heading their way. As the hours started to race by, it seemed less and less likely that they would be ready on time.

But if Colonel Henniker was worried, it seemed as if the rest of the Allied camp had already realized the First Airborne's failure and were ready to wash their hands of the survivors.

The Guards were already pulling back, evacuating their positions around Nijmegen, taking with them as much livestock as they could find. A Guards Major spotted his Quartermaster Sergeant loading a pig on a stretcher and asked him what he was up to. Cheerfully the NCO replied: 'It would be cruel to leave the thing in its lonely sty, sir, so we're taking it with us.' Thus they smuggled it through the line of watchful, suspicious redcaps.

Another Guardsmen, concerned that he might have to forego his dinner of pork cutlets, smuggled his piglet out in the back of his scout car. Unfortunately, it popped up its trotters just as the Dingo was passing by a group of MPs. One of them, an ex-Coldstream, stopped him and asked the driver what it was. Without hesitation the driver replied: 'A young Grenadier!' The ex-Coldstreamer, who obviously thought that all members of the rival regiment looked like pigs anyway, passed him on without any further comment. That afternoon it was recorded that the Irish Guards 'managed to get in some drill on the road'.

General Horrocks also seemed to have left the Airborne to its fate that afternoon. His main concern now was to keep Hell's Highway open. Four years before he had commanded the rearguard of a General Montgomery's Third Division. As the 'Iron Division' had retreated through Belgium, the country they had come to save from German aggression, he had felt 'acutely embarrassed' at having to leave the bewildered civilians to their impending fate. Then he had promised all and sundry: 'Don't worry – we'll be back!'

In September 1944, as his tank had just crossed the Belgian frontier, a young civilian with tears streaming down his face, had rushed up to him and cried: 'You came back!' That had been one of the great moments of his life.

Now the promise of that moment had vanished and for a while the heart went out of the General. He did not want to be reminded of the British Army's fresh defeat at Arnhem, a defeat which would set the end of the war back another six months or more. He concentrated on the task at hand.

It was the same at SHAEF. Early in the day Bill Downs of CBS could report to his listeners that 'the complete relief of the British Airborne west of Arnhem, which has held for eight days now, is definitely in sight.' At midday, however, SHAEF clamped a security blackout on the Arnhem operation. 'So long as the situation remains fluid,' its statement read, 'the only news to be given will be that authorized by Field Marshal Montgomery's HQ.' Responsibility had been passed neatly to the man who had dreamed up the disastrous operation.

In England, military commentators in the afternoon editions of the newspapers tried to persuade their readers that, 'Ominous conclusions need not be drawn from this development and, in fact, such news as is available, is, on the whole, reassuring'.

That afternoon SHAEF's Commander Eisenhower received several correspondents attached to SHAEF Forward to tell them that he wished to save manpower by reducing their numbers by one correspondent. 'Butch', Eisenhower's PR aide, thought 'it is one of the few times in history that a leading general has asked for a diminution of news coverage about himself. Red, as well as others with whom I have talked, think the Boss's decision is unusual.'

Within the perimeter rumours were beginning to circulate. The Second Army was coming across the Lower Rhine in real force this time. The First Airborne was going to launch one last desperate attack on the Germans. The perimeter was going to be shortened. As the officers began to be let into the withdrawal plan and went into long and secretive discussions of how they were going to do it, the rumours floated from foxhole to foxhole.

Glider Pilot Louis Hagen and three other NCOs were summoned to their CO at four that afternoon for briefing. In a confident voice the CO told them: '"It was going to be an orderly and organized withdrawal." All sections were to leave their sectors at a specified time with all their arms and ammunition. Our street was going to leave at ten fifteen. The men from the top corner house would move in to the next house, from there they would all move into the next, and so on until the entire glider pilot section were all in the house nearest the perimeter.' From there they would begin to slip along little woodland paths till they reached the river. Leaving their CO who 'fairly radiated optimism', the NCOs began to wolf down the rest of their rations to give themselves energy for the long, hazardous night ahead.

At Private Dukes' position around the shattered Oosterbeek Church, the last to be held, most of the men who stayed behind to cover the withdrawals were volunteers. 'Where there weren't enough volunteers', Dukes recalls, 'the lads tossed coins for it. The *winner* stayed behind.' In his section, every third foxhole would be held with the volunteers, the 'winner-losers' blasting off every last bit of ammunition to convince the enemy that the positions were being held in full strength. To Private Dukes, who had been through all this once before at Dunkirk, it seemed as if it were going to be 'no worse, but no better' than that great evacuation of 1940.

The First Border Regiment, which had run out of food and nearly out of water, was determined to go out the way it had come in – as a battalion. B and HQ Companies would lead the way, taking with them the walking wounded while A and C Companies held off the enemy under the command of the acting CO, Major Breese. When the van had safely reached the river, Major Breese would personally lead the rear party and any new wounded down there. Of the nine infantry battalions which had been flown to Arnhem on September 17th, the 34th Regiment of Foot, raised in 1702, was the only one to march out as a cohesive formation.

The South Staffs, which had gained two VCs in the cauldron, was too weak for such displays. It was now reduced to six officers and 133 other ranks, from the 45 officers and 720 men who had gone in so proudly that Sunday. They would come out as best they could.

Colonel Payton-Reid, the only surviving CO of the nine infantry colonels, who had lost both his A and B Companies and was defending his positions with a handful of weary survivors from the remaining two companies, knew that the 7th KOSB also would have to make the best escape it could without any concessions to regimental tradition. The men of Arnhem had done their utmost, and failed. Now all that remained was to save as many of their lives as possible.

On the other side of the river, as the dusk gave way to a pitch-black stormy night, ideal for escaping, Colonel Henniker began to grow more confident. Opposite the Oosterbeek crossing point, his British and Canadian engineers had found a railway yard in which they could concentrate their vehicles. From thence two young officers had taped a route over the marshy fields to the two floodwalls blocking off the river.

The first of the floodwalls was nearly twenty feet high and sloped at a forty-five degree angle. The second was not so high and not so sloped. Yet both would be tricky obstacles for the sappers dragging up the storm boats to negotiate in the darkness. Handropes were quickly fixed so that they could lever themselves upwards, but by the time the recce party was finished with this job, the first floodwall was covered in mud and as slippery as an ice-rink.

At the crossing point opposite Westerbouwing, the engineers took up their positions in a shattered apple orchard where the branches of the white, shell-stripped trees were lying around everywhere like severed limbs. They did not make any attempt to prepare the dyke in front of them. It was not as steep as the floodwalls. More important, German machine gunners, somewhere across the river, were sweeping it continually with fire. The engineers would wait to take their chance when H-hour came.

Behind them in the red-brick Dutch farmhouses, with the slaughtered cattle lying everywhere, the Fifth Dorsets prepared to send the paras swiftly to Nijmegen, to the meals and beds waiting for them there. That is, if the Canadian and British engineers could get them across the river. And three miles away, Major Thixton's convoy was already on its way to be 'seen and shot at'. It

314

was almost time now.

As the heavy guns of the 30 Corps, which would cover the withdrawal, crashed into action, Urquhart, his face blackened like those of the rest, and his boots muffled with rags, knelt in the crowded cellar. Around him lay the wounded. Beside him knelt the doctors who would be staying behind to look after them. The padre, who was also staying, said a brief prayer. Urquhart opened a bottle of whisky someone had found. RSM Lord, the majestic ex-Grenadier Guardsman who had done so much for morale in the cellar, passed out the last of the 'benzies'.

Then shaking the hands of those who would remain behind, Urquhart had a last look at the wounded who had served him and his Commander-in-Chief, Field Marshal Montgomery, so well. Despite the evacuation arranged by Warrack, fresh wounded were everywhere in the cellars, packed together, their bandages stained with blood that could not be stilled, their shattered limbs held by crude splints fashioned from bayonets, chair legs – anything that would do the job. Sadly the General passed through their ranks, saying good-bye to those who were aware still of what was happening, nodding to those whom morphia had put to sleep. Just before he left for good, a worn soldier struggled up, propping himself against the dirty white wall of the cellar, and murmured, 'I hope you make it, sir!'

The glider pilots were burying what was left of their mortar ammunition now. Louis Hagen and Sergeant Cooper were attempting to dig a hole to hide the 3-inch mortar bombs, determined that the Germans wouldn't find them, when a vicious burst of machine-gun fire struck Cooper. He fell back against the sagging door of their house, crying: 'They've hit me!' the blood pouring down his right arm.

Hagen realized the firing had come from the next house, held by the Poles. Angrily he burst through the waiting Poles and found an officer. The Polish officer asked how many had been killed. Hagen told him that only one soldier had been hit. A Pole pushed his way to the front of the rest, his eyes filled with tears. He had been the man who had fired the burst. But it was too late to worry about the Pole now; somehow or other they would have to get the seriously wounded Cooper to the river. It was time to go. Cautiously the glider pilots began to make their way through the wet pines, the sound of their dripping deadening the sound of their footsteps. They passed within fifty yards of the German POW cage on the shattered tennis courts. The Germans must have been asleep or cowering in their foxholes. At least they did not attempt to warn their comrades who were less than a couple of hundred yards away. The glider pilots passed on into no-man's land. Still there was no sound save for that of an occasional mortar and a burst of spandau fire; and all the time their own 30 Corps artillery miles to the rear on the other side of the river kept pounding the German positions.

The glider pilots' CO was absolutely confident he knew the route, but Hagen could see that the path was becoming increasingly difficult to follow through the dense wood. Still the Captain did not lose heart. 'We'll make it,' he whispered to Hagen, 'don't worry. Stick to me.'

Miraculously the pilots came upon their first real landmark – a shattered farmhouse. Hagen knew they would have to branch left down a lane now. Suddenly a German machine-gun opened fire to their front. They halted and then pushed on only to halt again. A fence had to be scaled. Just as Hagen began to take his turn, a bareheaded, bleeding officer loomed up out of the rain-swept darkness. 'Germans,' he gasped. 'Ambushed my men!'

Swiftly he explained that he and his platoon had run into hidden spandaus. He felt he was the only survivor and the way ahead was barred. The glider pilots' CO did not hesitate. He ordered the men to turn about. 'The men were remarkably silent and disciplined', Hagen remembers, 'and there was no shuffling or pushing.' With the men who still had sten guns bringing up the van, the glider pilots tried to find an alternative route to the river.

Led by an engineer called Major Brown, the 4th Parachute Brigade, once commanded by Brigadier Hackett (now a German prisoner) passed silently by a German mortar position, only ten yards to their right. Twisting and turning they followed the trail until they finally came upon their guides of the Glider Pilots Wing. A few minutes later they began to file down the muddy bank towards the Lower Rhine. The 4th Parachute Brigade had reached the river. There were exactly fifty-four of them left.

'It was all very ordered,' Private Dukes recalled. 'The officers told us what to do and we did it. It was every man for himself in a way, and yet it wasn't. I began to think that everything would work out okay.'

Fortified by the padre's last prayer – and the last tot of whisky – the Urquhart party slipped out of the Hartenstein Hotel with Mackenzie in the lead, making their way across the muddy grass to the shelter of the dripping pines. Although Urquhart knew it

318

was only a short distance to the river, the journey seemed to take a 'devil of a long time'. Once the group heard German voices and there was some talk of lobbing a grenade into the enemy post. But in the end they decided against it. They could not risk raising the alarm for the sake of killing a few of the enemy. They passed on.

One by one, the men who had set out with the burly General disappeared into the night including his faithful batman Hancock, who had been with him since 1941. Still they moved on, stopping every now and again as mortar bombs came howling down close by or sudden bursts of tracer split the night with their alarming morse-code.

The party started to squelch through boggy ground. Urquhart realized they had reached the low-lying polder on the southern edge of their perimeter. They were not far from the river now. Presently Mackenzie began to work his way along the semi-luminous light of the mine tapes. They dropped into a ditch and waded through the muddy water for a while, emerging to find themselves at the river's edge. Gratefully they dropped into the ooze to await their turn to cross.

The glider pilot party was passing across an open meadow now. Suddenly they began to see dead bodies on both sides of the marked path. Hagen came upon a wounded man

319

who begged piteously not to be left behind. Hagen and another NCO tried to lift him, but he screamed with pain as they touched him. They lowered him hurriedly. Then, as his eyes got used to the open darkness of the meadow, Hagen began to distinguish wounded men, moaning piteously, trying to drag themselves towards the river. 'Feverish pleading eyes looked up towards me,' he recalled later, 'arms clutched around my legs, it seemed that all wounded were frenzied by the fear of being left behind.'

For the first time since he had landed at Arnhem, he panicked. 'I dragged limp bodies along towards the beach – I ran around in circles searching for someone in command and pleading with uninjured men to give me a hand – I vomited and fainted.' Suddenly an authoritative voice brought him to his senses and ordered him to stop his antics; he was to continue with the rest towards the river. The wounded would be left where they lay. A doctor would remain behind to look after them. 'Exhausted and dazed by my impotence, and the ghastliness of the scene,' he dragged himself on as far as the Lower Rhine.

The first of Canadian Lieutenant Gemmell's boats was destroyed just before it hit the opposite bank at Westerbouwing. The second one, with Gemmell in charge, made it. His men spread out rapidly along the bank and waited tensely for the first arrivals. Heavy mortar fire was coming down now and despite the torrential rain Arnhem was blazing once again.

Suddenly Gemmell's heart missed a beat. Something was coming slowly and furtively towards them. His sappers gripped their weapons in sweaty hands and peered against the rain, while Gemmell ran forward. 'Who goes there?' he challenged, dropping on one knee in the mud.

'Friends,' a weary British voice replied.

A handful of men came forward through the rain. They were the survivors of the 4th Dorsets. The wounded and non-swimmers were hurriedly placed in the Canadian boat, while Major Whittle slipped into the water to swim with the rest. The operation had started.

The gravel-voiced Canadian correspondent, Stanley Maxted, whose recordings for the BBC were going to make the First Airborne's stand at Arnhem world-famous, had been called out of his foxhole at two minutes pas ten. Now, clutching the tail of the coat of the man in front he followed the 'file of nebulous ghosts' over the pock-marked, tree-strewn ground, into no-man's land.

'The back of my neck was prickling for that whole interminable march', he was to reveal later to his BBC audience. 'I couldn't see the man ahead of me – all I knew was that I had hold of a coat-tail and for the first time in my life was grateful for the downpour of rain that made a patter on the leaves of the trees and covered up any little noises we were making.'

Now they were among the glider pilots. 'At every turn of the way there was posted a sergeant glider pilot who stepped out like a shadow and then stepped back into a deeper shadow again.' Every so often they halted, once on account of a boy sitting on the ground with a bullet through his leg. They wanted to pick him up, but he whispered: 'Nark it. Gimme another field dressing and I'll be all right. I can walk.'

As he emerged from the trees of the wood, he 'felt as naked as if I were in Piccadilly Circus in my pyjamas, because of the glow from the fires across the river. The machine-gun and general bombardment had never let up. We lay down flat in the mud and rain and stayed that way for two hours till the sentry beyond the hedge on the bank of the river told us to move up over the dyke and be taken across.

'Mortaring started now and I was fearful for those who were already over on the bank. I guessed it was pretty bad for them. After what seemed a nightmare of an age we got our turn.'

He slithered over the mud-flat and waded into the Rhine. There was the shadow of an assault craft powered by an outboard motor. It came closer and 'a voice that was sheer music spoke from the stern, saying: "Ye'll have to step lively boys, it ain't healthy here!"'

On the 30 Corps side of the Rhine, Colonel Henniker paced the bank in the persistent, bitter rain, the water dripping off the edge of his helmet. He felt 'like a cat on hot bricks oppressed by the most gloomy forebodings'. It was half an hour since his sappers of the 43rd's own 260th Field Company had pushed off to row their assault boats across and still there was no sign of them returning. What had happened to them, he thought anxiously?

'Had they upset the boats and all gone silently to the bottom, weighed down by steel helmets and rifles? Had they rowed straight into the waiting Hun on the far bank? Or had they merely been washed downstream to God knows where?'

The minutes passed silently. Then the tense Colonel heard the sound of dipping oars. A boat loomed up out of the dripping night. It contained about a dozen men. Henniker strained his eyes. At first he couldn't believe them. But as they came closer, he saw he was not mistaken. They wore the well-remembered rimless helmets of paratroopers. 'Piss-pots', the men had called them when they had been first issued to replace the traditional British helmet.

'Never was there a more welcome sight', he recalled later. 'First one boat, then another, then another. About a hundred men came silently ashore with a few wounded... More and more boats were launched and then I heard the motors of the Canadian storm boats start. No music could have been more sweet!'

It was now shortly past ten and the Germans were aware something was happening within the cauldron. Harzer was informed by his men that: 'The British were using heavy mortar fire to interfere with relieving parties. It was further reported that a loud noise of engines could be heard from the south bank.'

Harzer ordered his artillery to start a counter-barrage, and turned in for the night. Tomorrow would be another day. The Tommies would break for certain then. It is recorded that he slept soundly, confident that on the morrow he would finish with the British *Fallschirmjaeger*.

In a pause in the fresh mortar barrage, Hagen and his friends joined the long line of men waiting in the darkness for the boats to take them across. New dead and wounded lay everywhere. An officer ordered them to spread out. The six-barrelled 'moaning minnies' might start again at any moment.

Just then a boat appeared out of the steady sheet of fine rain. It took a mere ten of the hundred or more in front of Hagen. With the rest he crouched in the deep squelchy mud of the river-bank, frozen and miserable. After the cover of the week-long street fighting, he felt hopelessly naked and exposed on the river bank. At any moment a chance mortar bomb might take his life after surviving the hell of the last terrible days. Suddenly he made his decision. He was no longer prepared to be 'heroic, playing at Dunkirk'. He turned to the CO and said that he was going to try and swim across.

The CO agreed with him. He shouted to the rest of the glider pilot section to follow him to a mole jutting out into the water, where the Lower Rhine narrowed somewhat. There the CO ordered the pilots to take off their boots and have a go at crossing under their own steam. 'We'll do it again, you and me,' he said to Hagen confidently.

By the time Hagen had slung his boots across his neck and his stern, the CO was already in the water and swimming strongly for the opposite bank. Hagen, a good swimmer who had learned to swim years before in Berlin, struck out after him. But to his horror, he found he could not catch up. The current was carrying the Captain downstream at a great rate. Then he had no further time to worry about the CO. Suddenly he found he was no longer making the proper strokes. His breath was coming in panicky gasps. 'Like a flash, it came to me that this was the one fatal thing to do and the best possible way to get drowned.' By an effort of will he turned himself over on his back and floated for a few moments; then he began to divest himself of his gear methodically – sten, boots, smock, personal kit, even his paybook. Finally he was ready to continue his swim. 'The difference was marvellous. I felt like I had when I'd been bathing a fortnight ago in the Thames... I looked around for Captain Z, but there was no sign of him at all.'

He swam on alone. Fires were burning on both sides of the Lower Rhine now casting their ruddy glow over the dark water. There was a steady, persistent rattle of spandau fire from the wood they had left just an hour before. But enclosed in what he felt was now 'warm water', he was beyond it all. He told himself with a sudden sense of complete detachment, 'I might never have been on the other side.'

Major Winchester of the Airborne Engineers acting as 'beachmaster' thought, in spite of the ever increasing volume of mortar fire falling on the men waiting on the muddy bank or crouched in the shellholes, that the 'discipline on the river bank was excellent'. More and more men were offering to give up their places in the boats to the non-swimmers and were taking their chance at crossing under their own power.

Captain Wood, one of the handful of survivors from the 2nd Battalion's fight on the bridge, took his chance with a sergeant from the Glider Pilots. Carrying their weapons, a German schmeisser and a Thompson sub-machine gun, but stripped down to their underclothing, they slipped into the water. The NCO made it half-way across and disappeared like a stone. Wood plunged on. Exhausted, dirty and gasping frantically for breath, he was pulled out by a Dorset, whose face was hidden by the night. He would never see it or learn the man's name. All he would be able to remember of him in years to come were his enormous leather dispatch rider's gauntlets. Before the Dorsets let him away to the waiting trucks, Captain Wood looked back at the bridge and Arnhem. To him, it looked 'like hell'.

Back at the abandoned positions, more and more of the rearguard finished the last of their ammunition and began to slip out of their foxholes. Their fire slackened. Hesitantly German night patrols followed up, wondering at the ease with which they took the Tommy positions, for which they had previously fought so hard.

The Reverend Thorne, who had been informed at the Oosterbeek Church that he could go with the rest, if he wished, was too tired to accept the offer. He fell into a deep sleep on a pile of cans in the corner of the kitchen. When he awoke again, the paras had gone and he was staring up at a puzzled young SS man.

The Reverend G.A. Pare, the chaplain to the First Glider Pilot Regiment, suffered a similar fate. Weakened by hunger and exhaustion, he fell asleep at the dressing station of the 181st Air-Landing Field Ambulance. When he awoke again, it was to a strange heavy silence. The RSM, who had remained behind with the wounded, told him that the Division had gone and an utterly weary Pare realized that it would be up to him to break the news to the wounded who had not heard the decision to withdraw the night before. Most of the Division's chaplains were dead, wounded or captured.

'Right – this party,' a subdued voice in the wet darkness snapped. Wearily Urquhart rose to his feet out of the mud and glanced at his watch in the same instant. It was a few minutes past midnight.

The HQ party squeezed aboard. But there was a hitch. The Canadian sapper cursed fluently. The boat had stuck. Hancock, who had reappeared, slipped over the side into the shallows and pushed. The boat started to move off. Hastily the undersized batman tried to scramble on board again. There was a loud protest from someone for him to 'Let go!' Hancock ignored the order. With the last of his strength, he struggled over the side. Machine-gun fire hissed flatly across the water towards them. Skilfully the Canadian zig-zagged his craft to avoid it. Then suddenly the engine spluttered and came to an abrupt stop. A confused attempt to restart the defective motor followed which seemed to Urquhart 'an absolute age'. At last the engine burst into throaty life again and they were on their way towards the other bank.

Suddenly the boat bumped into a wooden barrier. Out of the darkness a voice croaked: 'All right, let's be having you.' They dropped into the mud one by one and staggered up the steep bank towards the dark outlines above them. All around Urquhart other paras were scrambling up too. He took a grip of the slippery concrete, dug his foot in and attempted to heave up his fourteen stone frame. There was an ominous snap. '*Blast!*' the Divisional Commander cursed angrily.

'What is it?' Captain Roberts, his ADC queried anxiously.

'It's all right,' Urquhart said testily. 'It's only my braces.'

As Colonel Henniker, his steel helmet and cape gleaming with rain, welcomed them,

General Urquhart was holding up his trousers with irritated dignity. Swiftly Henniker ushered him up the line, while Roberts made his way to General Thomas's HQ to fix up some transport to take his chief to Browning's CP. Unshaven, his battledress torn and bloody, stinking to high heaven, he was (as General Urquhart records) 'not received with any warmth'.

As the last men on the opposite bank made a desperate scramble to get across before it was too late, throwing themselves into the water stark naked to attempt the swim across even if they could not swim a stroke, Colonel Payton-Reid of the 7th KOSBs touched the opposite side of the Rhine with one of the last boats. 'Wonder of wonders', he recalled later. 'we were on the south bank – safe and sound. Once there it seemed as though a haven had been reached and despite mud and fatigue, all trudged the four miles to Driel with light hearts... Until now I had always thought exaggerated these scenes on the cinema screen depicting the staggering and stumbling of worn-out men, but now I found myself behaving in exactly that manner...'

Soon the only infantry colonel to come out safely would be sitting down to a meal. But, despite his hunger, his mind would not be on the food. Instead he would be thinking back to 'the past, remembering all the acts of heroism and unselfishness I had seen

– I felt as I sat there what a proud and privileged thing it is to be a *SOLDIER*'.

4

Now they began to arrive at the Airborne seatail's at Nijmegen. In long queues they were filing, shivering and wet, past tables at which sat doctors who prescribed drugs and treatment for most of them. Louis Hagen was stopped at one of them and had a figure painted on his forehead by an orderly, who then prepared to give him a morphia injection. Hagen protested that he had not been wounded. Curtly the orderly answered: 'I'm treating for shock here, you'll feel fine in a minute.' He continued with the treatment.

But Hagen had had enough. Roughly he pushed the medic away. A struggle developed which was only solved when a doctor came up and Hagen could explain he was not shocked; only cold and wet. Another orderly was fetched. Together they removed Hagen's soaked, bloody uniform and it was slung on the large pile of wet, red-stained garments in the centre of the floor. Hagen was wrapped in blankets, sat on a chair with a little flickering oil stove beneath it. A cup of very sweet tea was pushed into his hands. Someone put a cigarette in his mouth. Hagen felt that he was 'in paradise'.

Not far away, Browning got out of bed to receive Urquhart. The knowledge that the Division had risked final annihilation that night had apparently not disturbed his sleep nor his usual concern with an immaculate turnout. As he came out of his bedroom, Urquhart thought 'he looked as if he had just come off parade instead of from his bed in the middle of a battle'.

Urquhart tried to pull himself together and report with some show of military briskness. 'The Division is nearly out now,' he said. 'I'm sorry we haven't been able to do what we set out to do.'

Browning poured him a drink and said: 'You did all you could. Now you had better get some rest.'

But Urquhart could not sleep. The meeting with his Corps Commander had been 'totally inadequate'. Yet it was not that which kept him turning and tossing in bed. 'Through my head', he wrote later, 'images tumbled over each other in a confusion of memories and ideas and plans. Behind them all the big questions loomed like some bewildering backcloth. Could we have been quicker off the mark at the beginning. What had become of Frost? What had happened to our fighter support? What had kept 30 Corps? How many officers and men of the Division had got out?'

As he finally drifted off into sleep, he felt that his questions were logical enough, 'yet oddly they seemed to belong to another life. They hung there in space...'

Now at the big red-brick schoolhouse, set back in a quiet, tree-lined street in Nijmegen, the men of the seatail began their tally of the exhausted survivors. The results were not good.

Of the senior officers, only Urquhart and Brigadier Hicks had come back. Hackett was a prisoner and Lathbury was missing. Colonels Smyth, Fetch and Sir W.R. des Voeux were dead. Colonels Frost, Lea, McCardic and Haden were wounded and prisoners. Colonel Dobie of the First Parachute Regiment was wounded and on the run. Twenty-five MOs had remained behind with the wounded. Only two of the fifteen padres had so far returned. The 1st, 3rd, 10th and 11th Battalions had ceased to exist. The 156th, the Borders and the KOSBs had less than a quarter of their original numbers left. And so the terrible tally of defeat went on until, at dawn, the counters knew that out of the 8,905 officers and men of the First Airborne Division who had gone in so confidently that Sunday, plus the 1,100 glider pilots who had taken them in on the first and second wave, only 2,163, with the addition of 160 Poles and 75 Dorsets had returned.

In the section set aside for Frost's Second Battalion, Warrant Officer John Sharp was responsible for the count. 'They started to arrive about twenty-three hundred hours,' he recalled much later, 'and I kept asking: "Has anyone seen the Second Battalion?" But no one had.'

The wet, weary survivors came stumbling in all night, but it took until dawn before the first man from the Second came in. By the time the count was over, Sharp found himself preparing billets for exactly seventeen men from the Battalion which had held the bridge. As the hard-boiled senior NCO remembers today: 'I don't think I was the only one there with tears in my eyes...'

5

On Thursday, 28th September 1944 Prime Minister Churchill stood up in Parliament to assess the state of the war. But his expected declaration that it would be over by the end of the year did not come. Informing the House about Arnhem, he stated that 'casualties have been grievous, but for those who mourn there is the consolation that the sacrifice was not needlessly demanded. "Not in vain" must be the pride of those who survive and the epitaph of those who fell.'

He went on in his finest rhetorical style to

deprecate very much people being carried away with premature expectation of an early cessation of the fighting. Then the great old man laid it on the line, giving the silent MPs the full significance of the defeat at Arnhem. 'I shall certainly not hazard a guess as to when the end will come.'

On the day that followed, during the debate on the Prime Minister's speech, Sir Edward Grigg claimed that: 'The men at Arnhem have given an example of splendid courage which will go down forever in the pages of our history. Arnhem will certainly now be part of British history for ever. None of us will ever forget.'

But on the day that Winston Churchill made his pessimistic assessment of the future course of the war, provincial papers were beginning to make some sort of victory out of a resounding defeat, thus ensuring that the Arnhem debacle would be soon forgotten. 'It is typical of the British soldier,' one leader-writer wrote, 'when ordered to evacuate and abandon some of his equipment, at least one dog-tired, blood-bathed hero calmly sat down under mortar fire and on his bag wrote "Shall be back – to be called for."'

But the 'blood-bathed heroes' were being rapidly forgotten. General 'Boy' Browning had just made a speech congratulating the survivors on 'the show they had put up', and was driving off with his escort of five paras, armed with tommy guns when he passed a dazed soldier who failed to salute. Browning's jeep squealed to a stop and the ex-Guardsman sent his aide hurrying to ask the survivor why he failed 'to salute the General'.

'But I haven't seen a general for a long time, sir,' the para protested. 'And I wasn't looking.'

The aide obviously thought the man's answer was unsatisfactory. He doubled back to the waiting Browning to consult the immaculate Corps Commander.

A few seconds later he returned to the para waiting there dumb and apprehensive. 'General Browning says,' the smart young aide announced, 'that you are not to be allowed to wear your red beret for the next fourteen days!'

Even at the highest level, it seemed to Urquhart that the powers-that-be did not understand what his men had gone through and even if they did, they wanted to forget it as soon as possible. On that Tuesday evening Horrocks and Browning gave him dinner. But it was a failure, although there was plenty of wine and chicken, rarities in those days. For Urquhart it was 'an ordeal even to have to face such food, let alone consume it'.

It was not only the food, however, which worried him. He seemed unable to understand Horrocks' account of why it had taken his 30 Corps so long to reach the trapped Airborne. Horrocks' habit of working on his listeners with his hands and his eyes, 'getting closer and closer to his victim' all the while, failed on Urquhart that evening. He 'found the 30 Corps Commander's hypnosis far from soothing', and he could not help 'wondering why 30 Corps had been so slow and unaware of the urgency, when they had a commander with such a capacity for dynamic human relations.'

The silent Airborne Commander noted that Horrocks, Browning and all the rest apparently enjoyed healthy appetites, whereas the good food nauseated him.

'It was a relief when the party ended.'

But there was one more meeting ahead of Urquhart before he would be sent home to be quietly and conveniently forgotten. At teatime on Thursday that week he arrived at Montgomery's HQ near Eindhoven. One of Montgomery's aides met him and informed him he was very worried because two of the Field Marshal's pet rabbits had escaped from their cage. The Airborne Commander's reaction at this grave news is not recorded.

Montgomery, however, greeted him with his usual brisk radiance. If he felt any disappointment at the failure of the Arnhem operation, which had put paid to his great plan, he did not show it to Urquhart. Thrusting out his hand, he snapped: 'Good to see you got back all right. Come and sit down and let's talk it over.'

The quiet warm September afternoon passed in sunshine while Urquhart explained what he had done at Arnhem, aided by curt questions on the part of the Field Marshal. The two men had dinner in his mess tent and Montgomery retired after his warm milk at his usual hour. Next morning Urquhart was taking a breath of fresh air when Montgomery came out of his caravan flourishing a piece of paper. 'This I would like to give to you,' he declared. 'I shall issue a copy to my public relations officer as well.' It was typewritten, but Montgomery assured the other General he had written it first in his own hand that morning.

Later, in the plane flying back to England, Urquhart was able to read the Field Marshal's letter. It said (in part):

'I also want to express to you my own admiration and the admiration of us all in 21st Army Group for the magnificent fighting spirit that your Division displayed in battle against great odds on the north bank of the Lower Rhine in Holland. There is no shadow of doubt that, had you failed, operations elsewhere would have been gravely compromised. You did not fail and all is well elsewhere. I would like all Britain to know that in your final message from the Arnhem area you said:

"All will be ordered to break out rather than surrender. We have attempted our best and we will continue to do our best as long as possible."

And all Britain will say to you:

"You did your best; you all did your duty; and we are proud of you."'

In the annals of the British Army there are many glorious deeds. In our Army we have always drawn great strength and inspiration from past traditions and endeavoured to live up to the high standard of those who have gone before. But there can be few episodes more glorious than the epic of Arnhem and those that follow after will find it hard to live up to the standards that you have set.

So long as we have in armies of the British Empire officers and men who will do as you have done, then we can indeed look forward with complete confidence to the future. In years to come it will be a great thing for a man to be able to say: "I fought at Arnhem"'

One hour later General Roy Urquhart had landed in Brussels, on the last leg of his journey back to the United Kingdom and obscurity. The Field Marshal, who was now stating that the operation had been 'a ninety-nine per cent success' and blaming the failure of the remaining ten per cent on the weather and a lack of American support, would never give him another operational command.

On that same Thursday Captain Muir, Lieutenants Skinner and Paull were leading a column of Airborne men towards Germany when a German corporal jumped out of a slit trench in front of the despondent British POWs. Before the SS officer who was in charge could stop him, he had fired a burst with a captured sten gun into the paras. Muir and Skinner went down dragging Paull with them. In that same instant, the blond SS officer grabbed one of his men's rifle and killed the corporal. But the damage had been done. Yet another two paras were dead.

Not far away, RSM 'Chalky' White, tramping towards the German border with another mixed bunch of POWs experienced a similar attack that left half a dozen paras dead or wounded on the road. The rest marched on 'too numb and downcast now' even to think of escaping.

The Ulsterman Tucker and the rest of the 2nd Battalion who had survived the bridge were being interrogated by German Intelligence on the other side of the border. In front of him a para was asked what the sand-coloured ribbon of the 'Africa Star' on his breast signified.

Cheekily he answered: 'It's my good luck mascot, mate.' The remark earned him an angry slap across the face.

Now the narrow country roads leading towards Germany were filled with some three thousand bedraggled and exhausted prisoners of the First Airborne Division. The shattered city for which they had come so far and failed to capture, was now left to the dead and those in hiding. And there were many of them. Corporal Wally Walton of the Military Police, who had escaped from the debacle at the bridge, was pushing a baker's cart through the littered streets, dressed in the old baker's spare clothes, trying to find a way out of the German cordon. Major Deane-Drummond was hidden in a cupboard, sunk in the wall and papered with the same paper. He had already killed one German in his first attempt to escape; now he would hide there for twelve days with nothing but a piece of bread and his water bottle to succour him. RSM Grainger, who had been wounded and taken to a local mental hospital with two other wounded paras, decided to use the German evacuation of the place to escape. Dressed in white blankets they joined the patients, 'some being led, some with their hands tied, and all of them dancing'. So the paras danced too. Grimacing and flinging up their arms in what the Regimental Sergeant Major hoped was the correct 'mental case' manner, they passed through the German cordon.

On that day, wandering behind the

German lines or trying to escape from German-controlled hospitals, there were two brigadiers, six colonels, and about sixty other officers and at least five hundred 'other ranks'. And on that same September day, the first of them to reach the British lines after the evacuation of the cauldron began his escape. It was none other than the ubiquitous Canadian, Lieutenant Heaps.

2

Heaps had noticed the 'port-hole', as soon as he had been herded into the cattle car, together with the para Sergeant Banwell and a glider pilot called Kettley. He waited till the crowded POW train had started, however, before clambering over the wounded paras and Dorsets to examine it. Putting both hands around the opening and bracing his leg against the side, the young Canadian had heaved. A rotten board gave way, revealing a narrow opening eighteen inches high and three feet wide, protected only by a few strands of rusty barbed wire. Kettley soon cut those through and the way to freedom was open.

Heaps asked if anyone wanted to go with them. Only one man volunteered, but since he was wounded in the leg they turned him down. The rest were too exhausted or shocked to take up his offer.

Heaps could wait no longer. He climbed through, took a deep breath and jumped. Next instant he was rolling down a steep grassy embankment to land at the bottom, all breath knocked out of him. Kettley and Banwell followed a few seconds later and lay there absolutely still while the train clattered by them. They caught a snatch of the German guards singing in the last coach. Then the train had disappeared into the night and there was silence.

The next few days passed in confused excitement. They contacted the Dutch Underground, manning a secret POW cage containing renegade Dutch SS men. They taught them how to use a Bren gun. They ambushed a German supply truck convoy and wrecked two trucks. They lost 'Tex' Banwell, who said he preferred to stay and fight as a partisan with the Dutch. Sergeant Banwell was to be captured by the enemy twice more before the war ended. Finally, on the morning of 1st October, the local Underground leader said that the resident 'British agent' would like to see Heaps and Kettley at the 'chicken coops'.

The coop he was led to that day turned out to 'be the most amazing chicken coop I have ever been in. The walls were covered with white, thick, sound-absorbing panelling.

343

There were two rooms and in the far room I could see a huge downy bed covered with sheets, with a big comforter lying neatly folded on the top. The rooms were brightly lit and the blinds drawn. In the room I was in there was a wireless set and an operator working it.' He paid no attention to the two paras. But the other man, a six-footer, wearing British officer's uniform, did.

'You are Lieutenant Heaps, aren't you?' he said with a faint trace of what Heaps took to be a French accent. 'I'm Captain King.'

The young Canadian officer had met the first link in the chain which would lead him eventually to the men of Room 900 and 'Saturday', the man who ran it.

Five days later – 'the most beautiful October 5th' in my life' – Lieutenant Heaps was across the Rhine and in safety. That same night he was invited to have dinner with Martha Gelhorn, Hemingway's third wife, a Major Fraser, and a tall, haggard Major, who had crossed that same river four years before in a coal barge on his way to Colditz from which he would later make a spectacular escape. The Major's name was Airey Neave, but he was better known in the professional escape network, which had helped Heaps to safety, by his code name – Saturday.

Heaps was being entertained by the Continent-based head of the Secret Intelligence

Service's top-secret Room 900.

When Major Neave had escaped from
Colditz in 1942 he was interviewed by a
mysterious but forthright Brigadier from
Intelligence who told him that he would not
be going back to the infantry. His experience
as the first man to have escaped from Germany's toughest POW camp was too valu-
able to be wasted on active military service.
Instead he was to join the tiny but efficient
staff of Room 900 at the War Office in charge
of secret escape routes from Occupied
Europe. The Brigadier's instructions had
been brief but determined: 'Remember that
many lives will depend upon you. For God's
sake, keep your mouth shut and get results!'

In the years that followed Neave got
results, helping to build up a Europe-wide
escape organization, based on a few professional British and Allied agents working with
the local Resistance movements, to spirit out
shot-down aircrew, wanted civilians and
escaped POWs. Each of these agents had a
cover-name: 'Horse' in Barcelona, 'Monday'
in Madrid, etc. So besides being 'Anthony
Newton' in the War Office, and 'Albert Hall'
to the Resistance, Major Neave became
'Saturday' within the hush-hush confines of
Room 900.

Now, after the failure of the Arnhem
landing he was ordered from France to his

new post in Holland to help organize the escape of the paras still trapped in Arnhem, whose situation had been pointed out, not only by Heaps, the first to escape, but also by the 'Voice' who was no less a person than Major Tatham-Warter of the 2nd Battalion.

The former CO of A Company had escaped from a German hospital and had contacted the Dutch Resistance who had hidden him in the neighbourhood of Ede. There it was still possible to communicate with the Allied-held side of the Rhine by a telephone link with Nijmegen Power Station: a link which Major Tatham-Warter had immediately taken over to become the 'Voice', which spelled out details of enemy movements, prisoners-of-war, artillery targets every night at six o'clock precisely to Saturday and his fellow Intelligence officers. Thus as the first days of October passed and it became clear that Montgomery's troops would not cross the Lower Rhine in force and link up with the men hiding in Arnhem, Neave gained the support of General Dempsey himself to attempt a large-scale mass escape of the trapped paras. But the ex-Colditz man needed four essential pieces of information before he could put his plan into operation: a safe area of concentration for the paras hidden over an area of thirty square miles; the means by which the paras would arrive at this area; a suitable gap on the

German Lower Rhine front through which they could pass; and a detailed account of the resources available to the paras. Neave realized that he needed a senior officer from the other side to brief him on the four counts. He telephoned the Voice and told him his problem, and on the other side of the Rhine the machinery was set into motion to expedite the escape of the first senior officer to break out of a German POW cage – Colonel Dobie of the First Battalion.

3

Dobie set off on his long and dangerous journey on the 16th October 1944. By evening he had reached his rendezvous – a hut at the edge of a wood – where he had met a British officer of the Special Air Service in charge of a 'strange party, working away in the light of their little oil lamp. The wireless, the winding of the power handle and its monotonous noise, the tap-tap of the buzzer, the quiet voice of "B", (an attractive blonde) as she decoded, the litter of equipment and weapons, the evening meal – all went to heighten the atmosphere and reality,' he recalled later.

On the following day, guided by the blonde, whose name he never learned (she was captured and shot a little later) he cycled through a gale for two hours until he was handed over to a new guide 'P'. A little later his new guide, a sturdy Dutchman who was going to row him across, took him to the Rhine and 'with a sudden pang', Dobie recollected, 'I remembered all those who had crossed it four weeks before going north full of high hopes and the bitter cost'. But there was no time for introspection now. Swiftly 'P' rowed him across and passed him on to the next guide, who took him to the Waal, still occupied here by the Germans. And then there was a hitch. The Dutch Resistance men informed him they couldn't get him across the river.

In his diary, Colonel Dobie noted that day: 'I was distressed at the thought of having to stay, so much depended on getting across, not only for myself now but all those chaps of ours. I said I would swim it. With a very worried and uncertain outlook I went to bed and slept hardly an hour.'

But his apprehension turned out to be un-necessary for a boat was found. Dodging a German patrol boat and nearly capsizing in mid-stream, his two very frightened Dutch helpers managed to get him across. A few hours later he was reporting at Dempsey's HQ and putting forward his ideas to Neave and his newly appointed deputy, Lieutenant Heaps, from his own Battalion. Pegasus One, the great escape, was on.

TWO

Ten o'clock on the night of 22nd October, 1944. At last the preparations were finished. At the lonely Dutch farmhouse near the riverside village of Randwijk, Saturday's headquarters for 'Pegasus One', the planners waited.

The last week had been hectic and nerve-wracking. Constantly plagued by rumours that the Gestapo was moving into the Arnhem area in force to search for the paras, they had worked out a complicated plan, which had been relayed to the 'Voice' bit by bit for discussion with the leaders of the Dutch Resistance. Now finally the details had been satisfactorily worked out and approved by the Dutch, and as Heaps, Dobie and Saturday smoked and chatted nervously in the kitchen of the farmhouse, they knew that some two hundred escapers were already on their way to the Lower Rhine.

In exactly two hours' time a Bofors anti-aircraft gun would fire fifteen tracer shells across the river in a straight line. This would indicate the line of advance for the paras. Then they would have to slip through the 'gap' – eight hundred yards of open ground

349

between two German posts, a mile short of the river. The Bofors signal would be repeated every half hour after that.

At the same time a small group of volunteers from the Screaming Eagles of the US 101st Airborne, which now held this section of the Rhine, would cross in order to cover the flanks against any German surprise attack. With them would go Colonel Dobie and Heaps to act as beachmasters for the forty assault boats of Major Tucker's Canadian engineers, who had helped to evacuate the cauldron nearly a month before.

But even now Saturday was worried that something might go wrong. If the Germans spotted the escapers and used flares to illuminate them as they waited for the boats on the opposite bank, the great operation might well turn into a massacre.

Outside it was very dark. There was no moon, but as Heaps stepped out of the door to take a breath of fresh air, he sensed the 'atmosphere vibrated with a tension and expectancy'. In the trees, the Canadian engineers crouched next to their assault boats waiting excitedly for midnight.

A pig in a barn near the river squealed suddenly and made him jump. He took a grip on his nerves and glanced at his watch. Still ten minutes to go. There was no sound now save for the remote explosions of a mortar 'stonk.' Dobie, who had just joined him, nodded at the fiery trails in the sky to the east. 'Moaning minnies,' he said drily.

Five minutes to go. The Canadians began to push their boats out of the concealment of the dripping trees. Another pig squealed as a big-footed Canadian stepped on it in the farmyard. But still the German side of the river remained silent. The machine-guns which they knew were sited at Wageningen did not open up to slaughter the paras who must be passing through the gap by now. Saturday joined the two para officers and strained his eyes to spot the red V to be flashed by torch from the other side: the signal that the escapers were in position. He could see nothing

Then with a crack that made the three of them jump, the Bofors opened up. White tracer shot flatly across the river, casting a brilliant glow in its hurrying wake. Dobie and Heaps doubled across the muddy field towards the boats. A red V flicked on-and-off almost immediately afterwards. Saturday cursed bitterly. It was nearly four hundred yards to the right of the planned crossing.

Hurriedly he rapped out new orders to the waiting Screaming Eagles. The paras sprang into their rowboats. As they disappeared into the night, Saturday thought the scraping noise of their rowlocks seemed 'uncomfortably loud'. Suddenly he started. There was a burst of uncertain rifle fire from the other bank. Had the Ede escapers run into a German patrol?

It had been a long eleven miles for most of the escapers. One body of forty men had reached the crossing point in two trucks only to bump into a company of German soldiers who had ridden through them on their bicycles, ringing their bells angrily. But that was all. Sweating nervously and praying their luck would continued to hold good, the party under Major Hibbert hurried to join the rest commanded by Major Tatham-Warter and Brigadier Lathbury.

Now the 147 escapers prepared for the last stretch and Major Tatham-Warter in the lead told himself that their chances of slipping through the gap were 'remote'; the Boche must surely see them. Besides, his men were a mixed bunch of Dutch, British paras, ten Americans – and one lone Russian who had appeared from somewhere or other. All were unfit and many of them had never seen the leaders of the group in daylight. As the Major wrote much later: 'It would have been a hazardous move with a highly trained company.' With this 'mixed bag' – his own private name for his group – it would be decidedly 'dicey'.

But men such as Major Deane-Drummond, who had survived thirteen days in the cupboard by rationing himself to four bites of bread a day and two sips of water every five hours, were determined not to be captured again. Already he had killed one German in his attempt to escape, and during his stay in the cupboard he had seen what captivity did to men. A glider pilot had betrayed military information in front of him, as he had peered out through a slit, in return for a hot meal given him by his German captors. 'What agonies of mind and tummy,' he recalled later. His disgust with the treacherous captain and the tantalizing smell had almost forced him out of his cramped hiding-place several times. But he had restrained himself and finally linked up with the escapers. Now he would stop at nothing to prevent recapture.

The long file of men, led by Dutch guides, moved cautiously into the wood which barred the way to the gap. The trees closed in on them like a tunnel. They could see little save the gloomy outline of the man ahead. There was no sound now save that of their own breathing and the occasional noise of some prowling animal in the deep thickets. The guides bumped into a deer. For a second they mistook it for a German. All along the column, tense strained men gasped with relief when the word was passed: 'Don't worry – only a deer.'

By eleven o'clock they had reached the gap. Here their guides left them. Now they would have to pass through two enemy positions, each containing infantry and, worse still, the feared 'moaning minnies' which would cut them to ribbons if they were discovered out in the open.

They dropped into a four-foot deep drainage ditch. Using it as cover, and bent double like asthmatic old men, they hurried down its length, hoping no alert German sentry would hear the noise they made in the pitch darkness. Now, half a mile in front, they could just make out the sheen of the Lower Rhine.

Major Tatham-Warter hissed a warning. The Germans kept a standing patrol in this area; they would have to be as quiet and as alert as possible. Everyone nodded his understanding, including the Russian who spoke no English. They began to crawl across the muddy open field towards the river.

'Nothing stirred on the river,' Deane-Drummond remembered long afterwards, 'save the gurgle of flowing water and a subdued swish from a nearby weir. A few marsh birds occasionally let out their plaintive cries and it was difficult to believe that the river was no-man's-land between the Germans and the Allies'.

Now they could see the other side through a layer of thin mist, curling over the surface of the Lower Rhine. But there was no sign of life anywhere. They edged closer and closer to the designated crossing point. Someone spoke too loud. Tatham-Warter's angry hiss to be quiet came too late. A German opened up with a *schmeisser* only fifty yards away. Lead hissed through the air. They dropped as one, their ears ringing with the sudden burst of fire.

For what seemed an age they lay there, not daring to breathe. Were they going to be discovered now after so much suffering and planning? Would they have to chance swimming for it? 'A thousand doubts went through my head,' Deane-Drummond recalled, as he wormed forward on his belly to see what was going on.

But nobody had been hit by the burst and they could hear the Germans withdrawing hurriedly across the field. Deane-Drummond thought they 'must have been even more frightened than we were.'

The question was now, where were the boats and their rescuers? Five – ten – fifteen minutes went by. Still no rescuers from the 43rd. They gave the agreed-upon signal time and time again. Nothing! The only sound was that of a German multiple mortar. Their imaginations began to conjure up a hundred and one frightening possibilities. Lying in the mud, a pale, emaciated Brigadier Lathbury, still weak from his spinal wound, felt sickeningly, 'that something serious had gone wrong...'

Heaps sprang out of the boat just after Dobie. The bank seemed to him 'quiet and foreboding'. He made a quick decision. Grabbing two American Screaming Eagles, he began to move cautiously down the bank eastwards. He spotted the signal winking feebly. He quickened his pace, followed by the two Americans. Suddenly a white Verey light hushed into the sky. Its icy unreal light illuminated the men crouched in the bushes everywhere. In that same instant Heaps and his two helpers dropped flat in the mud, hardly daring to breathe until the flare finally sunk to the ground. Swiftly he covered the couple of hundred yards to them. Now he could hear the muffled sound of feet crunching across wet grass – hundreds of them. They dropped again and waited, gripping their weapons. 'Then,' as Heaps wrote in the last month of the war, 'into sight on the very edge of the river came a very long line of men marching in single file. Some had civilian clothes on, others wore the torn remains of a battledress. I overtook them and ran towards the head of the column to be greeted by Major Tatham-Water's cheerful booming voice. It was the Pegasus column.'

On the other side, a tense nervous Saturday began his count as the first boat hit the bank and the Screaming Eagles hurried the paras between the white mine-marker tapes which indicated the route to the lonely farmhouse HQ.

Lathbury appeared first, a tall, skinny figure dressed in civilian clothes. The Voice, whom Saturday recognized immediately as soon as he opened his mouth, followed. Then two Dutch naval officers appeared out of the night. Saturday knew them too. Two years before they had been his comrades in that grim Saxon castle of Colditz. But he had no time to exchange reminiscences now. He had to get the escapers away from the river bank before the Germans tumbled to what was happening and opened up with their artillery. Strained and anxious, he hurried the weak men to the trucks which would take them back to the hospital in Nijmegen.

Heaps had been on the other bank seventy minutes now. He knew it was time he started back to the boats. The Germans would not remain so tame for much longer. Until now they had not fired a single bullet at the Pegasus escapers. But their luck could not hold much longer. He shot a quick look at his watch. It was now fifteen minutes past one. He had been walking around in front of the Germans for nearly all that time without a shot being fired at him. As he recalled later, 'it as almost unbelievable'.

Heaps took a last look round. It seemed as

if he had rounded up all the escapers. Slowly, his sten at the ready, still accompanied by his two American Screaming Eagles he began to back to the last boat. As he did so, his mind ran back to the last time he had been washed up on this beach, tired and exhausted. 'This time it had been different. The Rhine was becoming an old friend.'

By the time he reached the hospital at Nijmegen, the escapers, who had been hiding behind the German lines for over a month, were sleeping soundly, their bellies full with the first good meal they had had in weeks, helped down with plenty of issue rum. As Saturday wandered through the snoring wards, checking if everything was all right and carrying the bottle of champagne for the only officer to be wounded during the daring operation, he knew that he would now be able to bring out the rest of the paras.

2

Pegasus Two was born the following morning. In the Brussels 'safe house' rented by his organization he began immediate planning of the operation. But Saturday was undecided. He knew it might involve the 'possibility of serious casualties among men who were already wounded and who might be killed instead of spending the rest of the war in prison-camps.' He was also nervous about the security of the planned operation. Every dawn Dutchmen were crossing the Lower Rhine and Waal in such numbers that it was impossible for Field Security to check whether they were genuine Resistance men or German agents. Yet he knew too that the 101st's HQ had already contacted a Major Maguire, the First Airborne's Chief Intelligence Officer, who was eager to bring over no less than one hundred paras, pilots, and both Dutch and Airborne doctors. Despite his misgivings about security on the Rhine, Saturday decided to go ahead with the operation. Maguire and his men had to be saved.

But unknown to Saturday, his operation had already been compromised – in London.

In the last week of October Saturday reconnoitred a new crossing place – the tiny village of Heteren, four miles east of Randwijk. He decided this time that Major Tucker's engineers should use flat-bottomed storm boats, fitted with outboard motors to which a kind of primitive silencer had been attached.

October gave way to the first week of November. 'Ham', one of Saturday's agents who had taken over from the Voice, reported from Ede that the job of assembling the members of Pegasus Two was going well. But the Rhine, which was rising rapidly, due to the winter rains, was already running at a dangerous five knots an hour. Despite the obvious danger, however, and the report from London that the British Press had informed the world that there was some kind of civilian telephone link between German occupied Holland and that in Allied hands, the planning went on.

From the other side of the river 'Ham' radioed that there would be four main obstacles for the escapers, once they had left their assembly point: a barn, two major roads, a side road and a railway line, all to be crossed by men who were at the end of their tether thanks to hunger or serious wounds which had not yet completely healed.

Again Saturday wondered if he should continue with such a risky proposition. On the 16th November he wrote to a colleague in Brussels that 'the situation was critical'. But he knew that 'the hopes of the men who had waited so long could not be dashed'. Taking comfort from his own philosophy, which he had developed in Colditz that: 'escape is not only a technique but a philosophy. The real escaper is more than a man equipped with compass, maps, papers, disguise and a plan. He has an inner confidence, a serenity of spirit which makes him a Pilgrim,' he decided to go ahead. Pegasus Two would take place on the night of 22nd November at midnight precisely.

3

On the night of the operation, Heaps, Major Fraser of the SAS and Saturday ran into trouble right from the start. The night was dark, with a high wind and they thought they would be free from German interference. But they had hardly arrived in the deserted village when they ran into an enemy artillery bombardment. As they made a dash for the cellar of the house which they had picked as their HQ for the operation, one of the Canadian engineers fell, severely wounded. Still, Saturday consoled himself, as they clattered into the safety of the icy-cold dank cellar, the noise of the howling wind would cover whatever noise the Canadian boats made.

They spent the long night in the cellar in vain. No one could sleep. Every now and again one of the three would stir restlessly and walk over to the slit in the brickwork to stare into the darkness, hoping that there would be the red signal of the escape party winking at them from over the dark water. But no signal came. In the end Saturday said that perhaps they had missed the signal due to the bad conditions. They would try again on the following night. They crept away and spent most of the day asleep while the Canadian Corps' guns shelled Heteren to destroy its church tower so that the Germans would not be able to use it again for their own artillery observation.

In the late afternoon the three of them returned to the abandoned village to find interesting news awaiting them. The handful of US paratroopers they had left behind there reported a strange figure on the other side of the river. Several times he had come out of the bushes and shouted at them in an accent which the Screaming Eagles took to be Irish. According to the strange man, there were no Germans about; he was alone save for the company of two Dutchmen. Was the man a provocateur? The thought flashed through Saturday's mind. If he were, what did he want them to do? Go across in force to be annihilated? Or was he a member of the Maguire group? Had he news for them about the missing escapers?

In the end Major Tucker, the head of the Canadian engineers, made the decision for him. As soon as it was dark, he launched a storm boat and swept across the dark river, leaving Heaps behind on the mudbank armed with an American 'walky-talky'. Almost immediately the instrument started to squawk and Tucker 'garbled something to me about capturing Germans and Dutchmen (as Heaps expressed it later) and the conversation was mangled by odd shouts and weird cursing in a foreign language which I took to be Irish'.

Heaps gave up on the new instrument and waited till Tucker came back ten minutes later with the strange Irishman, an RAF Sergeant named O'Casey, and the two Dutchmen. Before he passed out completely with the aid of the big flask of rum Saturday had brought with him, O'Casey explained he had been in the Maguire party, some 120 strong, when they had bumped into a lone sentry who had fired his rifle and raised the alarm. Flares had hissed into the night sky on all sides. Machine-guns had opened up and the party had scattered wildly. In a panic, they had run into a wood, which had been sealed off by the Germans and then systematically mortared. As the mug fell from his lifeless fingers and O'Casey slumped into a drunken sleep, he mumbled that he thought that some of the men had escaped.

Saturday looked at the rest of his party aghast. What now? Heaps could read the shocked question in his eyes. 'Let's hang on,' he suggested. 'They might not all be dead or captured.'

Thus they waited. The hours passed leadenly while O'Casey snored heavily, his head slumped on his chest. Midnight came and went. Then they were alerted by a report that a faint light had been spotted on the other side of the river. Was it the signal?

Almost immediately a sentry on the river-bank telephoned to say that he had heard shouts and rifle shots coming from the area of the light. Heaps knew what that meant: some of the Maguire group might have slipped through the German trap after all.

A young paratroop lieutenant named Dixon approached the Screaming Eagle CO who was in the cellar with the British: 'Sir,' he said anxiously, 'there is only one sure way to get those men back on the far shore and that's by canoe. Let me go and I'll bring those British boys back.'

The CO frowned. 'The current's pretty swift, Dixon,' he said. 'What makes you think you can do it?'

The young paratrooper's jaw clenched firmly: 'I can handle anything with a paddle that floats, sir. I'm from Florida and I was brought up with a canoe on the bayous.'

'Okay, Dixon,' the Colonel answered a little wearily. 'Have a try at it.'

Heaps and Dixon ran out into the darkness. Minutes later Dixon was across and in touch with Heaps by means of the walky-talky. 'I've found a British paratrooper,' the tall American whispered, his voice distorted metallically by the instrument, 'and an airman too. I'm bringing them across.'

Quickly Heaps clicked the receiver off and edged even closer to the river. Kneeling, sten at the ready he peered into the thick darkness. Nothing. He cocked his ear into the wind and strained to catch the sound of Dixon's paddle. Again nothing. Worried by now, he pressed the walky-talky button and held it up to his ear. But his signals remained unanswered. The set was dead.

How long Heaps waited there in the cold at the river bank, he could never recollect afterwards. But as the night started to flood with the first dirty white of the false dawn and a bored German machine-gunner started to send his multi-coloured tracer skimming across the sullen water, the young Canadian knew it was time to go. Sadly he trudged back through the mud to the cellar. The American paratroop Colonel came out to meet him, humming softly to himself. When he saw the look on Heaps' tired face, the humming stopped. Mutely he raised his eyes in enquiry. Heaps shook his head.

Major Fraser of the SAS had followed him out. He stared out into the dawn haze across the river. But nothing stirred. Even the bored German machine-gunner had fallen silent now. The flat Dutch landscape lay grey, dull and empty. Another day of war had started.

Now Major Tucker's Canadian engineers began to drag their unneeded boats back to the cover of the trees, cursing sullenly when the clumsy craft got stuck. As the first German mortar of the morning 'hate' opened up

365

with an obscene belch, the rescue party started to squelch wearily through the mud to the rear. Pegasus Two had failed.

Now the last survivors of the great defeat were left to fend for themselves in a dying Holland, where famished, lean-ribbed horses collapsed in the streets to be hacked to pieces by hollow-cheeked housewives, greedy for meat, and pale-faced, consumptive 'good' girls sold themselves to German soldiers in the backstreets of Amsterdam for a loaf of hard Army bread or a tin of 'Old Man', the standard Wehrmacht meat ration.

And in the ruins of the city which the eager young men in their red berets had attacked so confidently that bright September Sunday morning one of the survivors, now a hunted and wounded man, hidden by two ancient maiden Dutch ladies, wrote his former commander a letter: 'Thank you for the party. It didn't go as we hoped and got a bit rougher than we expected. But speaking for myself, I'd take it on again any time, and so, I am sure, would everybody else.'

Far away in England, General Urquhart, recipient of that letter, finished his report on the Battle for the Bridge as 1944 gave way to 1945 and it seemed as if the long war would go on for ever. It ended with four simple words: 'We have no regrets.'

The publishers hope that this book has given you enjoyable reading. Large Print Books are especially designed to be as easy to see and hold as possible. If you wish a complete list of our books please ask at your local library or write directly to:

Magna Large Print Books
Magna House, Long Preston,
Skipton, North Yorkshire.
BD23 4ND

This Large Print Book, for people
who cannot read normal print,
is published under the auspices of

THE ULVERSCROFT FOUNDATION

... we hope you have enjoyed this book.
Please think for a moment about those
who have worse eyesight than you ...
and are unable to even read or enjoy
Large Print without great difficulty.

You can help them by sending a
donation, large or small, to:

**The Ulverscroft Foundation,
1, The Green, Bradgate Road,
Anstey, Leicestershire, LE7 7FU,
England.**
or request a copy of our brochure for
more details.

The Foundation will use all donations
to assist those people who are visually
impaired and need special attention
with medical research, diagnosis
and treatment.

Thank you very much for your help.